Haunted Spaces, Sacred Places

A Field Guide to Stone Circles, Crop Circles, Ancient Tombs, and Supernatural Landscapes

Brian Haughton,
author of *Hidden History*

New Page Books
A Division of Career Press, Inc.
Franklin Lakes, NJ

HAUNTED SPACES, SACRED PLACES
EDITED BY JODI BRANDON
TYPESET BY MICHAEL FITZGIBBON
Cover design by Lu Rossman/Digi Dog Design NY
Printed in the U.S.A. by Book-mart Press

Images on pages 81, 87, 95, 119, 169, 181, 235 are all publc domain.
To order this title, please call toll-free 1-800-CAREER-1 (NJ and Canada: 201-848-0310) to order using VISA or MasterCard, or for further information on books from Career Press.

The Career Press, Inc., 3 Tice Road, PO Box 687,
Franklin Lakes, NJ 07417
www.careerpress.com
www.newpagebooks.com

Library of Congress Cataloging-in-Publication Data

Haughton, Brian, 1964–
    Haunted spaces, sacred places : a field guide to stone circles, crop circles, ancient tombs, and supernatural landscapes / by Brian Haughton.
        p. cm.
    Includes bibliographical references and index.
    ISBN 978-1-60163-000-1
        1. Sacred space. 2. Haunted places. I. Title.

BL580.H38 2008
203'.5—dc22

2007048750

For Elina, Alice, and Christopher

Acknowledgments

Thanks to Michael Haughton and Elina Siokou for reading the manuscript, and to my agent, Lisa Hagan, of Paraview.

Contents

Introduction

Haunted Spaces, Sacred Places is an exploration of the archaeology, legends, folklore, and modern mysteries of 32 ancient monuments and sacred landscapes throughout the world, organized by geographical region. As with my previous work, *Hidden History,* the choice of ancient places was made to include a selection of both famous and relatively unknown sites, and also to encompass a wide geographical range.

There may have been a number of factors that marked a place as "sacred" in the mind of ancient man, varying from culture to culture and over different time periods. Nevertheless, one characteristic that must always have been of prime concern when constructing these ancient monuments or ritual complexes was the dividing up of the landscape, separating the sacred from the profane. Of course, the place may already have had natural characteristics that made it unique; recent research into geological anomalies and acoustics at ancient monuments is coming up with some interesting results. However, it seems more likely that it was something much less tangible, more "in the mind" of the inhabitants that made the place "special." Designing and building structures such as the ritual complex of monuments at Avebury (UK), the Bighorn Medicine Wheel (Wyoming, United States), and the standing stones at Carnac (northern France) may have been a way of "monumentalizing" or enhancing this aura of sanctity, but it was the place itself that possessed the sacredness. The buildings acted as an expression of this sacredness. Often, nothing at all was constructed at a sacred site, its own personal myth-history being enough for it to be venerated (Ayers Rock in Australia is a good example of this). In any attempt at understanding sacred places, perhaps a good way to begin is by examining some of the legends and lore that have become attached to the sites over time. However, the legends and even the archaeology of ancient sacred places are not sufficient in themselves for an understanding of how our ancestors viewed their sacred landscapes. In the words of American geographer Donald William Meinig, from his book, *The Interpretation of Ordinary Landscapes: Geographical Essay,* "any landscape is composed not only of what lies before our eyes but what lies within our heads." To gain even the slightest insight into what was going through the minds of ancient peoples when they designed or visited monuments such as the prehistoric temples of Malta or the vast Ohio Serpent Mound, we not only have to reunite ourselves with ancient values and traditions, but also attempt to cut ourselves off from our increasingly materialistic, technology-based, 21st-century worldview.

The stories connected with ancient sites can take many forms, from legends at least a thousand years old, such as that of the wizard Merlin transporting the bluestones to Stonehenge, to modern accounts of UFOs and Bigfoot at, for example, Mount Shasta, in California. There is a plethora of folklore connected with ancient sacred sites, especially the megalithic monuments of north Western Europe, a number of which are included in *Haunted Spaces, Sacred Spaces.* The folklore of ancient places has become fairly standardized over the years: They are inhabited by fairies, were built by giants or the devil, are haunted by ghosts, guarded by dragons, visited by spectral black dogs, or cursed by witches. Stones are said to conceal buried treasure, to dance at midday, to walk down to a stream at midnight to drink, to cause people to lose all sense of time, and to resist all attempts to move or to count them. The parallels between such folklore motifs and modern "paranormal" accounts reported at ancient monuments are obvious.

Indeed, though there is a significant record of folklore directly associated with ancient sacred places, the evidence for the occurrence of paranormal phenomena at these sites, reported in many books, on Internet sites, and in magazine articles, is largely unconvincing, much of the research remarkably uncritical, and the conclusions premature, to say the least. A good deal of the evidence for supposed "window areas," places that apparently attract or produce strange phenomena, is either media-generated or consists of exaggerations of local folk tales and legends, as is the cases with a large part of the material related to the San Luis Valley and Mount Shasta, and, to a certain extent, Mount Penteli, Greece, though in the latter area there are some genuinely unexplained elements to the accounts collected there. Such criticism does not mean to suggest that unexplained phenomena do not occur at such places, but there is no good reason to suppose that such things happen more or less often than anywhere else. Indeed, if the reports of strange lights, crop circles, and bizarre creatures at ancient sacred sites are indicative of anything, it is that these places are still regarded as significant enough to attract and generate myths thousands of years after their construction. The important question is whether these myths, ancient and modern, can tell us anything about the beliefs, ideas, and motivation of our ancient ancestors. It is in this sense that ancient sacred sites may be viewed as "windows" into the past.

But just how reliable is folklore as a guide to past events? Can legends shed any light on the construction and purpose of ancient sacred landscapes, such as at that around Stonehenge, and the ritual complex centered on Newgrange in Ireland? The majority of scholars of folklore and myth remain unconvinced that such tales can give us any genuine insights into the mind of ancient man. On many occasions the traditional tales surrounding archaeological sites are "modern" (post–18th century), as with the tale of the Witch at the Rollright Stones (Oxfordshire, UK). If this is the case, then it is obvious that although the lore may reflect contemporary ideas about the monuments, which is in itself important, it can tell us nothing relating to the purpose of the site it is connected with. Nevertheless, if research is undertaken combining folklore and legend with archaeology, as it was at Troy by Heinrich Schliemann, and is currently being done with the archaeology of Stonehenge, and the story of Merlin and the bluestones, then perhaps we can begin to create a richer ancient past, one inhabited by people rather than merely their artifacts and buildings.

Chapter 1

Newgrange and the Monuments of the Boyne (Ireland)

Interior of the monument, showing megalithic art.
Photo copyright Government of Ireland

Brú na Bóinne ("Palace on the Boyne") is an important area of Neolithic chamber tombs, standing stones, henges, and other prehistoric enclosures located next to a loop in the River Boyne, County Meath, just more than 30 miles north of Dublin, Ireland. It is surely no coincidence that the archaeological landscape of Brú na Bóinne is situated on the rich fertile soil of the valley of the Boyne, in close proximity to the Irish Sea, in what is the most accessible part of Ireland. The central feature of this vast ritual landscape is a cemetery containing around 40 passage graves. A passage grave is a tomb, usually dating to the Neolithic period (c. 4000–c2200 BC) in which the burial chamber is reached along a low passage. The major monuments within the *Brú na Bóinne* complex are the passage graves of Newgrange, Knowth, and Dowth, of which Newgrange is perhaps the best known and most impressive.

One of the greatest architectural achievements of prehistory, the vast Neolithic tomb/temple of Newgrange is one of the earliest roofed buildings in the world. Newgrange was probably built around 3200 BC, and consists of a passage running for 62 feet and a 20-foot-high chamber with a corbelled roof, constructed of large stone slabs without mortar. The passage and chamber are covered by a huge stone and turf mound about 262 feet in diameter and around 44 feet high, surrounded at its base by 97 large stones, known as kerbstones, some of which are elaborately ornamented with megalithic art. On top of the kerbstones is a high wall of white quartz. The large slab that now stands against the wall outside the passage entrance was originally used to block the passage when construction of the monument was complete. The passageway, which covers only a third of the total length of the mound, is lined with roughly hewn stone slabs and leads to a cross-shaped chamber with a magnificent steep corbelled roof. The recesses in the cruciform chamber are decorated with spirals and each contains a massive stone basin, two of which are carved from sandstone and one from granite.

Archaeologists believe these basins once held cremated human remains. The Neolithic builders who constructed the chambers took precautions to ensure that the inside of the structure remained completely dry. Sand, brought 10 miles from the shore close to the mouth of the Boyne, and a putty-like clay were packed into the joints between the roof stones. Additionally, the builders cut grooves into the roof blocks to channel rainwater away and prevent it from pouring into the passageway. Such precautions have implications for the function of Newgrange. If the monument was designed purely as a place to store the bones of the dead, there would surely be no need for these elaborate procedures to keep the remains dry.

Outside the base of the Newgrange mound is a ring of 12 (out of an original estimated 35 to 38) large standing stones, which represent the final building stage at the site. The circle was erected around 2000 BC, long after after the great passage tomb had gone out of use, although its presence shows that the area itself still retained some importance for the local population, perhaps connected with astronomy or ancestor worship.

Although there have been various investigations into Newgrange over the years, it was not until 1962 that the first major excavations at the site took place, under Professor Michael J. O'Kelly from the department of archaeology at University College, Cork. During excavations from 1962 to 1975, the massive passage grave underwent extensive restoration, including the rebuilding of the supposedly original facade of sparkling white quartz using a vertical steel reinforced concrete wall. The original white quartz found at Newgrange was not local to the area; it had come from the Wicklow Mountains, 50 miles away, and was probably brought down the River Boyne by boat. O'Kelly's restoration, however, has not been without its critics, who remain unconvinced that Neolithic builders had the technology to fix a retaining wall at such an angle as exists in the reconstruction. Some archaeologists believe that the reconstructed Newgrange represents O'Kelly's 20th-century idea of how the original monument *ought* to have appeared.

The passage graves of Newgrange, Knowth, and Dowth are justly celebrated for their wealth of megalithic (c. 4500–1500 BC) rock art. At Newgrange several of the stones inside and outside the monument are decorated with spiral patterns, cup and ring marks, serpentiforms, circles, dot-in-circles, chevrons, lozenges, radials or star shapes, parallel lines, and comb-devices. For some as yet unknown reason, a number of these stones are carved on their hidden sides so as not to be visible to anyone in the tomb.

The most spectacular piece of megalithic art at Newgrange is on the superb slab lying outside the entrance to the tomb. This recumbent megalith is profusely decorated with lozenge motifs and one of the few known examples of a triple spiral, the other two examples being inside the monument. Such motifs are found on stones in other passage tombs on the Isle of Man and the island of Anglesey in North Wales. Although these motifs were also used in later Celtic art, it is not known what they represent, though perhaps they recorded astronomical and cosmological observations.

One major aspect of the Newgrange monument that is often disputed is its primary function. Excavations inside the chambers revealed relatively few archaeological finds, probably because the majority had been removed in the centuries that the site remained open, from 1699 until it was examined by O'Kelly in 1962. The burials discovered consisted of two inhumations and at least three cremated bodies, all of which were found close to the huge stone basins, which, as has been mentioned, seem to have been used for holding the bones of the dead. Archaeological finds inside the monument have not been spectacular, though a few gold objects have been found, including two gold torcs (a piece of jewelry worn around the neck like a collar), a gold chain, two rings, a large phallus-like stone, a few pendants and beads, a bone chisel, and several bone pins. The lack of pottery finds at Newgrange is typical for passage grave cemeteries, which seem to have been places reserved for certain types of ritualistic activity involving a limited number of people.

The entrance to the Newgrange passage tomb consists of a doorway composed of two standing stones and a horizontal lintel. Above the doorway is an aperture known as the "roof box" or "light box." Every year, shortly after 9 a.m. on the morning of the Winter Solstice, the shortest day of the year, the sun begins its ascent across the Boyne Valley over a hill known locally as Red Mountain, the name possibly originating from the color of the sunrise on this day. The newly risen sun then sends a shaft of sunlight directly through the Newgrange light box, which penetrates down the passageway as a narrow beam of light illuminating the central chamber at the back of the tomb. After just 17 minutes the ray of light narrows and the chamber is once more left in darkness. This spectacular event was not rediscovered until 1967 by professor Michael J. O'Kelly, though it had been known about in local folklore before that time. In fact the monument was known locally as *Uaimh na Gréine* (the "Cave of the Sun"). The Newgrange light box reveals in spectacular fashion the knowledge of surveying and basic astronomy possessed by the Neolithic inhabitants of the area. It also illustrates that, for the people who aligned their monument with the Winter Solstice, the sun must have formed an important part of their religious beliefs.

Recent research into the acoustic properties of ancient monuments carried out by two separate teams, the International Consciousness Research

Laboratories (ICRL), and Aaron Watson, an archaeologist, and David Keating, an acoustic expert, found that Newgrange, along with other Neolithic chamber tombs, possessed the ability to amplify and alter sound. The researchers found that chanting, singing, and drumming inside these structures produced reverberating echoes that may have been utilized as part of ritual activity taking place in the monuments. The researchers were surprised to find that, although the tombs were of many different sizes, their resonant frequencies were very similar. An intriguing idea mentioned in Paul Devereux's *Stone Age Soundtracks* is that, if the blocking slab at the entrance to Newgrange was closed during rituals, the sounds created within would have been intensified. When these mysterious sounds escaped through the roof box they could have had a powerful psychological and physiological effect on those gathered outside, who perhaps interpreted them as the voices of spirits or gods.

There may also have been a visual side to these acoustic effects. Experiments at Princeton University in a replica of the Newgrange passage revealed that, if the chamber was smoky or misty, standing sound waves could be seen as they vibrated particles in the air. Perhaps this visual effect explains the zigzag, spiral, and concentric ring markings engraved on the stones at sites such as Newgrange. Although the research teams do not believe that monuments such as Newgrange were designed with acoustic purposes in mind, it certainly seems possible that Neolithic peoples discovered the effects and utilized them in their religious ceremonies.

Located just more than half a mile northwest of Newgrange and 1.2 miles west of Dowth, the great mound at Knowth was, like Newgrange, constructed about 3200 BC. There is evidence for even earlier activity on the site of the monument dating back to 4000 BC, in the form of the remains of a large wooden house. Excavation at Knowth began in the 1960s, overseen by George Eogan, currently director of the Knowth Research Project and professor emeritus of archaeology at the University College, Dublin, and Helen Roche. Knowth is the largest of the passage graves within the Brú na Bóinne ritual complex, and is at the center of its own miniature ritual complex, surrounded by 18 smaller satellite tombs. The mound at Knowth covers roughly a hectare, and is encircled by 127 kerbstones. It was constructed over two separate passageways, located on opposite sides of the mound. The western passage is 112 feet long and the eastern passage is 131 feet long, terminating in a cruciform chamber. As with the Newgrange passage grave, the three recesses in this chamber contained basin stones, in which the cremated remains of the dead were probably placed. Among the most important finds from excavations at Knowth are pottery, antler and bone pins, stone pendants and beads, a stone phallus, and an exquisite ceremonial flint mace head. After the passage tomb at Knowth had fallen into disuse a timber circle, probably a wooden henge, was constructed near the entrance to its eastern passage. Archaeological evidence in the form of a large number of votive offerings suggests that this area was used for ritual activity. This small wooden circle has now been reconstructed in its original position.

Knowth is best known for its megalithic art. In fact, the Knowth complex has the highest concentration of megalithic art in Europe. Around 250 decorated slabs have been discovered so far, from the main tomb and 12 of its satellites. Apart from the well-known passage grave motifs of spirals, lozenges, zigzags, and serpentiforms, there are also more rare designs including crescent shapes and rays. Generally, there is no consensus as to the meanings of these designs, though it is thought that the rayed design on Kerbstone 15 may represent a sundial or a prehistoric lunar calendar. The decoration on one of the megaliths inside Knowth has recently been touted by astronomer Dr. Philip Stooke of the University of Western Ontario (Canada), as the world's first map of the moon. But looking at the series of arcs carved into the stone it makes an unconvincing moon map. Based on the decoration of this stone and other motifs at Knowth, there have been claims that that the builders of this monument had unparalleled knowledge of the complicated movements of the moon, enabling them to predict eclipses and other astronomical events. In the opinion of Dr. Philip Stooke, speaking to BBC News Online, in April 1999, "They knew a great deal about the motion of the Moon. They were not primitive at all." I think Mike Pitts sums up ideas such as this succinctly when he writes in *Hengeworld* that "without science like mine, runs the clear subtext, these guys were savages."

Dowth is roughly the same size and was built around the same period as Newgrange and Knowth, though, because it has not been properly excavated, considerably less is known about it than its two more famous cousins. However, full-scale excavations at the site got underway in 1998 and are still ongoing. Though the huge mound at Dowth was badly damaged as a result of investigations in 1847 and 48 (though it had probably been pillaged by Vikings long before that), it is still an impressive monument. It has a diameter of around 280 feet and a height of 44 feet, and covers three fifths of a hectare. The mound is ringed by 115 kerbstones, some of which are decorated, and contains two west-facing chambers. The northern passage ("Dowth North") runs for 27 feet and leads to a cruciform chamber with a corbelled roof about 10 feet high. The mound's southern passage ("Dowth South") is much shorter at 11 feet, and leads to a circular chamber about 15 feet in diameter. Many of the megaliths in the passage and chambers are decorated with spirals, chevrons, lozenges and rayed circles, and sun wheel or flower motifs. It has been noted that on the evening of the Winter Solstice, the rays of the sun illuminate the passage of Dowth South, including three decorated stones, one of which contains the possible sun wheel motif. The majority of researchers believe this was intentional on behalf of the builders of the monument.

There seems to be no doubt that the sacred nature of at least two of these three passage graves and their immediate surroundings continued long after the monuments themselves ceased to be used. At Newgrange, various early Iron Age (c. seventh century BC) and Roman precious items, including gold coins, finger rings, beads, two gold pendants, and two brooches, have been discovered at the monument. Considering that some of the objects were in mint condition and that the Romans never invaded Ireland, many of these items must have been votive offerings, probably made by Romans or Romano-British visitors from Britain; perhaps they were ancient pilgrims venerating an already-3,000-year-old religious monument. Knowth came back into use again as a burial site in the Iron Age. There are 35 mostly female burials from the site from this period; 31 of these burials are in pits, and four in cists. They date from 190 BC to AD 250. One particularly interesting grave contained two decapitated males buried with gaming pieces, bone dice, a few bronze rings, and a pegged board game. One theory about the demise of these men is that they were executed for cheating at the game. Although the continued sacredness of Dowth is not attested to, mainly due to the fact that the site has not been properly excavated, there is evidence of its use long after the Neolithic period. At the entrance to the passage of the cruciform tomb is a souterrain dating to the first few centuries AD, with a 70-foot-long passageway leading to a series of chambers with a beehive chamber at either end. It is believed that these underground structures were used as places of refuge and/or as storage areas.

In 1993, due to their significant cultural and historical importance, Newgrange, Knowth, and Dowth were designated a World Heritage Site by UNESCO (United Nations Educational, Scientific and Cultural Organization). The monuments now attract in excess of 200,000 visitors per year, all of which come on guided tours from the Brú na Bóinne Visitor Centre, as there is no longer direct access to the site. For safety reasons, it is not possible to visit Dowth, though it can be viewed from the road. Anyone wanting to visit around December 21st to witness the magnificent Midwinter Solstice may, however, be in for a long wait. In 2006 there were around 27,485 applications to enter the tomb at this time. Consequently, admission to the Newgrange tomb chamber for the Winter Solstice sunrise is by lottery. To enter, it is necessary to fill out an application form, available at the reception desk in the Brú na Bóinne Visitor Centre. In late September, 50 names are drawn—10 for each morning the tomb is illuminated. Two places in the chamber are then given to each of the lucky people whose names are drawn.

Chapter 2

Stonehenge: Prehistory and Legend (England)

Close-up of Stonehenge, showing the huge sarsen stones.
Photograph by author

Huddled together like an isolated group of gray stone giants, the monument of Stonehenge, on Salisbury Plain, Wiltshire, southern England, has a legendary pedigree almost as rich as its archaeological history. In legend and folklore Stonehenge has connections with Merlin the Arthurian magician, giants, the devil, the Druids, miraculous cures, and, in more recent times, UFOs and crop circles.

Though the origin and the development of Stonehenge are fairly well known through archaeological excavation and survey, the purpose of the structure and how it related to the rich prehistoric landscape in which it was placed are not so well understood. There is evidence that the area of Stonehenge was regarded as somewhat special or sacred millennia before stone monuments were being constructed. Three large post holes and a tree hole were discovered during the construction of the modern parking lot at the site, as well as a pit, about 328 feet to the east. These extremely early features were dated to between 8500 and 7650 BC, the Mesolithic period, and, as no artifacts were discovered in association with them, they cannot have been rubbish pits. A ritual function is the most likely explanation, and it has been suggested that the holes may once have held 10–13-foot-high painted totem poles, similar to those erected by some North American Indian tribes. Indeed, looking at the evidence, it is diffcult to escape the conclusion that these Mesolithic pits and long-vanished posts represent the earliest evidence of the monument tradition in the landscape that was to culminate in the construction of Stonehenge itself.

The evidence so far recovered for human presence in the Stonehenge area after these "totem poles," during the period from 7500 BC to the beginnings of the Neolithic, around 4000 BC, is from scattered finds, mainly flint tools, rather than structures. However, a number of monuments were constructed in the early Neolithic period (c. 4000–3000 BC), one of the earliest of which is the causwayed enclosure (a type of large prehistoric earthwork) known as Robin Hood's Ball, 2.8 miles northwest of Stonehenge. Robin Hood's Ball was occupied, though not necessarily on a permanent basis, around 3700 BC. Other monuments in the area predating Stonehenge include the Winterbourne Stoke long barrow (communal burial chamber) and the Lesser Cursus (a long, narrow, rectangular earthwork enclosure). Thus, when the builders of the first stage of construction at Stonehenge began work, they were already operating in a sacred landscape, one that had seen habitation and ritual use for more than 5,000 years.

The first of the three major construction phases at Stonehenge was a circular "henge" earthwork completed about 2950 BC. A henge, in the archaeological sense, is a circular or oval-shaped flat area enclosed by a boundary earthwork. This feature was about 360 feet in diameter and had at least three entrances, the largest of which opened to the northeast. The monument was dug by hand using deer antlers and the shoulder blades of oxen or cattle, and modern excavations of the ditch have recovered antlers used in the construction that seem to have been deliberately left behind by the builders of the structure. One odd fact about this phase is that there were other animal bones, namely ox jaws, ox skulls, and the bones of red deer, placed in the bottom of the ditch near the entrance, which radio carbon dating showed to be between 50 and 850 years older than the antler tools used to dig the structure. It seems that the people who deposited these antique items had kept them within the family/clan group for a considerable time before burial; perhaps the bones were sacred objects removed from a previous ritual location and brought to Stonehenge.

Around 2800 BC, a ring of 56 equally spaced pits, known as the Aubrey Holes, were dug immediately inside the bank. The features are named after 17th-century antiquarian John Aubrey, and may once have held timber posts, though their function is still disputed. There is little remaining evidence for Phase II at Stonehenge, though, judging by finds of cremated bones from as many as 70 bodies, the site must have functioned as a cremation cemetery. One of these cremations contained a polished stone macehead, created from piece of black and white gneiss, a high-grade metamorphic rock not found locally, but existing in the north and west of Britain. This object may suggest that the body was brought some distance to be buried at Stonehenge and thus that the site possessed a reputation for sacredness at this time.

Phase III at Stonehenge, beginning around 2550 BC, involved the refashioning of the simple earth and timber henge into a unique stone monument. In the first stage, two concentric circles (sometimes known as the "Double Bluestone Circle") of 80 "bluestone" (dolerite, rhyolite, and tuff) pillars were erected at the center of the monument, with a main entrance to the northeast. These bluestones, weighing about 4 tons each, originate in the Preseli Hills (Pembrokeshire, southwest Wales), and were probably transported from there to Salisbury Plain over a route at least 185 miles long (see Chapter 3). Apart from the bluestones, a 16.4-foot-long greenish sandstone slab, now known as the Altar Stone, was brought to Stonehenge from somewhere between Kidwelly (near Milford Haven on the coast to the south of the Preseli Hills) and Abergavenny (in southeast Wales). It is thought that that the northeastern entrance to the enclosure was remodelled during Phase III so that it precisely aligned with the midsummer sunrise and midwinter sunset of the period. Outside this entrance, another feature, known as the Avenue, was added to the Stonehenge landscape. The Avenue (probably a ceremonial pathway) consists of a parallel pair of ditches and banks stretching for 1.5 miles from Stonehenge down to the River Avon.

There is a tantalizing glimpse of what may be a memory of the transportation of the bluestones over a great distance to Salisbury Plain in the most famous legend connected with Stonehenge. The story is found in Geoffrey of Monmouth's *The History of the Kings of Britain (c. 1136)* and describes how Aurelius Ambrosius, King of the Britons, desired to have a monument constructed to commemorate the massacre of 460 British nobles by the troops of Hengist the Saxon. On the advice of prophet and magician Merlin, the King sent his brother Uther Pendragon (the father of King Arthur), with an army of fifteen thousand men to bring back a stone structure called the "Giants' Dance" from a mountain called Killare (possibly Kildare) in Ireland. Merlin describes the Giants' Dance, according to Geoffrey of Monmouth's *The History of the Kings of Britain (c. 1136)*, as a "structure of stones there, which none of this age could raise, without a profound knowledge of the mechanical arts." Uther Pendragon's army were unable to budge the huge stones and so turned to Merlin, who, using "his own engines," dismantled the stones, which were then transported to Britain by ship. Whether or not this tale is a distorted memory of the actual journey of the bluestones from somewhere in "the west" is much debated, though the mention of "engines" is certainly intriguing. Nevertheless, it would be an inordinately long time for even a fragment of the event to have survived orally.

It had previosuly been thought that, around 2400 BC, the bluestones were dug up and replaced by enormous sarsen blocks brought from a quarry around 24 miles to the north, on the Marlborough Downs. However, recent work led by Mike Parker Pearson, professor of archaeology at the University of Sheffield, has suggested redating the sarsen phase to 2640–2480 BC, which would obviously affect the chronology of the site significantly. Thirty of these huge sarsens, each around 13.5 feet high and 7 feet wide, and weighing around 25 tons, were set up in a 98 foot diameter circle. On top of these were placed smaller sarsen lintels (horizontal stones) spanning the tops and held in place by mortice and tenon joints. Within this sarsen circle, a horseshoe-shaped setting of 15 more sarsens, making five trilithons (two large stones set upright to support a third on their top), was erected. Somewhere between 2280 and 1900 BC, the bluestones were re-erected and arranged at least three times, finally forming an inner circle and horseshoe between the sarsen circle and the trilithons, mirroring the two arrangements of sarsen stones. This arrangement is essentially the monument that we see the remains of today.

Between 2030 and 1520 BC, a double ring of oblong pits, known as the Y and Z holes, were dug outside the outermost sarsen circle, possibly to take another setting of stones. However, there is no evidence that the holes ever held stones or wooden posts, and they were eventually allowed to silt up naturally. The Y and Z holes seem to mark the end of significant activity at the site, and, after c1520 BC, there was no further construction at Stonehenge, and the monument appears to have been abandoned. Nevertheless, the site was occasionally visited, as is evidenced by finds of a crouched adult inhumation burial (770–410 BC), Iron Age (c800 BC– AD 43) pottery, 20 Roman coins, and the burial of a decapitated Saxon man, possibly the victim of an execution, dated to the seventh century AD.

From 2004 to 2006, sensational results were obtained from excavations led by Mike Parker Pearson at the henge site of Durrington Walls (in use between 3100–2400 BC), about 2 miles to the northeast of Stonehenge. Pearson's Stonehenge Riverside Project, a joint collaboration between archaeologists at the Universities of Sheffield, Manchester, Bristol, UCL, and Bournemouth, unearthed a huge settlement whose houses have been radiocarbon dated to 2600–2500 BC. These dates make the settlement contemporary with the beginning of the stone-built monument at Stonehenge, and archaeologists believe that the inhabitants of the Neolithic settlement, the largest ever found in Britain, were the builders of Stonehenge. The huge quantities of pig and cattle bones, pottery, and flint indicate not only intense occupation of the site, but also a high rate of food consumption. Parker Pearson believes the settlement was not lived in year-round but was used for huge ceremonial feasts at midwinter, which attracted people from a wide area. Parker Pearson also speculated that, after the feasts, certain members of the community would travel down Durrington Wall's ceremonial "avenue" to deposit their dead in the River Avon. They would then have traveled up to the Stonehenge Avenue and on to Stonehenge, where they cremated and buried the most important of their dead.

A vivid illustration of the importance of Stonehenge and its possible renown as a sacred healing centre during prehistory is the burial known as the "Amesbury Archer," discovered in 2002 at Amesbury, about 3 miles southeast of Stonehenge. Dated between 2400 and 2200 BC, this extremely rich burial included five Beaker pots, 16 beautifully worked flint arrowheads, boars' tusks, two sandstone wrist guards (to protect the wrists from the bow string of a bow and arrow), a pair of gold hair ornaments, three tiny copper knives, and a kit of flint-knapping and metalworking tools. One of the copper knives was of Spanish origin, and the gold may also have come from outside Britain. Studies of the skeletal remains by Jackie McKinley revealed that the Archer was a strongly built man aged between 35 and 45, though he had an abscess on his jaw and had suffered an accident when young that had torn his left kneecap off. Thus for much of his life the "Archer" would have walked with a pronounced limp. Research using oxygen isotope analysis on the Archer's tooth enamel found that he had grown up in the Alps region, either Switzerland, Austria, or Germany. Could this man have come to Stonehenge as an ancient pilgrim in search of healing? It is certainly an absorbing possibility.

There are traces of a belief in the healing properties of Stonehenge current in the 12th century AD, recorded by Geoffrey of Monmouth. Geoffrey states (*History of the Kings of Britain* 8:11):

> For in these stones is a mystery, and a healing virtue against many ailments…for they washed the stones and poured the water into baths, whereby those who were sick were cured. Moreover, they mixed confections of herbs with the water, whereby those who were wounded were healed, for not a stone is there that is wanting in virtue of leechcraft.

Such folkloric beliefs regarding the stones were still held in the locality of Stonehenge in the time of antiquary and writer John Aubrey (1626–97), who wrote that "pieces (or powder) of these stones putt into their Wells doe drive away the Toades, with which their Wells are much infected" (cited in L.V. Grinsell's article, "Legendary History and Folklore of Stonehenge," in *Folklore*). Indeed the alleged healing properties of ancient stones is not unique to Stonehenge: It is also found in connection with a number of other megalithic monuments (for example, to Mên-an-Tol, a holed stone in Cornwall, and the Long Stone, a standing stone in Minchinhampton, Gloucestershire).

Stonehenge shares a number of other folklore motifs with other prehistoric monuments, one of which is the "countless stones" also found at the Rollright Stones in Oxfordshire (see Chapter 6) and a stone circle known as Long Meg and Her Daughters in Cumbria (in the northwest of England). The earliest reference so far discovered to the belief that the stones at Stonehenge cannot be counted is in a sonnet by Sir Philip Sidney (1554–86):

> Neere Wilton sweete, huge heapes of stones are found,
> But so confusde, that neither any eye
> Can count them just, nor Reason reason trye,
> What force brought them to so unlikely ground.
> ("The Seven Wonders of England," 1: 598)

After his defeat at the Battle of Worcester on September 3, 1651, King Charles II spent time at the stones counting and recounting them, but was unable to arrive at a definite amount. *Robinson Crusoe* author Daniel Defoe (1659/61–1731) seems to be the origin of the tale that in order to accurately count the stones, a baker laid a loaf of bread upon every stone, but still could not reach the same number twice.

Another familiar theme in the tales surrounding megalithic monuments is the involvement of the devil in their construction. A sarsen boulder on the Hampshire-Wiltshire border, about 6 miles to the east of Stonehenge, and another in a field close to the village of East Knoyle, southwest of the monument, were said to have been dropped by the devil when flying over the areas to build Stonehenge. The "Giants' Dance," was, according to Geoffrey of Monmouth, the name by which Stonehenge was once known. This title reflects a common motif in the folklore of many prehistoric stone circles in which people are turned to stone for dancing or playing games on the Sabbath. Whether the name "Giants' Dance" predates Geoffrey of Monmouth is not clear, though in a letter to the archaeologist Leslie Grinsell in 1974 (and cited in his article, "The Legendary History and Folklore of Stonehenge"), Mr. R.S. Newall mentions that on very hot days when one approaches Stonehenge from a valley known as Spring Bottom, the stones of the monument appear to "dance off the ground in the shimmering hot air." Perhaps this optical illusion is the origin of the Giants' Dance name, though how far back in history or prehistory this effect was noticed, if at all, is unknown.

It seems that the modern versions of such folklore are the stories of UFOs, aliens, and crop circles sometimes attached to ancient monuments. Though many researchers would argue for the objective reality of such "paranormal" phenomena, and their intimate connection with ancient sites such as Stonehenge, the evidence, or lack of it, does not bear this out. Although UFOs have been reported in the immediate vicinity of Stonehenge from time to time, there is not an unusually high volume of reports, and there is also no evidence that the site itself attracts unusual phenomena. Similarly, crop circles (a phenomenon where an area of the crop has been mysteriously laid flat often into a circular or other more complicated pattern), though sometimes reported in the area of Stonehenge, are usually found to be man-made. One particularly spectacular example appeared on July 7, 1996, in a field just south of Stonehenge, and was given the name "the Stonehenge Julia Set." (A Julia Set is a specific kind of shape derived from fractal geometry.) The intricate design of the glyph, which measured 900 by 500 feet and contained 151 circles, and its impressive execution, persuaded most crop circle researchers that this particular design could not be the work of humans. Nevertheless, construction rings were discovered by investigators located in strategic spots around the formation, indicating the man-made origin of the crop circle. An interview on the circlemakers Website (*www.circlemakers.org*) also provides evidence that a group of circle "artists" were responsible for the design.

Chapter 3

The Sacred Megaliths of the Preseli Hills (Wales)

The Preseli Hills (or Mountains) in north Pembrokeshire (southwest Wales), are perhaps best known as the place of origin of the stones that make up the bluestone circle and inner horseshoe at the Neolithic and Bronze Age monument of Stonehenge, in Wiltshire, southern England. But Preseli, now within the confines of the modern

Pentre Ifan dolmen.

Pembrokeshire Coast National Park, is also home to a wide range of archaeological sites; in fact, the area represents an entire prehistoric landscape. There are Mesolithic remains going back about 9,000 years, a Neolithic stone-axe factory, Neolithic/Bronze Age funerary and ritual features such as chambered tombs, cairns, henges, and stone circles, as well as ancient settlements, hillforts, and trackways.

Preseli lies roughly 245 miles east northeast of Stonehenge and has been considered a likely source of the bluestones since the mid-19th century. The bluestones, so named because of their color when wet, consist primarily of spotted dolerite but also include rhyolite and volcanic ash. One hypothesized route for their transport to Wiltshire begins with the stones being first dragged down from Preseli to the sea at Milford Haven, possibly on sledges or wooden rollers, then floated on huge rafts hugging the southern coast of Wales, brought up the River Avon to the place where Bristol now stands, pulled overland to a point close to modern Warminster, floated down the River Wylye to Salisbury, and finally up the Avon River to West Amesbury, near Stonehenge. This was obviously a complicated and dangerous voyage, especially bearing in mind that the bluestones weigh up to 4 tons each. But perhaps it was the perilous journey itself that gave the stones special value. Unlike modern architects and builders, those who constructed Stonehenge may not have been thinking in terms of safety and efficiency. There have, however, been objections to the human transport idea, by some researchers; Aubrey Burl, for example, believes the bluestones were in fact moved to Salisbury Plain by glaciers. Most recently, in the February 2006 issue of *The Oxford Journal of Archaeology* a team from the Open University also backed the glacial hypothesis after analyzing and comparing prehistoric bluestone axes from England and Wales. They also put forward the theory that the bluestones at Stonehenge came from many different sources both within and outside the Preseli area.

Although it is indeed possible that there is a geological explanation for the presence of the bluestones at Stonehenge, there are one or two factors that favor human agency. The first is the presence of a group of skeletons known as the "Boscombe Bowmen," discovered in a single grave close to Stonehenge and dated to the Early Bronze Age (about 2300 BC). These individuals (three children, a teenager, and three men) have become known as "bowmen" from the amount of flint arrowheads found in their grave. Tests by scientists of the British Geological Survey on the strontium isotopes in the Bowmen's teeth show that they originated in a place where the rocks are very radioactive (in this case south Wales), but had migrated to southern Britain in childhood. Given that the Boscombe Bowmen were roughly contemporary with the transport and erection of the Welsh bluestones at Stonehenge, many reseachers believe that they may have accompanied the stones on their 245-mile trek to Salisbury Plain.

In 2005, work led by Professor Timothy Darvill and Professor Geoff Wainwright of Bournemouth University identified the primary quarry area for the Stonehenge bluestones at a remote site on Carn Menyn ("Butter Rock"), in the Preseli Hills. Geochemical analysis of the rocks from a small enclosure high up on the hill confirmed that bluestone from this spot were used to build part of Stonehenge. Intriguingly, there are a number of prehistoric sites located close to Carn Menyn, one of which is Bedd Arthur ("Arthur's Grave"), an oval or horseshoe-shaped setting of stones. This monument, which lies next to an ancient trackway leading to Carn Menyn, may be the remains of a henge, and there has been speculation that its horseshoe shape may have influenced the form of the inner horseshoe of bluestones at Stonehenge. There is a tantalising hint of an important lost stone circle in the area in Daniel Defoe's *A Tour through England and Wales* (1724), where the writer mentions seeing "near Kily-maen lwyd [llwyd], on a great Mountain, a Circle of mighty Stones, very much like Stone-henge in Wiltshire."

Bedd Arthur is one of many prehistoric monuments in and around Preseli associated with the legendary King Arthur. Others include the standing stones known as Cerrig Meibion Arthur ("The Stones of Arthur's Sons"), which, according to legend, mark the spot where King Arthur's sons were killed by a wild boar from Ireland, known as the "Twrch Trwyth," a natural outcrop called Cerrig Marchogion ("The Stones of the Knights [of Arthur]"), a chambered tomb known as Coetan Arthur ("Arthur's Quoit"), and a standing stone known as Carreg Fyrddin ("Merlin's Stone"), on the outskirts of the town of Carmarthen. This last monument supposedly marks the spot where Merlin once hid his treasure, and the Arthurian magician is said to have prophesized that a raven would one day drink a man's blood off the stone. In 1876 the vicar of Newchurch wrote that a man searching for treasure beneath Merlin's Stone was crushed to death by the megalith falling on him, and it took five horses to drag the stone back into position. There may be a connection here with the well known legend recorded in Geoffrey of Monmouth's (c. AD 1100–c1155) *History of the Kings of Britain*, where Merlin has a huge structure known as the Giant's Dance magically transported from Ireland to Salisbury Plain to become Stonehenge (see Chapter 2). Could this legend be a distorted memory of the journey of the bluestones from Wales, a confused oral tradition of a long, difficult journey from "the west"?

One has to assume that, if the bluestones were hauled all the way from Preseli to Stonehenge, there was something intrinsically special or sacred about them, the journey, or their place of origin. If the area of the quarry site on Carn Menyn was a venerated place, or the stones taken to Wiltshire came from a previously existing monument, then the bluestone structures at Stonehenge may have "inherited" some of that monument's sacredness. There are other examples of taking a piece of an already venerated place, not always an archaeological site, in order to endow a new place with its perceived value. The previously mentioned ritual deposits in the ditch of the first of the henges at Stonehenge is an example.

The most impressive of the many prehistoric monuments in the Preseli Hills is the spectacularly situated Pentre Ifan ("Ivan's Village"), the largest and best preserved dolmen (burial chamber) in Wales. Located about 3 miles east of the seaside village of Newport, Pentre Ifan dates from around 3500 BC. Its massive capstone, almost 17 feet in length and weighing 16 tonnes, is delicately balanced 8 feet off the ground on three upright megaliths. According to W.Y. Evans-Wentz, in his book, *The Fairy-Faith in Celtic Countries* (1911), local legend describes the "Tlwyth Teg," or Welsh fairy folk, as being seen around the monument. The fairies were described by one witness in the early 20th century as "little children in clothes like soldiers' clothes and with red caps." The Pentre Ifan structure is thought to have been used for communal burials and was once covered by a 120-foot-long trapezoidal earthen mound.

There are similarities between Pentre Ifan and the court tombs of Ireland, the earliest type of stone tomb found in the country, which were built mainly between 4000 and 3500 BC. The Irish court tombs were so-called because of the uncovered forecourt area ("court") in front of the tomb entrance, which also occurs at Pentre Ifan, and were probably used for some type of funerary rituals before burial. Excavations in 1935 at the Creevykeel court tomb in County Sligo, Ireland, showed that at least part of its function was funerary. Finds included four cremation burials, Neolithic pottery, flint arrow heads, polished stone axes, and other artifacts, including a chalk ball. However, although excavations at Pentre Ifan in 1936–37 and 1958–59 discovered a "ritual" pit with signs of burning and an irregular line of small stone-holes, no burials were discovered, and the number of artifacts recovered was very small. This is somewhat enigmatic, as is the north-south orientation of the structure, and the fact that the sloping angle of the capstone, which dips towards the Afon valley to the north, mirrors the slopes of Carn Ingli ("The Mountain of Angels") when seen from the site.

The sacred hill of Carn Ingli, actually an extinct volcano, takes its name from the sixth-century Celtic St. Brynach, who experienced visions and held conversations with angels in a cave on the summit there. High places are often considered as sacred, perhaps because of their lofty positions removed from the everyday world, and also as somewhere that it takes time and effort to reach. Carn Ingli was certainly one such place. This prominent hill, which has a spectacular Iron Age (c. 800 BC to AD 50) fortified settlement on its summit, was of obvious importance to the Neolithic inhabitants of the Nevern Valley area of the Preseli range. It is an interesting fact that, though none of the Neolithic monuments of the area are visible to each other, they all occupy a position in the landscape that allows clear views of Carn Ingli, looming above. The sacred hill must have been a central part of the ritual landscape of Preseli.

Researchers George Children and George Nash believe the different types of monuments in the Preseli Hills had distinct meanings for the Neolithic inhabitants of the area. In their opinion, the chambered tombs represent death or the final resting place of the body, and Gors Fawr stone circle, at the foot of the Preseli Hills not too far away from Pentre Ifan, may symbolize the beginning of that death—an enclosed liminal are where the dead could be viewed. The groups of standing stones, these researchers believe, define the processional route of the deceased person, between their journey from stone circle to tomb. In effect the person's remains were being moved around the ritual landscape from one monument to another, before reaching their final resting place in larger tombs such as Pentre Ifan, which had room enough to allow ceremonial activities to take place. Children and Nash think it possible that this circulation of remains may have been performed in imitation of the seasonal movements of hunter-gather ancestors.

When considering the remains of tombs such as Pentre Ifan, it is important to remember that the megaliths of such monuments were not exposed as they are today; they once had a covering mound and must have appeared as an organic part of the natural surroundings. For the Neolithic inhabitants of the Preseli Hills, and elsewhere in Britain and Ireland, the construction of such megalithic monuments was something that established their identity within this landscape, and, by using the monuments in the performance of rituals connected with the ancestors, they dramatized their own historical place in their chosen area.

Chapter 4

Maes Howe (Scotland)

Entrance to Maes Howe.

Among the finest ancient monuments in Europe, the chamber tomb/passage grave of Maes Howe is situated in Mainland Orkney, one of a group of 70 or so islands located 10 miles off the northern coast of Scotland. The Orkney Islands have been inhabited for at least 5,500 years and are home to an impressive range of prehistoric stone structures, the most important of which belong to the Neolithic period (c. 4000–2200 BC). One particularly fascinating group of Neolithic monuments on Orkney is located in the parish of Stennes and has become known as the "Heart of Neolithic Orkney." The main monuments in this group, now a UNESCO World Heritage Site, include Maes Howe, the prehistoric village of Skara Brae, the Ring o' Brodgar stone circle, and the Stones of Stenness, a stone circle and henge monument (roughly circular area enclosed by a ditch with an external bank).

Maes Howe has been dated to around 2800 BC, though it may have been built over an earlier structure. Its flat-topped grassy mound, which measures 115 feet in diameter and 24 feet high, lies on a circular platform enclosed inside an oval, rock-cut ditch. Inside the earthwork are a large central chamber, around 15 feet square, three side chambers, and a 36-foot-long entrance passageway. The stone-built chambers inside the tomb were constructed with extreme skill, the large dressed stones fitted together perfectly without the use of mortar. The plan of Maes Howe is similar in many respects to passage graves in Ireland, such as Newgrange. Another aspect of Maes Howe shared by Newgrange is its alignment, the entrance to both structures facing southwest, in the direction of the midwinter sunset. At the time of Midwinter Solstice the rays from the setting sun shine down through the entrance passageway at Maes Howe, illuminating the back wall of the central chamber. Also connected with this alignment is a 10-foot-tall standing stone known as the "Barnhouse Stone," located about half a mile to the southwest of Maes Howe, and directly aligned with its entrance and the sun at midwinter. The illumination of Maes Howe's chamber was part of local folklore long before the effect was discovered at the site by archaeologists, something else shared by Newgrange, where local legends also described the sun shining down the corridor of the tomb on the shortest day of the year. The accuracy of some of these legends is a valuable reminder of the importance of folk memories in connection with ancient monuments.

A fascinating new theory about the ditch encircling Maes Howe links it with another Neolithic monument, Silbury Hill, far to the south among the sacred sites around the village of Avebury in Wiltshire. When the Orkneys suffered floods in the winter of 2006 the ditch around Maes Howe was filled to the brim with water, dramatically illustrating archeologist Dr. Colin Richards's idea that the ditch was intended by its original builders to be filled with water, so acting as a visible barrier between the world of the living and that of the dead. As some researchers have theorized about the surrounding ditch at Silbury, perhaps the mirror-like effect of the water-filled ditch was utilized as the focus for ritual and ceremony at the site.

Another recently investigated aspect of Maes Howe, the Ring o' Brodgar, and a number of other stone monuments all over the world, is its acoustic properties. After studying the acoustics of Maes Howe, archaeologist and artist Dr. Aaron Watson found that sound behaved in a significantly different way inside the stone chambers than it did in the outside world. Watson concluded (quoted in Paul Devereux's *Stone Age Soundtracks* [2001]) that "the precise joining of the dry-stone walling creates a virtually unbroken surface from which sound can reflect. For this reason, sounds within this resonant cavity are heard quite differently, appearing fuller and louder." Watson believes that this effect was deliberately engineered by the Neolithic builders of the passage grave, and was intended to add another dimension to the sacred atmosphere of the structure when it was being used for shamanistic activities.

Recent work on the art of megalithic structures by Richard Bradley, professor of archaeology at the University of Reading in the UK, and Dr. Tim Philips, also at Reading, has revealed that the interior walls and ceilings of Maes Howe, and other tombs in Orkney, were probably painted. Illuminating the tombs using carefully positioned spotlights, the two researchers discovered clearly inscribed abstract motifs on the walls that probably represent the marking-out lines for tomb paintings that have not survived. Perhaps these paintings represent the visual aspect of shamanistic rituals held at Maes Howe, which also used sound to enhance the atmosphere. So, rather than being a silent and somber monument to the dead, on certain occasions the brightly painted interior of Maes Howe may have resonated with the sounds of singing, chanting, and drum beating, as part of rituals where shamans or priests attempted communication with the spirits of their ancestors.

When Maes Howe eventually fell out of use, it lay abandoned and forgotten for thousands of years, until the mid-12th century when Vikings crusaders Earl Harald Maddadarson and Ragnvald, Earl of Moer, forced their way into the tomb and looted it on their way to a crusade in the Holy Land. As they sheltered inside the monuments from a violent snowstorm, the Norsemen carved graffiti runes (the characters in several alphabets used by ancient Germanic peoples) on the walls of the main chamber. They carved 30 individual inscriptions in all, one of the largest collections of runes in Europe. The Vikings also left three engraved figures: an enigmatic dragon-like figure, a walrus with a fish in its mouth, and a knotted serpent. The Norse runes at Maes Howe confirm what is written in one of the Icelandic sagas known as the *Orkneyinga Saga,* compiled between AD 1192 and 1206. In this saga we have a fascinating semi-legendary interpretation of the first conquest of Orkney by Norway, and a description of the Norsemen's visits to Maes Howe, or "Orkahaugr," as they called it.

Very little is known of the original content of Maes Howe. When the tomb was originally investigated in 1861 by archaeologist James Farrer, only a single fragment of a human skull and some horse bones were recovered from the side chambers. Despite the lack of finds from the grave, the local paper, *The Orcadian,* for July 20, 1861, in true mid-19th-century fashion, carried unsourced reports that archaeologists had discovered two female mummies and also "the skeleton of a gentleman over ten feet long."

A similar story is told in Jo Ben's 16th-century *Descriptio Insularum Orchadiarum* ("Descriptions of Orkney"), where it is alleged that the skeleton of a 14-foot tall man was discovered in a tomb "on a little hill near to the lake." Ben also states that "money was found under the head of the dead man." These stories certainly have the ring of local folklore, perhaps retaining distant memories of a tradition of the burial of a powerful chief, possibly a Viking, within the chamber. The tradition may also be connected to another local piece of folklore about a strange creature called the Hogboy, from the Norse *haugbui,* ghost of the tomb, said to inhabit the grave of Maes Howe. Most of the mounds scattered over the Orkney Islands were formerly the dwellings of these supernatural creatures and a belief in the particularly bad-tempered example living at Maes Howe survived right up until the time of the excavation of the tomb, possibly even longer. Perhaps the Hogboy traditions at the site are remnants of beliefs in an ancestral spirit dwelling within the mound, possibly related to the burial of an early Norse prince inside the tomb.

Five of the Viking runes discovered at Maes Howe refer to a great treasure being discovered inside the tomb. One theory is that this treasure was roughly contemporary with the erection of the monument around 2800 BC, though whether the goods accompanying a Neolithic burial would have been rich enough to be regarded as a great treasure by the Vikings is doubtful. Just a few miles from Maes Howe lies a large Bronze Age cemetery known as "The Knowes of Trotty." This cemetery, which dates back around 4,000 years, consists of at least 16 barrows, or burial mounds, from which four beautifully crafted gold "sun discs," numerous amber beads, and burnt human bones have been recovered. These finds were unearthed from the largest of the barrows in 1858 by local anti-quarian George Petrie, and one wonders whether they may represent a part of the treasure mentioned by the Vikings.

Another theory regarding the treasure mentioned in the runes is that it belonged to a ninth-century early Viking chieftain burial within Maes Howe, an idea supported by archaeological evidence showing that the outer bank of the grave was partly rebuilt during the ninth century. The lack of sub-stantial remains from the Neolithic burials when the structure was opened in 1861 would also be explained by Viking reuse of the tomb. The Vikings would almost certainly have removed the earlier burials from the chambers before they buried their own dead.

Some researchers have interpreted the possible dragon carved at Maes Howe as the guardian of the treasure contained within, as dragons were often seen as the keepers of treasure in European folklore. Examples from England include a giant worm or dragon that guarded a supposedly vast treasure hoard at Cissbury Ring Iron Age hillfort, on the South Downs in Sussex, and others at the prehistoric barrow of Wormelow Tump (now destroyed) in Herefordshire, and at a large 12th-century castle mound called Money Hill at Gunnerton, Northumberland. One of the Viking carv-ings at Maes Howe also mentions another great treasure hidden to the northwest of the mound. Remarkably, in 1858, a hoard of more than a hundred Viking silver ornaments, the largest ever found in Scotland, was discovered near the parish church of Sandwick, only 7 miles northwest of Maes Howe. The hoard, which includes nine brooches, 14 necklets, 27 armlets, Arab coins, and various ingots and silver fragments, is believed to date from the mid-10th century AD. Though the treasure, known as the Skaill Viking Hoard (due to the proximity of the find spot to the Bay of Skaill), would appear to be a serious contender for the great treasure mentioned in the runes, the exact origin of the spectacular find is still in doubt. Many researchers believe that, rather than being a treasure buried to accompany a great Viking leader into the next world, the Skaill Viking Hoard was deposited in the ground for safe-keeping until its owner was able return to claim it.

The treasure of Maes Howe has also been linked with an account in the Old English epic poem *Beowulf,* probably composed sometime in the eighth century AD. The poem describes a great dragon lurking beneath the earth in a huge funeral barrow, jealously guarding its vast hoard of treasure for three hundred years. A thief breaks into the barrow through a secret passageway that runs underneath the mound, tricks the dragon, and makes away with a gem encrusted goblet. The dragon takes violent revenge on the neighborhood before being slain by Beowulf, who is himself killed in the struggle by a fatal bite on his neck. Some believe there are traces in *Beowulf* of the original Neolithic burial and its grave goods at Maes Howe, or perhaps the runes on the walls of the grave were written by Vikings who were familiar with the story of the dragon and its treasure from *Beowulf.*

According to popular tradition Maes Howe was sealed up again soon after the Viking runes were carved, an act linked with the description in the *Orkneyinga Saga* of two Viking warriors who went mad after staying in the dark tomb overnight. The roof of the structure did indeed collapse, probably soon after the Vikings broke in, blocking the chamber, but whether this was done intentionally, perhaps to imprison the belligerent Hogboy, is something we will probably never know.

Chapter 5

Avebury Ritual Landscape (England)

Huge stones at the southern entrance to Avebury henge.
Photograph by author

The area surrounding the village of Avebury, on the edge of the Marlborough Downs (in Wiltshire, southern England), boasts some of the most remarkable and important prehistoric monuments in the world. Avebury is one the richest of a number of areas in Britain and Ireland that became the focus of ceremonial and ritual activity during the Neolithic and Early Bronze Age (other examples being Stonehenge, 20 miles to the south, and Newgrange, north of Dublin in Ireland; see chapters 2 and 1, respectively). Similar to Stonehenge, Avebury has also become linked with modern as well as ancient mysteries, and is often connected in the popular imagination with crop circles, ley lines (hypothetical alignments of a number of places of geographical interest, often as ancient monuments), psychic phenomena, and UFOs.

The complex of monuments around Avebury covers an area of 8.7 square miles and includes the Avebury henge and stone circles, the Beckhampton and West Kennett megalithic Avenues, the huge manmade mound of Silbury Hill, the West Kennet Long Barrow (a Neolithic burial monument comprising stone-built chambers covered by a rectangular or trapezoidal earthen mound), Windmill Hill causewayed enclosure (ancient settlement), and a complex timber and stone monument known as "The Sanctuary." These major monuments are now part of what is collectively known as the "Avebury World Heritage Site," in recognition of their importance to our understanding of prehistoric life in the region and in Britain as a whole. The earliest monuments in the Avebury area, the Windmill Hill settlement and the 340-foot-long West Kennett Long Barrow, both date to around 3700 BC. These structures show that, long before the peak period of ritual activity and huge monuments in the area, lasting roughly from 3000 to 2200 BC, impressive ceremonial buildings were already being constructed by a sophisticated and organized culture.

The apparent heart of prehistoric Avebury is the enormous henge, which encloses part of the village of Avebury. This vast circular earthwork has a diameter of 1,378 feet and encloses an area of 28.5 acres, with four entrances (on the south-southeast, west-southwest, north-northwest, and east-northeast). Although massive, the henge at Avebury is not unique; others of similar size exist. The largest henge in Britain, at Marden (in the Vale of Pewsey, Wiltshire), encloses an area of 34.6 acres, and Mount Pleasant, in Dorset, is of a similar size to Avebury. The ditch of the henge at Avebury was once an enormous 69 feet wide and 33 feet deep, and even after centuries of weathering and vandalism the bank still stands 13 to 20 feet high and the ditch 13 to 16.4 feet deep. The henge encloses a massive stone circle placed within the circumference of the ditch, known as the Outer Circle, which consists of 95–100 standing sarsen stones, the largest stone circle in Britain. Some of these undressed megaliths weigh more than 60 tonnes, and, similar to the sarsens at Stonehenge, were brought, probably on wooden rollers, from quarries on the Marlborough Downs. Inside the Outer Circle are two smaller stone circles, the Northern and Southern Inner Circles, both almost 330 feet in diameter and consisting of 25–30 sarsen stones. Within the Northern Circle are various other settings of megaliths, the most impressive of which is the Cove, a small enclosure of three massive sarsen slabs open to the northeast. One of the stones that made up this setting fell in 1713 and was afterward destroyed.

Avebury henge and its interior stone settings were constructed in at least two stages over the period 2900–2600 BC, and the evidence indicates that it did not follow a single pre-designed plan but was an ongoing project between these dates. Leading away from the south and west entrances to the henge are the remains of two Late Neolithic (around 2500–2300 BC) rows of paired stones, the West Kennet and Beckhampton Avenues. Both Avenues are almost 50 feet wide, and consist of 5- to 10-foot-high sarsen blocks spaced every 65 to 100 feet or so. The West Kennet Avenue runs a serpentine course across the countryside for about 1 1/2 miles to the now destroyed timber and stone ritual site at the Sanctuary, on Overton Hill. Though little remains today of the Beckhampton Avenue, recent excavation and survey have revealed that, similar to the West Kennet stone row, it also follows an undulating course. The Beckhampton Avenue runs for at least a mile towards the Longstones (also known as the Devil's Quoits) at Beckhampton, the remains of a cove similar to the one inside of the Avebury henge.

The imposing and enigmatic flat-topped earthwork of Silbury Hill, the largest manmade mound in Europe, at 128 feet high, lies about 1.2 miles to the south of the Avebury henge. Silbury was probably begun around 2900 BC, though it did not achieve its final form until about 2500–2350 BC, which would make it contemporary with the two Avebury stone avenues, the Sanctuary, and the Beckhampton Cove. Despite various explorations and excavations at Silbury over the centuries (Professor Richard Atkinson's BBC-sponsored excavations from 1968 to 1970 are the most recent and the most comprehensive), we are still in the dark as to its function. Very few prehistoric artifacts have been recovered from the site, and no burials have ever been found. Perhaps the mound itself contains nothing at all and was constructed to mark a location believed by its Neolithic builders to be special or sacred.

Although the ritual constructions surrounding Avebury began as unconnected monuments, by the end of the Neolithic period it appears that the inhabitants of the area were attempting to integrate them into a single ritual landscape. The West Kennet and Beckhampton Avenues reaching out from the Avebury henge, demonstrate this desire in graphic terms. But how the monuments were used and what exactly their relationships were to each other almost 5,000 years ago is a more difficult question. It has been suggested that Avebury henge was erected as a meeting place for the inhabitants of the surrounding area, perhaps for seasonal fairs or festivals, with the majority of people watching ceremonies taking place while seated or standing on the huge earthen banks as the audience in a Roman amphitheatre would. However, the scarcity of prehistoric finds such as pottery and animal bone from excavations at Avebury suggests that entrance to the henge area was restricted; great gatherings inside the monument would have left a lot more "mess" than has been discovered. Curiously, some other henge monuments in Wiltshire, such as Durrington Walls and Woodhenge, have produced huge amounts of artifacts, which suggests that the similarity in design of such monuments does not necessarily indicate similarity of function. On the other hand, Stonehenge, as Avebury did, produced little in the way of archaeological finds, surely indicating the "sanctity" of both monuments.

Another similarity with Stonehenge (see Chapter 2) is the deliberate deposition of construction tools, such as antler picks, and other items, including animal bone and flints, in parts of the ditch of Avebury henge. As with Stonehenge, some of these items were already old when deposited, suggesting that the builders were forging a link with the past by placing objects from a previously sacred site in the new one. In this light, perhaps the construction of the monument, the hauling of the sarsen stones from the Marlborough Downs, their erection in and around the henge, and the digging of the huge bank and ditch, was thought of as one great sacred act. Certainly, by designing and constructing the henge at Avebury, its planners and builders were emphasizing a particular part of the landscape, marking it out as a sacred space different from that outside its huge banks. Within the henge, space is also divided by the various sarsen settings, which may have helped the visitor "experience" or understand the sacred area in certain preconditioned ways. A journey within the enclosure may have been a miniature version of the way in which the whole ritual landscape around Avebury could be interpreted or appreciated, perhaps while walking established routes such as those marked out by the West Kennet and Beckhampton stone avenues.

Some intriguing observations on the ways in which the various monuments in the Avebury landscape may have related to each other have been put forward by researcher and author Paul Devereux. After extensive research in the Avebury region, Devereux discovered that the monuments in the local ritual landscape appeared to be linked by engineered "sightlines" to Silbury Hill. In the opinion of Devereux, Silbury, or more particularly the "step" or terracing towards the top of the mound, was the focus of the complex of monuments in the area. Indeed Devereux thinks that Silbury may have been constructed to align with these monuments. It must be kept in mind, however, that some archaeologists believe the step on Silbury is the remains of an 11th-century Anglo-Saxon fortification on the hill, and not an original feature of the monument. An important alignment noticed by Devereux is one between the step on Silbury and the skyline formed by Windmill Hill, when seen from the western end of West Kennet long barrow. The alignment between this step and hills on the horizon behind and in front of it is also visible from other monuments in the area, such as East Kennet Long Barrow, the Sanctuary, and Avebury henge.

One particularly interesting sightline from a now-destroyed massive 80-ton stone called the Obelisk, in the Avebury henge, reveals the top of Silbury Hill sandwiched between Waden Hill in the foreground and the distant horizon. Devereux notes that at harvest time the cereal crop would have been high enough to completely block out this view of Silbury Hill. He relates this sightline to the theory, based on the presence of flying ants in the turf of the building, that construction of Silbury began at harvest time, and thus was possibly connected to harvest celebrations similar to the much later Celtic Festival of Lughnasadh, or Lammas. Such ideas of the interrelatedness of the monuments in the ritual landscape of Avebury are fascinating, though environmental evidence from the buried soil under Silbury Hill indicated a landscape of dry, open grass-land, and no evidence of soil disturbance that would signify cultivation until the end of the third millennium BC, long after the construction of the major monuments in the area. Consequently, if the harvest dependent sightline suggested by Devereux is to be accepted, it must have been uti-lized very late in the life of the ritual landscape around Avebury.

Another of Devereux's areas of research regarding Silbury involves the significance of apparent anthropomorphic features in some of the megaliths used in the Henge and the Avenues at Avebury. This field of research is also shared by Terence Meaden, who published his theories in his 1999 book, *The Secrets of the Avebury Stones.* Although archaeolgical evidence does not bear out Meaden's theory that Neolithic inhabitants of the area carved faces in the stones and his interpretation of the Avebury monuments in terms of a goddess-based Neolithic fertility cult, his con-tention that much can still be gained from the study of the shapes and positions of individual stones has much to recommend it. In what is probably the best book written about Avebury, *Avebury: The Biography of a Landscape* (2002), authors Joshua Pollard and Andrew Reynolds dis-cuss ideas broadly relating to the "personality" of the stones used in the monuments at Avebury. They note that some of the stones already had "histories" before they were incorporated into the ritual structures of the area. A number of sarsens, for example, had previously been used to polish stone axes; others had been heavily worked, indicating that they had been visited frequently before being transported to Avebury. Per-haps, as with the bluestones of Stonehenge, some of the sarsens were already part of a ritual location or monument before they were used at Avebury. Indeed, it may have been the perceived "sacredness" of par-ticular stones that made them natural choices for the builders of the Avebury monuments.

One of the most curious things about the Avebury megalithic monu-ments is the almost complete lack of legend and folklore associated with them, especially compared to sites such as Stonehenge and the Rollright Stones (see chapters 2 and 6). This may be due to the fact that the area of the Avebury henge and Avenues lies partly within the village, and the villag-ers' daily contact with the gigantic megaliths could have robbed them of their mystery. Alternatively, the actions of the church over the last 500 years to purge the site of pagan beliefs by persuading locals to pull down the stones may also have had an effect on the lack of development of legends connected with the site. As if to make up for the paucity of traditional legend, modern stories of ghosts, UFOs, and crop circles abound in the area. One particularly strange incident is recorded by Edith Olivier, a cousin of actor Laurence Olivier, in her autobiography, *Without Knowing Mr Walkley* (1938). Olivier states that one rainy evening in October 1916, she was driving between the Wiltshire towns of Devizes and Marlborough, and decided to stop at Avebury. She arrived at the village at dusk, and, after traveling along a mysterious avenue of stones, climbed onto the bank of the henge monument and saw what appeared to be the various booths, shows, and lights of a village fair. It was nine years before Miss Olivier revisited Avebury and mentioned her experience to a friend, only to be told that there had not been a fair held at the stones for at least 50 years. Olivier also found out that the avenue of stones she had walked along had apparently been the long-vanished Beckhampton Avenue. Olivier believed that on that rainy October night during the First World War she had somehow witnessed a scene that "must have taken place at least sixty-six years earlier." Whatever the objective reality of what Olivier saw, she also claimed on another occasion to have glimpsed the towers, domes, spires, and battlements of the mythical land of Lyonesse, beneath the sea, while standing on the cliffs at Land's End, Cornwall.

These days, Avebury and its surrounding Wiltshire countryside is almost as well known for crop circles as it is for prehistoric monuments. The term *crop circle* is used to describe often-complicated geometric patterns created in fields by the flattening of crops, mainly wheat, but also barley, canola, rye, corn, linseed, and soy. Though some people prefer the explanation that the designs in the fields are messages from aliens or perhaps from other dimensions, others believe in natural explanations such as vortexes, ball lightning, or plasma. Skeptics, on the other hand, are convinced that the circles are all manmade hoaxes, nothing more than performance art on a massive scale. Crop circles began appearing in numbers in the late 1970s, in the English counties of Hampshire and Wiltshire. In England in 2000, 175 crop circles were recorded, 70 of which were found within a 15-mile radius of Avebury. A number of these "agroglyphs," as they have been dubbed, have been discovered in the fields of standing corn around Avebury henge, Silbury Hill, and the West Kennet long barrow, leading some researchers, such as Freddy Silva, to postulate a connection between the crop circles and the ancient monuments.

On the night of July 28–29, 1999, an elaborate triangular formation containing 33 circles appeared in a field next to the Avebury henge. As is often the case, the design was thought too intricate to be the work of humans, and a paranormal explanation was soon mooted. However, not long after the circle was discovered, a group of crop circle hoaxers known as "Team Satan/circlemakers" claimed that they had been sponsored by the *Daily Mail* newspaper to create the formation. There is much controversy over claims by Team Satan/circlemakers that they have created not only the Avebury formation but many others in the area over the years.

However, it cannot be denied that the vast majority of crop circles are hoaxes and that crop circles have now become a lucrative industry. Rod Dickinson of "circlemakers" is quoted as saying that the *Daily Mail* paid the farmer whose field had been used to create the Avebury crop circle £6,000 ($12,535) for the equivalent of about £100 ($209) worth of crops. Indeed it has been said that one farmer in the area of Stonehenge made around £30,000 in a month by charging a couple of pounds each for tourists to visit a crop circle that had appeared in his field. There are even "Crop Circle tours" now, mostly originating in the United States, combining crop circles with visits to ancient sites, such as Stonehenge, Avebury, and Glastonbury. Nowadays, it would probably be more accurate to described crop circles as a business rather than a "phenomenon," and, either way, there is no evidence they have any connection whatsoever with the prehistoric monuments around Avebury.

Chapter 6

The Rollright Stones and Their Legends (England)

The King's Men Stone Circle.
Photograph by author

In the neighbourhood of Oxford there are
Great stones, arranged as it were in some
Connection by the hand of man. But at
What time; or by what people; or for
What memorial or significance, is unknown.

Though the place is called by the inhabitants
Rollendrith.
(*De Mirabilibus Britanniae*, 11th century)

The Rollright Stones is the collective name for a group of prehistoric
monuments located next to an ancient ridgeway known as the Jurassic
Way, on the border between the counties of Oxfordshire and
Warwickshire, in the English Midlands. The name "Rollright" derives
from *Hrolla-landriht*—"the land of Hrolla." The complex of monuments
at the site consist of three main elements: the "King's Men," a circle of
about seventy stones, probably dating to around 2500 BC; the "King
Stone," a solitary weathered monolith dated to 1792 BC; and the
"Whispering Knights," the remains of the burial chamber of a Middle to
Late Neolithic portal dolmen, estimated to date to between 3800 and
3000 BC. There are also two further monuments, both almost completely
destroyed, a round cairn (a roughly hemispherical burial mound constructed primarily of stones), and a ditched round barrow (a hemispherical
burial mound). Though by no means as grand and well preserved as the
Avebury or Stonehenge ritual landscapes, the Rollright monuments possess their own unique atmosphere, and have attracted a wealth of folklore over the centuries involving witches, fairies, invading "Danes," and
the famous prophetess Mother Shipton.

The skeleton of the earliest structure in the Rollright complex, the
Whispering Knights portal dolmen, consists of four vertically set stones
between 5 feet to around 8 feet in height and a fallen capstone, oriented
southeastward down a gradual slope. The covering earthen mound has
long since vanished from this monument, perhaps during Roman occupation of the site, testified by pottery discovered in excavations in the area.
Some researchers have contested the identification of the Whispering
Knights as chambered tomb, though the discovery of a fragment of human skull within the chamber by T.H. Ravenhill at least testifies to its
use for burial.

Around a thousand years after the construction of the Whispering
Knights, the builders of the King's Men planned and erected their stone
circle within sight (about 1150 feet to the west) of the portal dolmen. The
King's Men is an almost-perfect circle of 70 heavily weathered oolithic

limestone monoliths with an internal diameter of around 105 feet. It is thought that the circle may once have contained as many as 100 stones creating an almost continuous wall, with an entrance on the south-southeast formed by two outlying portals, one now collapsed. Unfortunately, a number of stones have fallen, been removed, or been damaged over time, and in 1882 some of the fallen stones were re-erected possibly in the wrong positions by the local landowner. There are similarities between the Rollright stone circle and those of Swinsdale and Long Meg and Her Daughters in Cumbria (North West England). These circles also have stones positioned outside their circumference, which are astronomically aligned, as also seems to be the case with the external portal stones at the King's Men, which Aubrey Burl suggests were aligned to the major rising of the southern moon at midsummer. Burl also suggests another possible connection between the Midland circle and those of Cumbria when he posits that the King's Men may have been a "depot" from which Cumbrian stone axes were exchanged. Indeed a fragment of a greenstone axe, probably from Cumbria, was discovered at Rollright, although the theory that the stone circle was constructed primarily as an arena for axe distribution remains unproven.

On the other side of the ridgeway (now a modern road), about 230 feet northeast of the King's Men, stands the King Stone. This 8-foot-high gnarled pillar attained its odd curved profile in the 19th century, as a result of the actions of Welsh drovers (someone who drives sheep, cattle, or horses on foot to market), who would hack pieces off to keep as charms. It is not certain what function the King Stone fulfilled, though it may have been a marker for an associated cemetery. Support for this theory is suggested by the remains of a round cairn, 56 feet across, just to the northwest of the Stone, which has been radiocarbon dated to around 1800 BC, and a small round barrow to the west, inside of which were an infant's cremated bones and a collared urn (a type of Early and Middle Bronze Age pottery cinerary urn) dating to about 1750 BC.

However, Aubrey Burl is of the opinion that the King Stone functioned rather as an outlier to the King's Men stone circle, set up as a signpost to guide travelers or pilgrims approaching along the Jurassic Way to the circle. Of course, the King Stone may have begun life as a marker for the King's Men and later became the focus for burial monuments. Without more information from archaeological excavation and survey, it is difficult to be sure how the monuments in the Rollright ritual landscape related to each other and how they were used.

One rather unorthodox attempt to understand prehistoric monuments in terms of the 'energy fields' supposedly associated with them was set up by researcher Paul Devereux in the late 1970s. Based at the Rollright Stones, the "Dragon Project" was begun in 1977 and involved interdisciplinary work undertaken by volunteers at prehistoric sites in the UK and in other countries. The project utilized dowsers, psychics, astronomers, and a variety of scientific tests such as ultrasound, infrared photography, magnetometer, and Geiger counter monitoring. Although magnetic and radiation anomalies were recorded on some occasions, there was no evidence for the presence of particularly exotic energies connected with prehistoric sites.

Another source of information on the Rollright Stones is its very rich store of folklore; indeed the monuments in the area seem to have attracted more legends than almost any other prehistoric site in England. The earliest known belief about the stones—that they were petrified men—is first mentioned in Camden's *Britannia*, written in Latin, in 1586:

> ...an ancient Monument...to wit, certaine large stones placed in a round circle (the common people usually call them *Rolle-rick* stones, and dreameth that they were sometimes men by a wonderful *Metamorphosis* turned into hard stones)...For, without all form and shape they bee, unequall, and by long continuance of time much impaired. The highest of them all, which without the circle looketh into the earth, they use to call *the King*, because hee should have beene King of England (forsooth) if hee had once seene *Long Compton*, a little towne so called lying beneath and which a man if he goe some few paces forward may see: other five standing on the other side, touching as it mere one another, they imagine to have been knights mounted on horsebacke and the rest the Army. But loe the foresaid portraiture. These would I verily thinke to have beene the Monument of some Victory and haply erected by Rollo the Dane who afterwards conquered Normandy.

(from the first English language translation of *Britanniap* by Philemon Holland, 1610)

Writing in the journal *Folklore* (September 1902) Percy Manning mentions perhaps the earliest appearance of a well-known rhyme about the Rollright Stones, added as manuscript notes to his copy of Dr. R. Plot's *Natural History of Oxfordshire* (2nd edition, 1705):

> Said the Danish General,
> If Long Compton I cou'd see
> Then King of England I shou'd be.
> But reply'd the ["British" erased] Saxon General,
> Then rise up Hill & stand fast Stone-
> For King of England thou'lt be none.

By the mid-19th century the "Saxon General" had been replaced by a witch. The witch confronts a conquering king at Rollright, who is a few steps away from the crest of the ridge from where the village of Long Compton, lying in the valley below, is visible. According to the most complete version of the tale, collected by Arthur Evans from local people and published in *Folklore* in 1895, the witch stopped the King in his tracks by saying:

> Seven long strides shalt thou take, and if Long Compton
> thou canst see, King of England thou shalt be.

Realizing that the village would certainly be visible from the edge of the hill the King strode forward shouting:

> Stick, stock, stone, As King of England I shall be known!

Taking seven strides forward, the King was suddenly confronted by a long mound of earth rising up magically before him (the mound of earth that still stands next to the King Stone) and blocking his view of the valley below. The witch then said:

> As Long Compton thou canst not see
> King of England thou shalt not be.
> Rise up, stick, and stand still, stone,

For King of England thou shalt be none,
Thou and thy men hoar stones shall be
And I myself an eldern-tree.

And so the King and his army became the King Stone and King's Men stone circle, and the witch became an elder tree. The Whispering Knights were said to be huddled together plotting treachery against the King when they were also turned to stone by the witch. The witch in this tale was sometimes identified as the mythical prophetess "Mother Shipton," probably for no other reason than the proximity to Rollright of a village called Shipton-under-Wychwood. As this folktale shows the stones have a connection in the popular imagination with witchcraft, though how far back this connection goes is not clear. Writing in the magazine *3rd Stone* (Winter 2000/2001) folklorist Jennifer Westwood has shown that both the witch and the related elder tree elements of Rollright folklore are of comparatively recent date, there being no evidence for either motif earlier than the mid-19th century in stories from the site. In fact, in versions of the petrifaction tale from earlier in the 19th century, it is not a witch but a "magician" who turns the King and his army to stone. The witch element at Rollright seems to have become popular due to the fact that the village of Long Compton and the surrounding area had a reputation for witchcraft in the 19th century, though the region does not seem to have been noted for its witches during the witchcraft persecutions of the 16th and 17th centuries.

In September 1875, an old woman of Long Compton named Anne Turner was stabbed to death with a pitchfork by a feebleminded agricultural laborer called James Haywood, who believed her to be the head of a local witch coven that had cursed him. The local belief in witches was still strong in 1945, when another murder occurred, this time on Meon Hill, near Lower Quinton, a few miles to the northwest of Rollright. On Valentine's Day, a hedger named Charles Walton was found pinned to the ground with a hayfork, with a cross carved into his chest and neck. The murder was never solved, although some suspected a ritual or "witchcraft"-related killing (though no evidence was ever produced for this). Over the last few decades the Rollright Stones have attracted followers of modern witchcraft, or "Wiccans," as well as other pagan and ritual magic groups that still hold ceremonies within the stone circle today.

Fairies are often connected in folklore with prehistoric monuments, and the Rollrights are no exception. In the late 19th century Arthur Evans was told that a man named Will Hughes, from the village of Long Compton, had once seen fairies dancing around the King Stone and described them as "little folk like girls to look at." Will Hughes's widow, Betsey (whose mother had apparently been "murdered as a witch"), a woman between 70 and 80 years of age when interviewed by Evans, told him that when she was a little girl working in the hedgerows there was a gap in the bank close to the King Stone, from where fairies emerged to dance at night. Betsey and her friends had often placed a flat stone over the hole in the evening to keep the fairies in, only to find it turned over the next morning.

The folklore of the Rollright Stones contains three of the standard motifs connected with megalithic monuments. The first is that whoever removes a stone from the site will suffer the consequences, well illustrated by the tale of the farmer who took away the capstone of the Whispering Knights to act as a bridge across the brook at Little Rollright. After an exhausting ordeal using "a score of horses" to drag the stone down to the brook (according to Arthur J. Evans's article in the March 1895, issue of *Folklore*), the farmer and his helpers laid it across to form the bridge. But every morning the stone was found lying in the grass, having somehow turned over in the night. Deciding that the stone was more trouble than it was worth, the farmer managed to return it using only a single horse to pull it up the hill.

Another common element in megalithic folklore is the idea that it is impossible to accurately count the number of stones at a site. The story about a baker who placed a loaf of bread on every stone in order to count them correctly has already been mentioned in connection with Stonehenge; it is also present at Rollright, but with the added twist that, no matter how he laid them out, the baker always found one stone without a loaf at the end. The third element is that the King Stone and the Whispering Knights are said to go down the hill at midnight to drink from a spring in Little Rollright Spinney. The Banbury Stone, Worcestershire, the Whetstone at Kington in Herefordshire, and the Hoarstone at Enstone in Oxfordshire are other examples of drinking stones.

Unfortunately, the recent history of the Rollright Stones, now owned by the Rollright Trust, has been far from pleasant. Over the past few years the stones have been repeatedly vandalized. In March 2004, many of the Kings Men were daubed in yellow paint, and on March 23, 2006, the warden's hut at the site was broken into and burnt to the ground. The latest act of mindless vandalism occurred in September 2007, when the monument plaque at the King Stone was wrenched off the railings and broken, and the information board daubed in graffiti. More seriously, a tire was forced over one of the stones in the King's Men circle, filled with wood and set alight, blackening a large part of the stone and causing cracks to appear around its circumference. What provokes such moronic acts is unclear, but George Lambrick, chairman of the Rollright Trust charity, has said that they are now considering "installing some kind of CCTV system here to deter further attacks" (according to the online magazine *Heritage Action Journal*). Such action may indeed be necessary if we are to preserve what is left of the ancient ritual landscape at Rollright before it is too late.

Chapter 7

The Sacred Hill of Tara (Ireland)

The *Lia Fáil* (Stone of Destiny).
Photograph by Przemslaw Sakrajda

A low grassy limestone ridge in County Meath, lying in the valley of the River Boyne, about 30 miles northwest of Dublin, is one of the most important ancient sites in Ireland. The sacred Hill of Tara (Irish *Teamhair na Ri*—"Hill of the Kings") was also called *Druim Caín* ("the beautiful ridge") or *Druim na Descan* ('the ridge of the outlook'). The latter title is particularly appropriate, as it is said that on a clear day one may see as much as a quarter of the Irish mainland from its summit. The Hill has been an important place since at least the Neolithic period (fourth–third millennium BC), and it is from here that 142 High Kings of Ireland are said to have ruled the land, up until AD 1175, with the end of the reign of Rory O'Connor, the last native High King of Ireland. Many of the monuments spread across Tara are mentioned in ancient texts, poetry, and oral lore, and up until the early 20th century, it was said that the music of the fairies could still be heard drifting down from the hilltop.

There are about 25 visible ancient monuments on the Hill of Tara in the form of embankments, ditches, grassy mounds, and a few megaliths. In the 1990s Dublin-based archaeological research institution the Discovery Programme detected at least 80 more by using non-intrusive archaeological techniques such aerial photography and topographical, geophysical, and geochemical survey. Before the Discovery Programme began its survey at Tara in 1992, the only serious archaeological work at the site had been the excavation of the Rath of the Synods and the Mound of the Hostages in the 1950s. The excavations at the Mound of the Hostages were performed in 1955 and 1956 by Seán P. Ó Ríordáin, University College Dublin (UCD) professor of Celtic archaeology, and completed in a third season during 1959 by Ruaidhrí de Valera, Ó Ríordáin's successor as professor of archaeology at University College. It would be almost 50 years before the findings of these excavations at the Mound of the Hostages were published, in the form of an extensive study prepared by Dr. Muiris Ó Suilleabháin, head of the UCD School of Archaeology, in 2005.

The Mound of the Hostages, the oldest structure on Tara, was named by 19th-century scholars attempting to identify monuments at Tara with semi-legendary places and people mentioned in 11th-century Celtic manuscripts. In this case, they connected the site with Niall of the Nine Hostages, one of the legendary kings of Tara, who had taken prominent citizens hostage from each of the five provinces of Ireland and also from Britain. However, the megalithic monument is actually a small passage grave covered by a stone cairn, and dates much farther back in time than such Celtic heroes. There is evidence that the area where the Mound of the Hostages stands was in use *before* the construction of the monument.

Traces of a Neolithic ditch underlying the western part of the cairn suggest that a Neolithic enclosure existed on the site before the tomb was erected, and Neolithic pottery shards and radiocarbon dates from charcoal beneath the mound indicate activity at the site around 3800–3700 BC. In total, 58 radiocarbon dates were obtained from material excavated at the Mound of the Hostages, which makes our knowledge of the sequence of events at the monument fairly detailed. The construction of the tomb and the first phase of its use has now been radiocarbon dated to 3350–3100 BC. The passage of the structure, 13 feet in length and 3.3 feet wide, was subdivided by sillstones into three compartments, which contained cremated and unburnt human bone representing a total of more than 250 individuals, deposited in the tomb between 3350 and c1750–1500 BC. There were also 62 burials (55 adults, three children, and four infants) placed inside three cists (small stone-built coffin-like boxes) built against the outside of the tomb chamber. The burials in the Mound of the Hostages were accompanied by an assortment of rich grave goods including beads, stone pendants, pins and tubes made of bone and antler, a ceremonial battleaxe, bronze daggers, and pottery including two intact Carrowkeel bowls (a type of pottery often found in association with cremations in Irish passage graves). There seems to have been a hiatus of activity at the site between the last Neolithic deposits in the tomb chamber c. 2900 BC). and the Early Bronze Age period, with burials in the chamber beginning again 2281–1943 BC and in the mound 2131–1533 BC. We don't know whether, during these missing centuries, Tara lost some of its importance and funerary activity shifted elsewhere, or if burials were made at another location on the Hill, or even if the meaning of the monument somehow changed. In fact, this latter idea of the change in the significance of the Mound of the Hostages over time is entirely possible, especially bearing in mind the monument was in use for at least 1,600 years.

The last burial was inserted into the Mound of the Hostages between 1750 and 1500 BC. The interment was that of a young male, age 15–16, who was buried unburnt in a flexed position, with bronze, jet, amber, and segmented faience beads, a razor, and a probable awl. The beads have strong parallels with contemporary examples from the south of England, and this has led some researchers to suggest that the body may have been brought over from England, to be buried, though of course the beads themselves may have been imported. It is, however, an intriguing possibility that important people may have been brought from Britain or elsewhere in Ireland to be buried at the sacred hill of Tara. The amount of human remains at the Mound of the Hostages and its long period of use testify to its importance as a site where the memory of the ancestors was a vital part of the life of the inhabitants, and this memory was perhaps kept alive by funerary rituals at the site.

One upright megalith at the side of the Mound of the Hostages passage was found to have pecked decoration showing concentric circles, cup-marks, wavy lines, and other designs. Some researchers have proposed that these symbols have astronomical significance, and that they show the sun, moon, or stars, or that the stone represents some kind of prehistoric calendar. One recent theory, put forward by Sean Keir Moriarty after visiting the site on numerous occasions, is that the designs on the megalith represent a map of the monuments on the Hill of Tara, the way they would have appeared in antiquity.

To the south of the Mound of the Hostages stands a granular limestone megalith known as the *Lia Fáil* ("Stone of Destiny"). Blatantly phallic in shape, this 3.3-foot-high stone is thought by some to have served as a prehistoric fertility symbol. The stone, at least half of which lies below the surface, has been moved several times over the years. It was transplanted to its present location to mark the mass grave of the 400 United Irish rebels who fell at the battle of Tara on May 26, 1798. According to Irish legend the Stone was one of the four sacred treasures brought to Ireland in the distant past by the semi-divine race known as *Tuatha dé Danann* ("People of the goddess Danu"), the other treasures being the *Claíomh Solais* ("The Sword of Light"), the Spear of Lugh, and the Dagda's Cauldron. The *Lia Fáil* was supposed to have been used as a magical coronation stone for all the kings of Ireland, and when the rightful king of the country stood upon it, it would roar three times in approval. The *Lia Fáil* is actually one of two stones named the Stone of Destiny. The other stone was, according to some stories, taken from Tara by King Fergus of Scotland in the ninth century AD and it remained at Scone, a few miles north of Perth, until the end of the 13th century, when King Edward I of England took it to be set up at Westminster Abbey. In 1996 the Stone was returned to Scotland, and it is now kept at Edinburgh Castle, until it is needed again for coronation ceremonies at Westminster Abbey. However, there has obviously been some confusion between the stories of the two Stones of Destiny, especially as the Stone of Scone is an oblong block of red sandstone rather than a pillar. The *Lia Fáil* is believed to have originally stood in front of the entrance to the Mound of the Hostages, and, similar to the two pillar-shaped stones that stand in front of the eastern and western passages at Knowth, also in the Boyne Valley, it may have been contemporary with the tomb.

The *Lia Fáil* stands in the middle of the *Forradh* ("King's Seat"), one of two linked ringforts (fortified settlements); the other is *each Chormaic* ("Cormac's House"), located within a large hill fort known as *Ráith na Rig* ("the Royal Enclosure"). Cormac Mac Airt was an Irish king who reigned at Tara for 40 years in the third century AD, though, as these structures have not been excavated, it is not clear if there is evidence for a real connection between Cormac and the ringfort. To the south of the Royal Enclosure lies a ringfort known as *Ráith Laoghaire* ("Laoghaire's Fort"), where King Laoghaire is said to have been buried fully armed and in an upright position in order to see his enemies approach.

Just outside the Royal Enclosure to the north is the previously mentioned *Ráith na Seanadh* ("Rath of the Synods"), an elaborate 300-foot-diameter ringfort with four concentric banks and ditches, dated by finds of Roman coins and a lead seal to the second to fourth centuries AD. The monument acquired its name when it was reputed to have been the meeting place for three successive centuries of Synods (councils or assemblies of church officials or churches) held by St. Patrick, St. Ruadhán, and St. Adamnan. Between 1899 and 1902 a series of enormous trenches was dug into the Rath of the Synods by members of the British-Israel Association of London, in search of the Ark of the Covenant. The group caused serious damage to the monument before protests by leading public figures, such as revolutionary and feminist Maud Gonne, Irish nationalist Arthur Griffith, and poet W.B Yeats, led to the "excavations" being stopped.

Located to the north of the Rath of the Synods is a pair of parallel banks running for 700 feet and known as *Tech Midchúarta* (the "Banqueting Hall"). Despite the name (which originated in medieval literature) this feature, which probably dates from between the fifth and eighth centuries AD, is thought by archaeologist Conor Newman, director of the Discovery Programme, to be a processional road. Newman believes this sacred avenue controlled not only the approach to the summit of the Hill, but also the way in which the ceremonial complex was viewed and thus interpreted by the person walking along it. One of the most recent discoveries at Tara is a huge oval-shaped structure, measuring around 575 feet east to west, and 689 feet north to south, marked out by 300 post holes, each 6.5 feet wide. Conor Newman believes the mysterious structure dates from 2500 to 2300 BC. Though some people have labelled it a "temple," its exact date and function will remain enigmatic until it is excavated.

In legendary tales Ireland has sometimes been connected with the lost land of Atlantis through the mysterious sunken island of Hy-Brasil, located somewhere out in the Atlantic. Some believe the island (supposedly named after an Irish king called Bressal) may actually have been Atlantis. In his 2004 book, *Atlantis from a Geographer's Perspective: Mapping the Fairy Land,* geologist Ulf Erlingsson goes one step further and identifies Ireland itself as Atlantis, with Tara as its capital. Although Erlingsson's Ireland scenario is interesting, the author demonstrates a basic misunderstanding of European prehistory when he talks of a "megalithic empire" as a single megalithic culture extending all over Europe and North Africa. There is no evidence that anything of the sort ever existed, and the distribution of megalithic monuments in Europe does not bear the idea out. Furthermore, if Ireland was the centre of the Atlantis "megalithic" empire, then you would expect its earliest megalithic structures, such as the court tomb of Creevykeel, County Sligo, and the later passage tombs of Newgrange and Knowth, to be the earliest in Europe, which is not the case. Current evidence suggests that the Almendres Cromlech megalithic complex (near Évora, Portugal), the Cairn of Barnenez (in northern Finistère, Brittany), and the Gantija megalithic temple complex (on the Island of Gozo, Malta) are at least contemporary with if not earlier than the Irish examples.

Since 2006 the ancient sacred site of Tara has been under threat from the construction of a new motorway (the M3) whose route is scheduled to dissect the Tara–Skryne Valley, passing within 1.37 miles of the

Hill. There have been calls for the rerouting of the M3 way from the Tara, not only because of the visual impact the motorway will have, but also because the massive building project will destroy many important archaeological sites in the area. The ancient monuments on the Hill of Tara did not exist in isolation, and may soon be deprived of all historical context if the building of the M3 through the Tara-Skryne Valley goes ahead as planned.

Chapter 8

Glastonbury: A Confusion of Legends (England)

The town of Glastonbury stands on a peninsula in the Somerset Levels, an area of wetlands 31 miles south of Bristol in southwest England. The area is dominated by the steep, conical Tor, a prominent landmark rising island-like from the surrounding level landscape. The small size of the town belies its prominent place in the legends and myth-history of Britain. Apart from the mysterious Tor, there are Iron Age lake villages in the area, the seventh century Glastonbury Abbey, and links with Joseph of Arimathea, King Arthur, and the Holy Grail. Unfortunately, such a mass of

Glastonbury Tor and the tower of St. Michael's church.

tradition, myth, and fiction have become so entangled with the real history of Glastonbury that sifting the truth from the legend is an almost-impossible task.

In contrast to the colorful legendary history of Glastonbury, the archaeological remains so far uncovered from the town and its immediate surroundings are fairly unremarkable. Recorded prehistoric finds include a Neolithic ax on Wearyall Hill, to the southwest of the town, and Bronze Age flints and bronze artefacts (including axes, palstaves, spearheads, a dagger, and a pin) from the Turbaries to the west of the town. The theory that Glastonbury Tor itself may have been shaped by man into its current labyrinthine appearance in the Neolithic period, perhaps for use as a ritual maze, is an intriguing possibility as yet unproven. Although the most widely accepted explanations nowadays is that the terraces on the Tor are either natural geological features or medieval strip lynchets, the idea that it was sculpted as a prehistoric religious center is not entirely without merit.

Archaeological excavations at the summit and the shoulder of Glastonbury Tor by Philip Rahtz from 1964 to 1966 discovered no evidence for prehistoric structures, though there were a number of interesting finds including Upper Palaeolithic (c. 30,000–c. 8000 BC), Mesolithic (c. 8000–c. 4500 BC) and Neolithic (c. 4000–c. 2200 BC) flints, a Neolithic greenstone ax, Roman pottery, and tile fragments. Such archaeological evidence suggests occasional visits to the site, perhaps for ritual activity, rather than occupation.

Four miles west of Glastonbury, the "Sweet Track," a raised plank walkway that ran across a reed swamp over a distance of 1.2 miles, was constructed in 3806 BC. A later "lake settlement"—or, to be more exact, marsh settlement—discovered in 1892 by Arthur Bulleid, and in use between 250 and 50 BC, was constructed 3 miles to the northwest of modern Glastonbury, and is renowned for its remarkable preservation of timber, wooden utensils, basketry, and a dug-out canoe. A linear earthwork known as "Ponter's Ball," lying to the east of Glastonbury, may have an Iron Age or earlier origin, though the evidence so far recovered from the site dated from the 12th century AD.

Between the fifth and seventh centuries AD, there was a settlement on the summit of Glastonbury Tor. The activity was mainly centred on the sixth century and included timber buildings, a significant amount of animal bone (mostly cattle), hearths (suggesting bronze working), shards of imported Mediterranean pottery, a small iron-cored bronze head thought to be part of a pail handle or cauldron escutcheon, and two north-south oriented inhumation burials of young people. There has been considerable debate over what kind of settlement these finds indicate. One theory, influenced by the naturally defensible position of the Tor, and the large amount of meat bones at the site (suggesting feasting), is that the Tor was used as the stronghold of a local chieftain. Alternatively, the remote location of the Tor has indicated to some archaeologists, including its excavator Professor Philip Rahtz, that it may have been home to a small Celtic Christian monastic site, though north-south oriented burials are not usually found in Christian contexts. Evidence in the form of the foundations of small, square buildings, and a wheel-headed cross carved from Doulting stone show that the Tor was reoccupied from AD 800 to 1100, possibly as a Saxon monastic retreat. The 69-foot-high St. Michael's Tower, which now stands alone atop Glastonbury Tor, was part of a church built in the 1360s dedicated to the Saint. The previous 12th-century church erected on the site was destroyed in an earthquake in 1275.

Although it presents itself as "traditionally the earliest Christian sanctuary in Britain" on the official Website of Glastonbury Abbey, the history of Glastonbury Abbey is far from clear. Nevertheless, we do know that Glastonbury was one of the first monasteries in England, probably established in the seventh century. It was recorded in 1086, in the Domesday Book (a written record of a census and survey of English landowners and their property in 1086), as the richest monastery in the country. A disastrous fire in 1184 destroyed many of the buildings and most of the ancient treasures kept at the monastery. After the fire, a program of renovation and rebuilding was undertaken that cumulated in the ruins that survive today. In September 1539, during the Dissolution of the Monasteries ordered by King Henry VIII, the Abbey was stripped of its valuables, and its Abbot Richard Whyting was hanged, drawn, and quartered as a traitor on Glastonbury Tor on November 15, 1539.

Whyting's severed head was subsequently displayed over the gate of the by then deserted Abbey.

On current historical evidence, the foundation of Glastonbury Abbey in the form of a Benedictine monastery, under Beorhtwald, its first Saxon abbot, can be dated no further back than AD 670. Although tradition states that an older wattle and daub Celtic Christian church stood on the site, no evidence of this structure has been discovered yet. Such dates would make the Abbey's origin and development as a sacred or religious site later than, and consequently secondary to, that of Glastonbury Tor. The archaeological evidence for the history of the Abbey contrasts somewhat with the prestige bestowed upon it in medieval legend.

Much of the legend and some of the history of Glastonbury Abbey originates with William of Malmesbury's *De Antiquitate Glastoniensis Ecclesiae* ("Enquiry into the Antiquity of the Church of Glastonbury"), begun somewhere between 1129 and 1135. When William of Malmesbury wrote his "Enquiry," Glastonbury Abbey was on the point of ruin, with its buildings in a dilapidated condition and the monks barely having enough to live on. It was Henry de Blois, the Abbot at Glastonbury, who brought William to the monastery, initially to compose biographies of various saints associated by tradition with the monastery. For some reason William was unable to complete these works and instead produced his *De Antiquitate Glastoniensis Ecclesiae*. In this "history," William calls the Abbey "the oldest church in England," and records that Pope Eleutherius sent the missionaries, Faganus and Deruvianus (Phagan and Deruvian), from Rome to the island of Britain to preach the Gospel, at some time in the second half of the second century AD. William also said that he had seen documents that stated that "no other hands than those of the disciples of Christ erected the church of Glastonbury."

William of Malmesbury was one of a number of professional historians and hagiographers used by various monastic communities to create semi-legendary histories of their monasteries and lives of their saints. Connections with important saints and histories stretching back to the foundation of Christianity were desirable for a monastery dependent on its prestige to attract pilgrims and donations. These concerns were so vital to the existence of Glastonbury Abbey that, when the monks made copies of William of Malmesbury's book, they inserted false passages into the work that described Joseph of Arimathea as the leader of a group of twelve disciples of Jesus who came to Britain in AD 63. During the later Middle Ages this myth was gradually built up, so that, by the late 15th century, Glastonbury was touted as the birthplace of British Christianity, where Joseph of Arimathea erected the first church to house the Holy Grail.

There was also a story that Joseph had earlier visited Glastonbury along with the child Jesus, a legend that later inspired William Blake (1757–1827) to compose the poem that became the words to the English hymn "Jerusalem." By the late 15th century there was a story circulating that Joseph had brought two silver flasks containing Christ's blood and sweat to Britain, and that these two relics were buried in his grave. This tale has shades of the legendary Holy Grail, and there is no record of any shrine marking the spot of the grave, which there surely would have been if the incident had any basis in fact.

Perhaps the most famous story concerning Joseph of Arimathea and Glastonbury tells of him bringing the Holy Thorn to the town. According to one version of the legend, Joseph is said to have sailed over the flooded Somerset Levels to Glastonbury and, on disembarking, planted his wooden staff in the ground, where it miraculously flowered into the Glastonbury Thorn. This hawthorn flowered twice annually, once in spring and again around Christmastime, and apparently attracted pilgrims during the Middle Ages. It was chopped down during the English Civil War (1642–1651) by the Puritans (supporters of Parliament, as opposed to the king), who disapproved of superstitious relics. In one tale, the roundhead Puritan soldier who destroyed the tree was blinded by a flying splinter. Fortunately, cuttings of the original Holy Thorn were taken and planted elsewhere in Glastonbury, and some survive today in the grounds of Glastonbury Abbey, at St. John's Church, and at Chalice Well. Every year at Christmas a sprig of the Glastonbury Thorn is cut by the local Church of England priest and the eldest pupil from St. John's school and sent to the queen. This custom apparently dates back to the time of King James I of England (1566–1625), when James Montague, Bishop of Bath and Wells, sent a branch to Anne of Denmark, queen consort of James I. In 1965,

Queen Elizabeth II erected a large wooden cross amid the ruins of Glastonbury Abbey that reads: "The cross. The symbol of our faith. The gift of Queen Elizabeth II marks a Christian sanctuary so ancient that only legend can record its origin."

The origins of the Glastonbury Thorn story do not seem to go back any further than a poem of 1502, which mentions three hawthorns on Wirral (Wearyall) Hill that flowered at Christmas. By 1645 it was said by some that the Holy Thorn had grown from a thorn taken by Joseph from the Crown of Thorns. Hearse's *History and Antiquities of Glastonbury* (1722) describes a Mr. Eyston being given information on the Thorn by a local innkeeper:

> ...I was told by the innkeeper where I set up my horses, who rents a considerable part of the enclosure of the late dissolved abbey, that St. Joseph of Arimathea landed not far from the town, at a place where there was an oak planted in memory of his landing, called the Oak of Avalon; that he (Joseph) and his companions marched thence to a hill near a mile on the south side of the town, and there being weary, rested themselves; which gave the hill the name of *Weary-all-Hill*;...whether it sprang from St. Joseph of Arimathea's dry staff, stuck by him in the ground when he rested there, I cannot find, but beyond all dispute it sprang up miraculously! 'This tree, growing on the south ridge of Weary-all-Hill (locally abbreviated into Werrall), had a double trunk in the time of Queen Elizabeth....

One theory still entertained today is that Joseph of Arimathea may have been a tin merchant who brought the young Jesus with him on a trading voyage to Britain. However, this story is a relatively recent invention and originates with English hagiographer, antiquarian, and author, the Reverend Sabine Baring-Gould, who introduced the idea in 1899 in his *Book of Cornwall*. Baring-Gould had connected Joseph with the tin mines of Cornwall, but in a 1922 pamphlet the Revd. Lionel Smithett Lewis, Vicar of St. John's at Glastonbury for more than 20 years, and deeply interested in stories of Joseph of Arimathea's connection with Glastonbury, appropriated the idea and attached the myth to his own town. By the time it reached its final edition in 1955, Smithett Lewis's *St. Joseph of Arimathea or the Apostolic Church of Britain* ran to about 200 pages, including 13 appendices, and included a claim that Glastonbury was the burial place of the Virgin Mary.

Glastonbury Abbey was at the center of some controversy in 1918 with the publication of the book *The Gates of Remembrance,* written by Frederick Bligh Bond. In 1908 Bligh Bond had been appointed director of the archaeological excavations at Glastonbury Abbey, but in *The Gates of Remembrance* claimed that he had used automatic writing (involuntary or unconscious writing believed by some to derive from "spirits") to locate the Edgar Chapel, which he had discovered during his excavations at the site. Bond revealed that the main communicators were a Captain John Allan Bartlett and later a monk named Johannes Bryant, and that his "spirit" guides (who called themselves "The Watchers") had directed him exactly where to excavate. Bond was told by his guides that Joseph of Arimathea and 11 disciples had founded a settlement at Glastonbury, and he expected to find remains of their occupation of the site.

The publication of another book in 1919, *The Hill of Vision,* also based on "psychic" communications, added to the strain on Bond's relationship with his employers the Church of England, and he was removed from his position as director of excavations in 1921, and in 1924 sacked from the project entirely. Bligh Bond's "psychic archaeology" at Glastonbury Abbey remains controversial to this day, with some believing that he was indeed guided to his discoveries with the assistance of discarnate entities. Archaeologists, however, believe that a well-trained architect who specialized in ecclesiastical structures had no need of mediums and automatic writing to make the discoveries he did.

In Geoffrey of Monmouth's works the *History of the Kings of Britain* (c. 1136) and *Life of Merlin* (c. 1150), Geoffrey writes that the wounded King Arthur was taken to "the Isle of Avalon," an enchanted otherworldly place, to be healed. Geoffrey does not indicate a location for Avalon, nor does he say that it is an earthly place. Nevertheless, in 1191, monks at Glastonbury Abbey made the sensational claim that they had discovered the remains of King Arthur and Queen Guinevere buried in a hollow oak in the churchyard of the Abbey, with a lead cross stating (in Latin):

"Here lies buried the renowned King Arthur with Guinevere his second wife, in the Isle of Avalon." Gerald of Wales (c. 1146–c1223) stated in his "On the Instruction of Princes" that the monks had dug for Arthur's grave at the request of King Henry II, who had been told where to dig by "an ancient Welsh bard." The supposed remains were later moved, and apparently lost during the Reformation, though the lead cross survived and was illustrated in Camden's *Britannia* (1590). However, the wording on the cross shows it to be a medieval forgery. Scholars now believe that the "discovery" of the graves was a hoax, not only to substantiate the antiquity of the Abbey, but also to raise funds for rebuilding after the damaging fire of 1184.

The origin of much of the legend surrounding Glastonbury Tor is to be found in a 16th-century Welsh text called the *Life of St. Collen*. In this text, St. Collen has settled in a hermitage on Glastonbury Tor and one day overhears some locals talking about Gwynn ap Nudd, king of the fairies and lord of Annwn (the Underworld). Collen rebukes them for speaking of such superstitions, stating that fairies were merely demons. Soon after, Gwynn summons Collen three times to come and meet him on the summit of the Tor at midday. Eventually Collen agrees, bringing with him a container of holy water. The saint is led through a secret door in the hill and finally comes to a magnificent castle full of musicians, horse-riders, and beautiful courtiers, where Gwyn awaits him seated on a golden throne. Collen is offered food and drink but refuses, remembering that fairy offerings are extremely dangerous. Instead, the saint sprinkles his holy water all around him, whereupon everything vanishes. Collen then finds himself standing alone on the grassy, wind-swept Tor. Since this time the Tor has often been represented as an entrance to Annwn (perhaps Avalon?), as is the case with many hills or mounds associated with the fairies.

A more recent theory regarding the Glastonbury landscape was put forward in 1927 by local sculptor and mystic Katherine Maltwood, and published in her 1935 book, *A Guide to Glastonbury's Temple of the Stars*. Maltwood believed that the landscape around Glastonbury had been sculpted around 5,000 years ago into a vast astrological zodiac, with its hills, rivers, and hedgerows representing astrological figures. This enormous star map apparently measured around 10 miles across and 30 miles around. However, two independent studies of the supposed giant zodiac done in 1983 using historical research and landscape analysis, one by Ian Burrow and the other by archaeologists Tom Williamson and Liz Bellamy, concluded that there was no evidence whatsoever for the existence of a Temple of the Stars in the Glastonbury landscape. The researchers showed that Maltwood had included a number of modern features in her "prehistoric" zodiac and had also failed to take into account how the landscape around Glastonbury in Neolithic times differed significantly from that of the early 20th century.

Chapter 9

The Sunken Land of Cardigan Bay: A Welsh Atlantis? (Wales)

Panorama of Cardigan Bay.
Photograph by Graham Well

There are many fascinating tales in Welsh literature and folklore of sunken lands, both on the coast and in lakes. These lost lands can be cities, towns, palaces, or fertile plains, and each story may have several versions dating from various periods. One example is Kenfig, which lies in Swansea Bay, in southeast Wales. The medieval town of Kenfig was engulfed by the ever-changing and drifting dunes of Kenfig Burrows, and nowadays only its Castle Keep is visible. According to legend, the bells of the sunken church tower can be heard on misty nights just before a storm. Llangorse Lake, in the stunning Brecon Beacons National Park in Mid-Wales, was said by Gerald of Wales (c. 1146–c. 1223), in *The Journey through Wales,* to contain a drowned city beneath its waters. English churchman and writer Walter Map, in a manuscript of anecdotes and tales held by the Bodleian Library in Oxford known as *De Nugis Curialium* ("Trifles of Courtiers"), recounts a similar folk-tale about a palace or town within Llangorse Lake that was submerged because of the wickedness of the prince and his subjects. Perhaps this tale is a folk memory of the small man-made island, or "crannog," which was constructed as a fortified palace by Brychan, king of Brycheiniog, on the lake during the late ninth century, and destroyed in AD 916 by a Mercian (from the Midlands of England) army.

On the northwestern tip of mainland Wales near Llandudno, there once stood Llys Helig, the palace of sixth-century Prince Helig ap Glanawg. One night during a feast at the palace a huge wave surged over Llys Helig and left the whole area underwater. At very low tides, it is said that the ruins of the old palace can still be seen under the water. There are various later embellishments to the myth of Llys Helig, including a tale that it was Glanawg's daughter Gwendud's unfaithfulness in love that caused the flood.

Perhaps the best known of these sunken lands, and one that is sometimes known as "the Welsh Atlantis," is *Cantre'r Gwaelod* ("The Lowland Hundred"). This legendary ancient drowned kingdom is said to lie beneath the waters of Cardigan Bay, on the Welsh coast between Ramsey Island and Bardsey Island. According to the legend, Cantre'r Gwaelod was a fertile land, 40 miles in length and 20 in breadth, with 16 fortified towns, including its principal city of Caer Wyddno ("the fort, or palace, of Gwyddno"), all protected from the sea by a dyke and sluices. One night around the year AD 600, when Gwyddno Garanhir ("Longshanks") ruled the area, there was a severe storm that whipped up huge waves that crashed against the sea walls and threatened the kingdom. The keeper of the dyke was a man called Seithenhin, apparently a drunkard, who on this night negligently left the sluice-gates open so the sea came rushing in, flooding the land, and drowning the towns and most of the inhabitants. It is said that when the sea is calm and the waters clear the submerged buildings of Cantre'r Gwaelod can still be glimpsed beneath the waves, and the sounds of its church bells can be heard faintly ringing out from the depths of the sea. There are many versions of the same story in existence, but where do these tales originate, and do they have any basis in fact?

In the popularly known form just described, the legend of Cantre'r Gwaelod may not go back any further than the mid-17th century, when the antiquary Robert Vaughan made the connection between it and Sarn Badrig ("St. Patrick's Causeway"), an 11-mile-long submerged pebble reef running out into Cardigan Bay. Vaughan believed that this natural feature was man-made and described it, according to Jennifer Westwood's book *Albion*, as "a great stone wall, made as a fence against the sea." In the following centuries, details were added to the unexplained "causeway," including the tale of Seithenhin, the drunken sluice-keeper who allowed the land to be overwhelmed by the sea, and the story that the sound of the church bells of Cantre'r Gwaelod can still be heard today. The earliest reference to the drowning of Cantre'r Gwaelod comes from the *Black Book of Carmarthen*, dating to about the mid-13th century, and one of the earliest surviving manuscripts written entirely in Welsh. The book contains a collection of poetry, and in one of these poems are the following lines:

> And look upon the fury of the sea;
> It has covered Maes Gwyddneu.
> Accursed be the maiden
> Who released it after the feast;
> The fountain-cupbearer of the raging sea...
>
> The cry of Margaret from the back of the bay Horse;
> It was the mighty and generous God who did it;
> Usual after excess is want...
>
> The grave of Seithenhin the presumptuous,
> Between Kaer Kenedir and the shore;
> How magnificent a lord.

From these ancient verses we can see that there are considerable differences between this original account and the 18th and 19th-century versions. For one thing, the roles of the two main protagonists are reversed: It is Seithenhin, not Gwyddno, who seems to be the lord of Cantre'r Gwaelod (here called "Maes Gwyddneu"—"the Plain of Gwyddneu"). There is also a maiden called Mererid (Margaret), the "fountain cupbearer" whose mistake it is that allows the sea to flood in. There are other tales from Welsh and Irish folklore of an overflowing well or fountain that forms a lake, one of which comes from *The Book of the Dun Cow* dated to the 11th or 12th century, one of the oldest known manuscripts in Ireland. In this story, known as "the Death of Eochaid man Mairid," Eochaid's daughter is put in charge of a magic well, but one day forgets to replace the cover, so that the well overflows, drowning Eochaid and all but two of his children, and forming Lough Neagh in present-day Northern Ireland.

A similar tale involves a man called Llyn Llech Owen, who lived on Mynydd Mawr ("Big Mountain"), in Carmarthenshire (southeast Wales). Owen had a magic well, which he always kept covered with a large flat stone when he was not taking water. The story goes that one summer evening, Owen Glyndwr (c. 1359–c. 1416), the last Welshman to hold the title Prince of Wales, was traveling through the area on his horse, and became tired and weary from the journey. He discovered Owen's well, removed the stone, and took a long draught of the cool water. Glyndwr then resumed his journey refreshed and stayed at the nearby Dyllgoed Farm. However, he had neglected to replace the stone cover back over the well, and during the night was woken by the sound of flowing water. Looking out of the window in disbelief, Glyndwr saw a large lake where the well had been. He quickly jumped out of bed and went outside, saddled his horse, and rode to the edge of the lake. Owen then galloped round and round the water to stop further flooding. Hence the lake was called the Lake of Owen's Flag (*Llyn Llech Owen*).

The transition from the early forms of the Welsh flood tale of Cantre'r Gwaelod, in which it is a well that overflows, to the later story of the drowned land can perhaps be explained by a misreading of the Black Book of Carmarthen poem, and the adaption of the legend to the conventions of the many sunken city stories of the coasts of England (particularly Cornwall), Germany, France, and the Low Countries (Belgium,

The Netherlands, and Luxembourg). The tradition that cities were over-whelmed by floods as divine retribution because of the evil ways of their inhabitants is probably derived from the biblical stories of Noah's Flood and the destruction of Sodom and Gomorrah. The various Welsh flood tales are so similar that it is probable that they go back to a common origin in early Celtic literature. But is the common origin a purely ficti-tious one, or was there an actual cataclysmic flood somewhere in the realms of the Celtic world on which most or all of these accounts are based?

Although the idea that the myths contain folk memories of gradually rising sea levels at the end of the last Ice Age is an attractive one, it is extremely unlikely that stories could have survived, even in vague form, by being handed down for 10,000 years or so. There have, however, been one or two intriguing "sightings" of Cantre'r Gwaelod over the years. In 1770, Welsh antiquarian William Owen Pughe reported glimpsing the ruins of the lost land 4 miles off the Welsh coast between the rivers Ystwyth and Teifi in Cardigan Bay. In the 1846 edition of *The Topographical Dictionary of Wales*, Samuel Lewis records a feature in Cardigan Bay he calls Caer Wyddno:

> In the sea, about seven miles west of Aberystwith in Cardiganshire, is a collection of loose stones, termed Caer Wyddno, "the fort or palace of Gwyddno;" and adjoining to it are vestiges of one of the more southern causeways or embankments of Cantrev Gwaelod. The depth of water over the whole extent of the bay of Cardigan is not great; and on the recess of the tide, stones bearing Latin inscriptions, and Roman coins of various emperors, have been found below high-water mark: in different places in the water, also, are observed prostrate trees. The truth appears to be, that the inundation swept away only a small part, and not the whole, of the land now covered by the waters of the bay, as Ptolemy the geographer, who lived in the second century, marks the promontories by which Cardigan bay is bounded, and the mouths of the rivers, in nearly the same relative situations which they occupy at present...

Geological research has, however, found such "causeways" to be natural formations, shingle and boulder ridges or reefs separating the river beds of a submerged land surface. Intriguingly, at low tides the remains of a preserved sunken forest have been recorded in Cardigan Bay on the coast between Borth, near Aberystwyth, and Ynyslas. The oldest sections of this prehistoric forest date back to 3500 BC, though the part at Borth is though to date to around 1500 BC. It is likely that observing these submerged tree trunks and roots, which have been visible at least since the time of Gerald of Wales (who mentions them in his writings), and the three reefs extending into Cardigan Bay, gave people the idea that a submerged land lay beneath the Bay. The original ancient Celtic folktale motif of the flooding of a well due to the negligence of its guardian also contributed to the final form of the myth of Cantre'r Gwaelod.

Though there is practically no physical evidence of this fabled civilization said by folklore to lie under the sea, a conservation group called "Friends of Cardigan Bay" believe there is some truth to the tale and have begun a project to study the ecology of the sea bed in the area. Perhaps this project, the first serious ecological research into Cardigan Bay, will one day show that the land of Cantre'r Gwaelod was more than just a legend.

Chapter 10

Ancient Dartmoor and Its Legends (England)

Dartmoor is a vast expanse of moorland in the county of Devon, southwest England. The moorland, now protected by National Park status, covers an area of 368 square miles, and includes some of the wildest and bleakest country in England. Perhaps it is not surprising then that Arthur Conan Doyle chose to set his dark atmospheric crime thriller *The Hound of the Baskervilles* on Dartmoor. Much of the Dartmoor National Park lies over a granite plateau and is characterized by numerous exposed granite hilltops, known as "tors." The highest of these tors, and also the highest point in southern England, is High Willhays, at 2037 feet above sea level.

Beardown Man, prehistoric menhir.

It has often been said that Dartmoor is the finest open-air archeological museum in the country, and, with more than 10,000 listed archaeological sites, this is hard to dispute. The presence of man in this wild, blustery part of England can be traced back to Mesolithic hunter-gatherers, who roamed the area around 10,000 years ago and left their flint blades, arrowheads, and traces of temporary camps in the landscape. The majority of the rich prehistoric remains on Dartmoor date back to the late Neolithic and early Bronze Age periods (c. 3000–2000 BC), and include stone rows, circles and avenues, standing stones, hut circles, cists (known on Dartmoor as "kistvaens"—box-like stone coffins), and extensive field systems known as "the Dartmoor reaves." Unfortunately, organic remains, including unburnt human bone, do not survive in the highly acid soil of Dartmoor, so our picture of prehistoric life in the area is far from complete.

One of the most impressive series of prehistoric monuments on Dartmoor is located next to the river Plym at Drizzlecombe, east of the village of Sheepstor. This "intriguing ritual complex," as Aubrey Burl calls it in his 2005 book, *A Guide to the Circles of Britain, Ireland and Brittany*, contains impressive arrangements of stone circles, rows, cairns (artificial piles of stones), standing stones, cists, and pounds (ancient walled settlements). The plan of the entire series of monuments forms a giant trapezoid, with a narrow north-to-east top, a wider base, and long sides, in proportional to each other. Though the meaning and function of this arrangement are long lost, it is likely that it was the inhabitants of the adjacent settlement who constructed this sacred landscape in stone.

Merrivale ("the pleasant valley"), located on a spur of high ground above the river Walkham, between the towns of Princetown and Tavistock, is home to another ritual complex. The monuments at Merrivale were once known locally as the "Potato Market" and "The Plague Market." The names date back to the year 1625, when there was an outbreak of bubonic plague in the area, and 575 residents of the nearby town of Tavistock died. In order to get food to the townsfolk without contamination, the moorland farmers would travel to the ancient site and leave provisions there.

The Merrivale complex consists of two stone circles, a stone avenue, double and single stone rows, standing stones, a large cist, and hut circles (the remains of ancient houses). The narrow double stone row at Merrivale (it is only 3.6 feet wide) is aligned almost east–west and runs for almost 600 feet. There have been suggestions that the stone rows at the site were astronomically aligned, perhaps to provide a calendar for the year, enabling a more accurate planning of farming and ritualistic activity. The solstices, the bright orange star Arcturus, and the Pleiades star cluster have all been put forward as possible targets of the stone alignments. But why the need for such precision? As I have noted in other chapters, such vast arrangements of stone are huge undertakings, considering that there were enough natural signs for the Bronze Age inhabitants of the area to understand the time of year. Another objection to the astronomical hypothesis is that to make alignments "fit" the intended pattern, some researchers have used monuments dating from many different periods, sometimes hundreds of years apart; consequently, their theories are unlikely to have any validity.

The Nine Stones, also known as the "Nine Maidens," and the "Seventeen Brothers," is a stone circle located on Belstone Common not far from the East Okement River, to the south of the village of Belstone. Despite the name, this monument, the outer wall of a vanished Bronze Age burial chamber, has 11 closely set upright stones, with others lying prostrate, and has a diameter of 25 feet 8 inches. The tallest stone of the ring is a mere 3 feet in height. There is a tradition that a group of maidens danced on the Sabbath (Sunday) and, for their punishment, were turned to stone and also compelled to dance at noon every day for eternity. In some versions of the tale, if the stones hear the sound of Belstone church bells, they will come back to life. Another variation of the story, and one that tallies more with the actual number of stones in the circle, is that of the Seventeen Brothers who danced on Sunday and suffered the same fate as the maidens.

Many stone circles throughout the UK, Ireland, and France are associated with a dancing legend (Stall Moor Circle on Dartmoor is another example), and most of them involve the tradition of people being turned to stone for some misdemeanour or other. Intriguingly, there are other examples connected with the dancing legend that are also called the "Nine Maidens" or "Nine Ladies" (the Nine Maidens in Cornwall, for example), often regardless of the actual number of stones in the circle. Legends of punishment for dancing on the Sabbath can be traced back to 17th-century fire-and-brimstone preaching, though why the number 9 is so prevalent in these tales is not clear.

One fascinating theory for the ubiquity of the number 9 was put forward by B.C. Spooner, writing in the December 1953, issue of the journal *Folklore*. Spooner noted that the hour most connected with stone circles in tradition was noon, "the hour of the sun and the sun's meridian, of the full strength of the noonday devil, the still hour of Pan." Noon is derived from the Latin *none hora*, the ninth hour after sunrise, when the Office of *Nones* was to be recited. By AD 1100 the hour of noon had been changed from 3 p.m. to midday, and became known as *None* in France and *Noon* in England. That Nine Maiden and Nine Ladies stone circles should be associated with midday, noon, rather than the number 9, seems a perfectly reasonable suggestion, though the number 7 also occurs frequently in the folklore of megalithic monuments (The Seven Sisters, Lissyvihheen Killarney, Ireland, for example). There is a parallel here with the Greek myth of the petrification of Niobe, whose seven sons and seven daughters were killed by Apollo and Artemis for their mother's disrespect to the goddess Leto.

Apart from its abundant prehistoric remains, the heather covered wilds of Dartmoor are also home to a plethora of antiquities from later periods. These include Anglo-Saxon settlements, ruined castles, medieval abbeys and manor houses, ancient churches and bridges, and the remains of tin, copper, lead, zinc, and silver mines. It is often from Dartmoor's historical sites that many of the best-known legends of the area come, and prominent amongst these is that of "Childe the Hunter." This legend was first recorded in the early to mid-1600s, and tells of a wealthy Saxon Lord of the Manor of Plymstock, named Childe, who was caught in a blizzard on the wilds of Dartmoor. Lost and unable to continue in the bitter cold, Childe was forced to kill his horse, disembowel him, and shelter inside his belly. But this act did not save him, and a few weeks later his body was discovered frozen to death inside the horse's carcass. Childe had stated in his will that, wherever he was buried, the local church should inherit his land. The monks of Tavistock Abbey, on whose lands the body had been found, acted quickly and, after narrowly avoiding being ambushed by a rival party from Plymstock, buried the remains of Childe at the Abbey and inherited his land.

A stone cross monument known as "Childe's Tomb" was erected in the place where the squire's body was apparently recovered inside the horse, on the southeast edge of Foxtor Mire. This cross still stands next to a Bronze Age cist, and the legend may indicate confusion between the story of Childe and a folk memory attached to the prehistoric tomb. Childe the Hunter is usually identified as Ordulf, son of Ordgar, an 11th-century Anglo-Saxon Earl of Devon, though whether the dramatic story of his death is fiction or reflects a genuine account is unknown. The tale of Childe the Hunter certainly has elements that seem to have originated in a dispute over land between the towns of Tavistock and Plymstock.

It is said that Sir Arthur Conan Doyle was inspired to write the Sherlock Holmes novel *The Hound of the Baskervilles* after hearing tales about Dartmoor while staying at the Duchy Hotel in Princetown (now the High Moorland Visitor Centre). The legend of Squire Richard Cabell from Brook Manor, north of Buckfastleigh in Dartmoor, was probably related to Conan Doyle by journalist and barrister Fletcher Robinson. Robinson's coachman was called Harry Baskerville, though the name may also originate with Birmingham printer John Baskerville, a friend of Conan Doyle when he lived in the city in the late 1870s. Squire Cabell, who died in the 1677, was rumored to have murdered his wife, and apparently had an evil reputation in the district. There was a legend that, when he died, howling black dogs breathing fire raced across Dartmoor ready to drag his soul to hell. It was also said that after his death the wicked squire could be seen leading a phantom pack of hounds over the moors at night, usually on the anniversary of his death, or that he rode in a black coach pulled by headless horses and driven by a headless coachman.

Cabell lies buried in the mausoleum known as "the Sepulchre" in the churchyard at Buckfastleigh. There are various pieces of folklore attached to the Sepulchre, an eerie, red glow was said to surround the tomb, and a host of demonic creatures were reported to cluster around the Sepulchre, attempting to reach through the iron bars and grab the squire's soul. Stories of the "hell hound," the ghostly black dog of British and Irish mythology, certainly influenced Conan Doyle's *Hound of the Baskervilles,* but it is not the only example of the dreaded creature on Dartmoor.

The ancient structure of Fitzford House, near Tavistock, is home to a bizarre headless ghost. According to local tradition, the Lady Frances Howard (who died in 1671), wife of the owner of Fitzford House, Sir Richard Granville, had murdered her first three husbands. Because of these wicked acts, she was condemned to ride out every night at midnight in a coach of human bones with skulls at the four corners, driven by a headless coachman and pulled by four headless horses. A spectral black hound, sometimes said to be Lady Howard herself, with a single eye in the middle of its forehead, also accompanies this terrifying apparition. When the phantom coach arrives at Okehampton Castle, a ruined 11th-century structure overlooking the River Okement, it is the strange task of this dog to pluck one blade of grass from the castle mound and bring it back to the gate of Fitzford House. The hound must continue to do this every night until all the grass has been plucked from the mound, which of course will never happen as the grass grows faster than the dog can work.

In some versions of this tale, the coach stops to pick up the souls of the dying, which surely indicates that, as with so many spectral coach and black dog tales, Lady Howard and her phantom coach are the personification of death itself. As Devon folklorist Theo Brown has pointed out, Lady Howard did not in fact own a coach, and, as the country folk of Devon in the late 17th century would not have known what such a vehicle looked like, much less encountered one, the phantom coach motif must have been added to her story at a much later date.

Another ghostly black dog is testified to by the names of two hamlets in the parish of Washford Pyne: Upper and Lower Black Dog. Theo Brown was told the story that there used to be a tunnel leading from the old well at the crossroads where the Black Dog Inn now stands to the ancient earthworks at Berry Castle, almost a mile to the south. At the time of the Civil War (1642–1651), the entrance to this fabled tunnel was guarded by a phantom black dog. There are many more spectral black hounds haunting the lanes and byways of Dartmoor. As elsewhere in the UK, the origins of such phantoms can be traced back to the folk myth of the *Herlething* (Wild Hunt) of northern, western, and central Europe, where a spectral procession of huntsmen and their hounds pass noisily over countryside at night reveling, hunting, and destroying all in their path. The form and personnel of the Wild Hunt varied from place to place; the Dartmoor version was known as the "Whish-Hounds" (or "Wisht Hounds") or the "Yeth Hounds," and it was said that they were the souls of unbaptized children. An ancient road called the Abbot's Way and the valley below Dewerstone Rock are said to be favorite haunts for these terrifying spectral hounds.

Chapter 11

The Tower of London
(England)

Founded almost 1,000 years ago, the Tower of London is known mainly for its grim history of imprisonment, torture, and execution. It also has a reputation for being one of the most haunted places in Britain. But are the legends of royal hauntings and bizarre encounters at the site based on real sightings or local folklore?

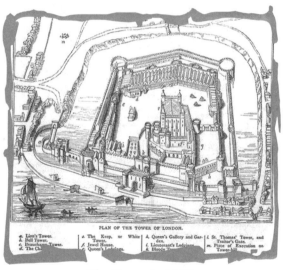

The Tower in 1597.

According to the ninth-century *History of the Britons,* attributed to Nennius, and Geoffrey of Monmouth's *History of the Kings of Britain,* written around 1136, the city of London was founded by Brutus of Troy, the grandson of Aeneas. Brutus named this new city *Troia Nova* ("New Troy"), which gradually changed to "Trinovantum."

The city was later rebuilt by King Lud, who named it *Caer Lud* ("City of Lud") after himself, and, in time, this name became *Caer Llundain,* and finally London. Unfortunately, this romantic history of the founding of London is not corroborated by archaeological and historical evidence. The Trinovantes were a pre-Roman Celtic tribe of Britain, whose territory encompassed the modern-day counties of Essex and southern Suffolk and parts of what is today Greater London. *Trinovantes* probably means "the Vigorous People," and has nothing to do with Troy. The name *London* derives directly from the Roman *Londinium.*

The mythological origins of the Tower of London are described in a fascinating tale in *The Mabinogion,* a group of stories from medieval Welsh manuscripts, parts of which probably date back to older Iron Age traditions. The tale involves Bran the Blessed ("Bendigeidfran" in Welsh; probably "Blessed Crow"), the giant king of Britain, who invades Ireland and is fatally wounded in the foot by a spear during a battle. At the end of the battle only seven of Bran's followers remain alive. Before he dies, Bran orders his head to be cut off and carried to *Gwynfryn* ('White Hill') in London, thought to be the site of the Tower, where it is to be buried facing in the direction of France. As long as the head of Bran the Blessed remains buried in this place, no invaders from across the seas can come to the island of Britain.

According to the *Welsh Triads,* it was King Arthur, desiring that Britain should be guarded by his strength alone, who uncovered the talismanic head of Bran. The story of Bran's head, which may indicate the sacred origins of Tower Hill, was once thought to have some connection with the tradition of keeping ravens at the Tower to guard the country against invasion. If the name *Bran* signifies "crow" or "raven" then there could perhaps be a link between them. Recently, however, Geoff Parnell, official Tower of London historian, has undertaken detailed research into the raven mythology of the Tower of London. Parnell was able to trace the tradition of ravens at the Tower of London no further back than 1895, so it would seem on present evidence that rather than ravens being at the Tower for hundreds, if not thousands of years, the connection is no more than a piece of Victorian romance. Though some researchers have connected the "White Tower" with the "White Hill" of the legend of Bran, the name seems to have originated in 1240, when Henry III (1216–72) had the exterior of the building whitewashed, though this does not, of course, mean that Tower Hill and the White Hill are not the same place.

Although known as the "Tower of London," the Tower is, in fact, a whole complex of buildings, situated on the northern bank of the River Thames, on the eastern side of central London. The original stronghold was begun within the southeast corner of the old Roman walls by William I, following the Norman conquest of England in 1066. Around 1078, work on a huge imposing stone tower (the White Tower) was begun using Norman masons and local labor. The enormous square Tower was not only an imposing physical structure (it measured 118 x 106 feet across, and was 90 feet tall) that dominated the London skyline, but also a visually striking psychological reminder of the power of the Norman crown. The Tower was never intended to function primarily as a royal residence. It was built as a fortress-stronghold, as much for protection from the people of London as against any overseas danger. Almost from its inception, the Tower was used as a prison. The first to be detained there was Bishop Ranulf Flambard of Durham in 1100, though he escaped a year later.

The White Tower itself and the complex of buildings, walls, and walkways that grew up around it have served many different functions over the centuries. Apart from a prison and a site for executions, the Tower has also been used as a royal palace, a treasury (the Crown Jewels have been kept at the Tower since 1303), a mint, a royal observatory, a zoo, and finally a museum.

But it is as a prison and a place of execution that the Tower is most infamous. A list of those imprisoned and executed in the Tower reads as a "Who's Who" of English history. The more famous include the two "Little Princes" (nephews of Richard III, probably murdered in the Tower in 1483), Sir Thomas More (beheaded in 1535), two wives of Henry VIII—Anne Boleyn (executed by a French swordsman in 1536) and Catherine Howard (beheaded in 1542)—the "Nine Days' Queen," Lady Jane Grey (only 17 years old when she was beheaded in 1554), Guy Fawkes (tortured in the Tower in 1605), and Sir Walter Raleigh (imprisoned in the Tower from 1603 to 1616).

The Tower was also used as a prison during the two World Wars. In WW I, 11 German spies were shot in the Tower's East Casemates Rifle

Range, and, in May 1941, Rudolf Hess, the Deputy Führer of the Third Reich, spent five days as a prisoner in Queen's House, the place where Anne Boleyn had been held more than 400 years earlier.

With such a grisly history, it is natural that the Tower of London has acquired a reputation as being the most haunted building in England. Perhaps the most illustrious of the many royal ghosts said to roam the corridors of the Tower is that of Queen Anne Boleyn. Her ghost has apparently been seen often, both on Tower Green where she was executed, and in the Chapel Royal, in the White Tower, where she was buried. In 1864, a sentry of the King's Royal Rifle Corps was on duty at the Queen's House, when, encountered a misty white figure. He challenged the "person" but received no reply, so he thrust his bayonet into the figure; it went straight through it. At this, he fainted and was duly court-martialed for being found asleep at his post. At the hearing, the sentry described the spectre: "It was the figure of a woman wearing a queer-looking bonnet, but there wasn't no head inside the bonnet." Due to the testimony of two witnesses who had described the whole scene exactly as the sentry had, the man was found not guilty and was acquitted. Apparently this same misty phantom was seen by other sentries in later years, though why it is attributed to the ghost of Anne Boleyn is never stated. Perhaps the mist swirling up from the River Thames had something to do with these sightings.

In the book *Ghostly Visitors* (1882), author "Spectre Stricken" (a pseudonym for English clergyman and spiritualist William Stainton Moses) writes about another, more spectacular sighting of Anne Boleyn witnessed by a Captain of the Guard who had been attracted to the Chapel Royal by a mysterious light:

> Slowly down the aisle moved a stately procession of Knights and Ladies, attired in ancient costumes; and in front walked an elegant female whose face was averted from him, but whose figure greatly resembled the one he had seen in reputed portraits of Anne Boleyn. After having repeatedly paced the chapel, the entire procession together with the light disappeared.

Where this story originated is not certain, but, as *Ghostly Visitors* seems to be the only source for the sighting, it is perhaps best to regard it as a piece of colorful folklore, if not outright fiction. Lady Jane Grey, Queen of England for just nine days, is said to appear at the Beauchamp Tower, again as a white shape, on the anniversary of her execution (February 12, 1554). One of the most recent sightings was made on February 12, 1957, when a guard at the Tower, called Johns, glimpsed her on the battlement above the place where he stood. Apparently he alerted a colleague, who also saw her. As with all such "anniversary ghosts," Lady Jane seems to have disregarded the 1752 Calendar Reform, when Great Britain switched from the Julian Calendar to the Gregorian Calendar, omitting 11 days in the process.

The ghost of Sir Walter Raleigh, the famous courtier and explorer beheaded at Whitehall on October 29, 1618, after being kept prisoner in the Tower for 13 years, also walks the Tower. One yeoman on guard in the Byward Tower, one February night in 1983, was in the guardroom in the early hours of the morning when he saw the handle of the door rattle. Thinking it was due to the strong winds, he disregarded it, but, when he glanced through the glass door, he saw, peering into the room from the doorway, the figure of Sir Walter Raleigh, exactly as depicted in a portrait in the Bloody Tower. The figure lingered for a short while before vanishing. About a year and a half later, another yeoman witnessed the same apparition in the same place. The ghost of Sir Walter is also said to haunt "Raleigh's Walk," where he used to exercise during his long imprisonment.

On May 27, 1541, 67-year-old Margaret Pole, Countess of Salisbury, was executed on Tower Green by order of Henry VIII. Her son, Reginald Cardinal Pole, had enraged Henry by publishing a book, *Pro ecclesiasticae unitatis defensione* ("On the Unity of the Church"), denouncing the king's policies, from the safety of France. The King's revenge was swift and fatal: Margaret and two of her sons, as well as other relatives, were executed. In popular accounts of the execution, the defiant Margaret Pole refuses to kneel at the block and challenges the executioner to cut off her head. The headsman pursues the old lady round and round, hacking away at her as she screams in terror, until she is finally decapitated in a welter of blood. After such a dreadful ordeal, it is not surprising that the ghost of Margaret Pole is seen on the anniversary of her death re-enacting the bloody execution in the area where she was beheaded.

However, as Jennifer Westwood and Jacqueline Simpson make clear in their valuable work *Lore of the Land,* the only known contemporary account of Margaret Pole's execution, written by the Spanish ambassador Eustace Chapuys, is a little different:

> When informed of her sentence she found it very strange, not knowing her crime, but she walked to the space in front of the Tower, where there was no scaffold but only a small block. She commended her soul to God, and desired those present to pray for the King, Queen, Prince and Princesses. The ordinary executioner being absent, a blundering garçonneau [young lad] was chosen, who hacked her head and shoulders to pieces.

A horrible ordeal, without doubt, but hardly the bizarre chase around the execution block given in popular ghost lore, which Westwood and Simpson quite rightly sum up by commenting, "Such a travesty must surely set the proud and courageous countess turning in her grave."

An extremely peculiar apparition from the Tower, and one that did not involve the ghost of a person at all, was witnessed by Edmund Lenthal Swifte, the Keeper of the Crown Jewels. The bizarre incident occurred in October 1817, as Swifte, his wife, their young son, and his sister-in-law were eating their evening meal in the candle-lit sitting room of the Jewel House, on the west side of the Martin Tower. As Swifte later recounted in the journal *Notes and Queries* (1860):

> I had offered a glass of wine and water to my wife, when, on putting it to her lips, she paused and exclaimed, 'Good God! What is that?' I looked up, and saw a cylindrical figure, like a glass-tube, seemingly about the thickness of my arm, and hovering between the ceiling and the table; its contents appeared to be a dense fluid, white and pale azure, like to the gathering of a summer-cloud, and incessantly mingling within the cylinder. This lasted about two minutes, when it began slowly to move before my sister-in-law; then, following the oblong-shape

of the table… passing behind my wife, it paused for a moment over her right shoulder…Instantly she crouched down, and with both hands covering her shoulder, she shrieked out, 'O Christ! It has seized me!'

Swifte approached the form and struck out at it, but his blow seemed to hit the wall. The strange apparition then floated toward the end of the table before vanishing. Curiously, Swifte stated that neither his sister-in-law nor his son had seen this strange object, despite it passing in front of them. In the correspondence in *Notes and Queries* that followed the publication of the story, one explanation proposed for the strange apparition was that someone had been projecting images into the room. Two girls then living in the Tower were supposed to have been making "phantasmagorial experiments," and it was thought that they might have been responsible. However, Swifte protested that the thick curtains hanging in the room would have made projections from outside impossible. If it were a "projection," wouldn't everyone have seen it?

Another possibility, mentioned by J.A. Brooks in *Ghosts of London,* is that "primitive methods of sanitation" at the Tower in the early 19th century, and its proximity to the Thames, could have generated enough methane gas to "give a cold flame effect," perhaps akin to that created by marsh gas though whether such an effect could take on the form of a glass-tube containing a dense liquid is another matter. One problem with the case is that Swifte did not publish the details until 43 years after the event, and one wonders how reliable his memory could have been after that amount of time.

Today the Tower of London is principally a tourist attraction. But according to UNESCO, the skyscrapers surrounding the site are threatening its historical value, and so the 900-year-old Tower complex is on the verge of being placed on the United Nation's Heritage in Danger List. UNESCO believes that new developments in the vicinity of the Tower do not respect the location of the site, and that the planning policies of London to protect the tower are not, according to am October 2006, BBC online article, being "applied effectively." The situation is extremely serious and it seems that, unless something drastic is done, the ancient Tower that once dominated the skyline for miles around will soon be completely smothered by the concrete tower blocks surrounding it.

Chapter 12

The Stone Alignments of Carnac (France)

Standing stones in the Kermario alignment.

Carnac is a town on the south coast of the Brittany region, in north-western France. The area surrounding the little town is renowned for being one of the greatest centers of megalithic remains anywhere in the world, containing a vast concentration of dolmens (single-chamber mega-lithic tombs), tumuli (earth and stone burial mounds), stone alignments, and single menhirs (large upright standing stones). The megaliths of the

Brittany region cover a period of almost 3,000 years, from the earliest Neolithic (c. 4800 BC) to the beginning of the Bronze Age (c. 2200 BC). There are roughly 5,000 menhirs at Carnac, though archaeologists believe that there were once as many as 10,000. Most of the missing stones were plundered centuries ago for building stone; others have fallen over and been removed, even in modern times, for houses, walls, or road-building.

The rows of menhirs at Carnac run in parallel alignments for about 2 miles to the north of the town. The stones in these alignments can be up to 20 feet high and weigh up to a staggering 20 tons. In constructing the avenues the builders used rough, unhewn blocks, the majority obtained from natural outcrops rather than quarries. There are four main groups of these standing stones, each avenue of menhirs running at a slightly different angle from southwest to northeast. The Ménec Alignments, named after a nearby village, share a common attribute with the other stone rows of Carnac—that is, that the stones in the avenues start tall (some over 12 feet high) and the avenues wide. As the Ménec Alignments run east, the height of the stones decreases steadily (the smallest stone is just 2 feet high) and the width of the avenue narrows. There are 1,099 standing stones arranged in 11 parallel avenues at Ménec, which stretch for almost three quarters of a mile before terminating at a barrel-shaped cromlech (stone circle). There is another cromlech at the beginning (western end) of the Ménec Alignments.

The Kermario ("House of the Dead") Alignments consists of 10 columns of menhirs containing a total of 1,029 stones, and run for about 0.8 of a mile. Remains of cromlechs have been identified at the avenue's eastern end by aerial photography, and, at the western end, there is a dolmen considerably older than the alignment. The Kerlescan Alignments consist of 13 rows of 555 stones, the tallest of which is about 13 feet high, and run for about half a mile, again with a barrel-shaped cromlech at the western end, and another one, 255 feet in diameter, as well as a dolmen, to the north. The last of the major avenues at Carnac, and also the smallest, is known as the Petit-Ménec Alignments. These three curved rows of moss-covered avenues stretch for almost 1,000 feet, and are now located in woodland. Only 250 menhirs survive today, due to the pillaging of the megaliths in the 19th century to build the Goulphar Lighthouse, on Belle Ile, the largest of the South Brittany islands.

When Scottish antiquary James Miln (1819–81) carried out the first extensive excavation at Carnac in the 1860s, he noted that fewer than 700 of what he calculated were 3,000 stones were still standing. Many of the fallen menhirs were re-erected at the end of the 19th century, though often probably not in their original positions. Consequently, determining the purpose of the vast lines of standing stones is made all the more difficult. Unfortunately, we don't know if what are now interpreted as individual alignments of menhirs once formed a single group of avenues, but have been become separated over the centuries as stones were removed. The undulating, serpentine shape of the alignments as seen today may be more of a result of the re-erection of the stones rather than part of their original design. Nevertheless, the stones at Carnac were once identified by writers such as the Rev. John Bathurst Deane, in his 1833 book *The Worship of the Serpent*, as giant serpent temples ("dracontium") designed for snake-worship. In past centuries the alignments have also been attributed to Egyptians, Phoenicians, Celtic druids, or even Caesar's army, who supposedly set them up as giant tent pegs to protect their shelters against the strong local winds. Such explanations, of course, reflect the tastes and agendas of the day rather than any genuine archaeological research.

There is also a certain amount of folklore that has grown up around the Carnac stones over the years. The most famous account is that the lines of menhirs represent a Roman legion turned to stone by Merlin, the magician of Arthurian legend. In a different version of the petrified army tale (also known from the Rollright Stones in England; see Chapter 6), it is the Roman army pursuing the centurion Cornelius, because of his conversion to Christianity, who are turned into stone through his prayers. Another tradition also ascribes the petrification of the Roman army to Cornelius, though under the name St. Cornély, Carnac's patron saint, who had been chased by the Romans to Brittany after they had expelled him from the papal throne in Rome. This element of the folklore of the stones is probably a misinterpretation of events in the biography of the real Pope Cornelius, who lived in the third century AD.

A fascinating verbal tradition connected with the Carnac Alignments was recorded by the Abbé Mahé in 1825. He was told that each generation would add a new stone to the avenues every year in June, and on the night before the ceremony, all the menhirs were illuminated. This tradition was also told to Breton scholar Jacques de Cambry (1749–1807) by an old sailor at Carnac, but in this version it was in the time of "the ancients" that the stones were added. Writing in the journal *Folklore* in 1894, M.J. Walhouse mentions visiting Carnac five years previously and being told by a young guide that "on certain nights a flame was seen burning on every stone, and on such nights no one would go near; the stones are there believed to mark burial places." This intriguing piece of folklore may indicate a stripped down version of the original ceremony for adding a stone to the alignments, but whether this rite was actually performed millennia ago is impossible to tell, though the tale does indicate that a vague sense of the sacredness of the avenues seems to have survived into modern times. In connection with this rite, author John Michell has suggested that, as so many of the Carnac stones have Christian crosses carved into them or added onto their tops, the cross may have replaced something else that was once put there, perhaps a fire basket containing some kind of beacon light.

Stories of vast treasures associated with prehistoric sites, especially barrows (burial mounds), are common. Examples from England include barrows at Minchinhampton in Gloucestershire and Priddy in Somerset, and there are also numerous similar tales from Ireland, Scotland, and Wales, as well as from northern France (Normandy and Britanny). Such a huge amount of treasure is said to be concealed beneath one of the menhirs in the Carnac avenues, that the other stones were only erected to confuse the treasure seeker. It is said that the key to finding out the identity of this stone is, for some reason, in the Tower of London. Many of the Carnac menhirs are rumored to conceal treasure, though it is said that anyone who has tried to search for it has died.

One of the more recent theories put forward to explain the function of the Carnac megaliths was suggested by French engineer Pierre Méreaux. He believed that the location and orientation of the menhirs at Carnac reflected seismic fault lines and that the dolmens, with the large, flat capstone balancing on top of its uprights, would have functioned as primitive seismic detection devices. Méreaux set out his theories in his 1992 book, *Carnac: Des Pierres Pour Les Vivants,* but, as France is not a particularly active seismic zone, the earthquake detector conclusion seems hard to justify. It is important to remember that the avenues at Carnac should not be viewed in isolation; such alignments are found in England, Ireland, Denmark, Corsica, and many other areas. British archaeologist and author of *From Carnac To Callanish: The Prehistoric Stone Rows of Britain, Ireland, and Brittany* (1993), Aubrey Burl, believes that multiple stone alignments, such as those at Carnac, developed from early processional avenues leading to stone circles. Consequently, the avenues could have been used as processional routes to cromlechs that served as focal points/sacred centers, perhaps as part of rites connected with the changing of the seasons.

Another of the theories put forward to explain the function of the Carnac alignments suggests that they were vast calendrical devices designed to help ancient farmers with planting and harvesting crops. A similar hypothesis, and one that has attracted a great deal of support today, is that the Carnac alignments possess astronomical significance. As far back as 1887, H. de Cleuziou had suggested a connection between the Carnac avenues and the directions of sunsets at the solstices, but it was not until the early 1970s that the possibility of significant astronomical alignments was properly investigated. From 1970 until 1974, former professor of engineering at Oxford University, Alexander Thom, worked with his son Archie, carrying out a detailed investigation of the Carnac avenues. Thom's theory, published in a series of papers detailing the astronomical alignments of the stones, is that the menhirs were set up to record the extreme positions of the moon's orbit, and that this information was utilized by the Neolithic inhabitants of Carnac to predict eclipses. The explanation put forward by Thom is intriguing, and, if true, would suggest, as Thom noted, that the prehistoric population of the time had been carrying out accurate astronomical observations and record-keeping for perhaps a century or more in order to plan this vast giant observatory in stone.

However, the erection of thousands of megaliths seems a huge undertaking in order to accomplish a task that could be achieved by simply observing nature over a period of time or, if need be, planting a few wooden poles in the ground at the appropriate points. Additionally, as stated elsewhere in this book, an obsession with time and calculation is a product of a modern technology-dominated age, and reflecting this obsession back to the peoples of the Neolithic period is dangerous to say the least. Thom has proved that there are astronomical alignments at Carnac, no doubt. But whether astronomy was the primary function of the stone avenues, or indeed why such precision would be so important to the Neolithic inhabitants of the area, are questions that need to be addressed if we are to accept an astronomical function for the Carnac stone rows.

One of the many problems with assigning functions to the Carnac stones—and megalithic monuments in general—is that we do not know for sure whether the remains we see today are a representative sample of what existed during the Neolithic and Bronze Age periods in the area. This point is borne out by the fact that, close to some menhir alignments, researchers have discovered traces of a variety of wooden or wood and earth structures, which may have been just as important as the stone structures in the area. Rescue excavations of stone alignments at Saint-Just, Ille-et-Vilaine (Brittany), in the 1990s, revealed post-holes interspersed with standing stones, as well as five post-holes that turned out to be the remains of a Neolithic house-like structure. Perhaps then, when detailed excavation is one day undertaken at the Carnac avenues, the thousands of menhirs remaining will be shown to represent the more durable, though not necessarily the most important, of what once existed in the Neolithic/Early Bronze Age at Carnac, and thus are only a part of the rich picture of prehistoric life in the area.

Chapter 13

Chartres Cathedral (France)

Chartres Cathedral from the front.
Copyright Atlant.

The Cathedral of Our Lady of Chartres (*Cathédrale Notre-Dame de Chartres*) is located in the center of the medieval town of Chartres, on the west bank of the Eure River, about 50 miles southwest of Paris. Visible from a great distance as it looms above the surrounding wheat fields on a natural mound, the majestic architectural masterpiece we see today represents one of the most complete and best-preserved gothic cathedrals ever built.

The town of Chartres is named after an Iron Age Celtic tribe called the Carnutes, a people of north-central Gaul (France) who seem to have controlled the area between the rivers Seine and Loire. The Carnutes founded a settlement on the banks of the River Autura (modern Eure), which was captured by Caesar after the 52–51 BC revolts and named Autricum. Under the Romans, the town was the capital of the region until the third century AD; the remains of two aqueducts and an amphitheatre in the modern town of Chartres testify to the importance of Roman Autricum. The ancient settlement of Autricum was burnt by the Vikings in AD 858, and during subsequent centuries belonged to the Counts of Blois and the Counts of Champagne, until it became the property of the French Crown in 1286.

The site of the cathedral itself probably began life as a sacred well, possibly connected with the Druids, just before the time of the Roman occupation. The area of the Carnutes was, according to Caesar, an important center of the Druids. He describes the Druids as assembling "at a fixed period of the year in a consecrated place in the territories of the Carnutes" (*Gallic Wars 6:13*). However, we do not know if this sacred place was the future site of Chartres Cathedral or the other chief fortified town of the area *Cenabum* (the modern Orleans). The sacred well, now known as the *Puits des Saints-Forts* ("Well of the Strong Saints"), still exists inside the ninth-century crypt of Saint-Lubin under the choir of the cathedral, though it has now been filled in. The well apparently received its name in the reign of Holy Roman Emperor and King of France, Charles the Bald (823–877). During the Norse siege of 858, two Christian Saints, Altin and Eodald, were allegedly murdered by the invading Vikings and thrown down into the 108-foot-deep well.

In the fourth century AD, a Christian church was built on the site, but was destroyed in 743 by Hunaud, the duke of Aquitaine. After rebuilding, the church was again destroyed, this time by the Vikings in 858, after which Bishop Gislebert began reconstruction of the cathedral, the remains of which survive as the crypt of Chartres Cathedral today. Gislebert's cathedral fell victim to another fire in 962 and in 1020 was burnt to the ground. After this destruction, Fulbert, bishop of Chartres, along with the architect Béranger, began work on a completely new cathedral, which was finished in 1037. This structure, which included a wood-framed roof, was almost completely destroyed in 1194, when yet another fire devastated the city of Chartres. Most of the Cathedral of

Our Lady of Chartres that we see today was built over a 30-year period during the mid-13th century. On October 24, 1260, it was dedicated in the presence of King Louis IX and his family.

Perhaps the most impressive features of Chartres Cathedral are its two spires. The south spire (built in 1145) is 378 feet high, and the Clocher Neuf (built in 1513), on the cathedral's northwest corner, rises to 350 feet. Chartres is also justly famous for its 152 (of the original 186) 12th- and 13th-century stained-glass windows. These remarkable windows, the most complete collection of preserved ancient stained-glass windows in France, are particularly celebrated for their vibrant blue color (known as "Chartres Blue"), chiefly in a representation of the Madonna and Child known as the "Blue Virgin Window." During World War II, much of the stained glass was removed from Chartres and kept safe in the surrounding countryside against attacks by German bombers. When the war ended, the precious windows were brought back to the cathedral and replaced.

Laid into the floor of the Gothic nave of Chartres, the vaulting of which is a staggering 121 feet high, is an early-13th-century labyrinth. The Chartres labyrinth is an 11-circuit design divided into four quadrants, a type that was fairly common in Gothic Cathedrals, though many have been destroyed or removed over the years. The labyrinth at Chartres is known as a "Prayer Labyrinth," and has a diameter of 42 feet. It was designed for pilgrims to walk the 860-foot route as a form of repentance, or as a pilgrimage/contemplative journey in an attempt to become closer to God. If the pilgrims were seeking redemption they would often crawl along the route on their knees. In some cases, walking the labyrinth would symbolize an actual pilgrimage to Jerusalem, and came to be known as the "Chemin de Jerusalem," or Road of Jerusalem. The four quadrants of the labyrinth are symbolic of Christ's cross, and the six-petal rosette design at the center has a deep symbolic meaning, including that of representing the six days of Creation, the Virgin Mary, the Holy Spirit, or simply enlightenment.

One of the more puzzling names attached to the Chartres labyrinth was *La Lieue* ("The League"). A league is a distance of about 3 miles, but the length of the path is only 860 feet. However, as stated previously, during the Middle Ages some pilgrims would walk the labyrinth on their knees, which would take about an hour, or the time required to walk 3 miles.

In AD 876, Charles the Bald made a gift to Chartres cathedral of a sacred relic known as the *Sancta Camisia* ("The Veil of the Virgin"). This relic, which had been given to Charles by the Byzantine Empress Irene (c. 752–803), is a cloak that is believed by some Christians to have belonged to the Virgin Mary, which she was apparently wearing when she gave birth to Jesus. The presence of the Holy Cloak began the cult of the Virgin at the cathedral and made the town of Chartres a popular destination for religious pilgrims. Apparently, when the cathedral burnt down in 1145, the *Sancta Camisia* miraculously escaped damage, which was seen as a sign that a new and greater cathedral should be built on the site. The remarkable survival of the relic was proclaimed a miracle by a papal legate and Cardinal from Rome, and consequently donations and contributions to the building project flooded in from all over Europe. The *Sancta Camisia*, a long white piece of silk, is now housed inside a reliquary in an apsidal chapel of the cathedral.

One of the most intriguing mysteries at Chartres Cathedral is the *Virgo Paritura* ("Black Virgin"). A Black Madonna or Black Virgin is a statue or painting of Mary in which she is depicted with dark or black features. There are hundreds of examples in churches, cathedrals, and sanctuaries from Catholic areas throughout Europe, many of which are in France. The majority of these objects date to the medieval period (12th to 15th centuries) and are constructed of wood, though occasionally stone examples are found. There are two Black Madonna sculptures at Chartres, the first—"Our Lady of the Pillar"—is located on a 6-foot-high pillar in the nave and is a copy of the original 13th-century gilt statue. The second Black Madonna at Chartres is located in the crypt of the cathedral and is also a copy; the original peat wood sculpture was burned in 1793, during the French Revolution. This Madonna, known as "the Madonna Sous Terre" ("the Madonna Under the Earth"), who wears a crown of oak leaves and holds the Christ Child in her lap, is still venerated by thousands of pilgrims from all over the world.

Scholars of comparative religion as well as a number of popular authors, including Louis Charpentier and Jean Markale, have argued that the Black Madonnas are, in reality, pre-Christian mother or earth goddesses in the guise of Christianity. In connection with this theory, Charpentier and Markale also believe that the original Black Madonna in the crypt of Chartres was based on a Druidic image of the Virgin forever giving birth, set up on the site of the sacred well in the crypt of the cathedral. These authors also consider it likely that Chartres was built on the site of a "dolmenic chamber" (a dolmen is a single-chamber megalithic tomb), in the opinion of Charpentier built to capture "earth energies," and that the Druids worshipped at this ancient structure.

Although this is all fascinating, it is complete speculation. Although Christian shrines and churches were often built over prehistoric monuments, there is no evidence that Chartres is sited over a megalithic tomb. Continuity of belief and religious practice at the site is also hardly likely, because dolmens date from the fifth to the end of the third millennium BC and there are no records of the Druids before the first century BC. Furthermore, there has never been any proof of a worldwide "mother-goddess" cult, and the idea is now considered mistaken and outdated in the light of archaeological discoveries of Neolithic weapons and fortified defensive structures throughout Europe. The notion that patriarchal invaders attacked and defeated the harmonious goddess-centered culture, and replaced it with their own male-dominant culture, also falls down when one wonders where, if all cultures were matriarchal, the patriarchal cultures came from.

In his book *The Mysteries of Chartres Cathedral* (first published in English in 1972), Charpentier was one of the first to connect those staples of modern "alternative history" books—the Knights Templar and the Ark of the Covenant—with Chartres. There is an intriguing carving on the exterior of Chartres Cathedral, by the north door, which may possibly represent the Ark of the Covenant as a chest being transported on some type of wheeled vehicle. Does this carving indicate some kind of link between the cathedral and the Ark? Many researchers into the Ark of the Covenant believe that the sacred object was probably kept at Chartres after being taken from Jerusalem by the Knights Templar, though they have never produced any hard evidence to back up this theory. Charpentier claims that the Knights Templar built the Cathedral as a repository for ancient wisdom, using their knowledge of sacred geometry. He also connects the "sudden" appearance of Gothic architecture with this knowledge that the Templars brought back from the Holy Land. However, Gothic architecture did no appear suddenly. The style was developed from the previous architectural genre, Romanesque, as can be seen, for example, in the design of the Abbey of Cluny, in the region of Bourgogne, east-central France, which was founded in AD 909.

Due to the sublime artistry of its design, its exquisite sculptures and stained-glass windows, as well as the mysteries of its labyrinth and Black Madonnas, Chartres has become one of the most famous Gothic structures in the world. In recognition of this historical and cultural importance Chartres cathedral was added to UNESCO's list of World Heritage Sites in 1979.

Chapter 14

The Sacred Town of Aachen (Germany)

Aachen Cathedral.
Photograph by Aleph.

The town of Aachen (French—"Aix-la-Chapelle") is situated in North Rhine-Westphalia, on the westernmost tip of Germany, bordering The Netherlands and Belgium. The earliest evidence for human activity in the area extends all the way back to the late Neolithic period (late fourth to third millennium BC), when there was a flint mine in operation on the Lousberg, a hill on the northwestern edge of Aachen. No traces of further human presence have so far been discovered until the arrival of the Romans, who incorporated the sulphur-rich hot springs at Aachen (said to be the hottest in Europe) into two bath complexes, which were probably used from the first to the late fourth century AD. These baths, the Büchelthermae and the Münsterthermae, together with a large temple complex and the living quarters for the legionaries, formed an important health or healing center. There was also a Roman necropolis, in use in the third and fourth centuries AD, to the northwest of the baths and settlement.

The Romans named the military spa town Aquae Granni ("the waters of Grannus"). Grannus was a Celtic healing god, often associated with healing springs, so it seems probable that Celtic tribes had been using the thermal springs at Aquae Granni before the arrival of the Romans in the first century AD. According to Roman historian Dio Cassius (born c. AD 165), the Roman emperor Caracella (AD 188–217) visited the temple sanctuary of Grannus when ill during the war with Germany in around AD 214. However, he was unsuccessful in obtaining a cure. The Romans called the Celtic god "Apollo Grannus," after the Greco-Roman sun-god, who was also known as a healing deity, which may explain the connection with the Celtic Grannus. Grannus was worshipped over a large part of Europe, and sites dedicated to him are usually associated with sacred mineral springs, such as at Trier (Germany) and Grand (Vosges, in eastern France).

It was on such a sacred foundation that the town developed, and at Christmas 768, the year of his coronation, Charlemagne came to Aachen for the first time. Charlemagne (Charles the Great) was king of the Franks, a confederation of West Germanic tribes. By AD 800, he would become the undisputed ruler of Western Europe, with his empire encompassing present-day France, Switzerland, Belgium, and The Netherlands, and parts of Italy, Germany, Austria, and Spain. Charlemagne may initially have been attracted to Aachen partly by its thermal springs and partly for strategic reasons, and it soon became one of his royal residences, and a center of Western culture and learning. The Aachen Rathaus (city hall), built between 1333 and 1350, stands on the site of the

Charlemagne's imperial palace, itself built over the ruins of the old Roman baths, and the oldest part of it, the intriguingly named "Granusturm" ("Granus Tower"), dates back to the time of the original palace. From the coronation of Otto I in 936 until the Reformation in the 16th century, more than 30 Holy Roman emperors and German kings were crowned at Aachen.

The best known monument at Aachen is its great cathedral, often referred to as the "Imperial Cathedral." A local legend states that the people of Aachen ran out of money during the construction of the cathedral and made a pact with the devil, who supplied the townsfolk with the much-needed cash. In exchange, the devil was to claim the soul of the first living being to walk through the door of the magnificent new cathedral. The devil hoped for a bishop or perhaps even the pope, but was tricked, as the cunning townsfolk caught a wolf in the nearby woods and sent it running through the cathedral doors. Not realizing the ploy, the devil grabbed the wolf and ripped the soul from its chest, only to discover that he had been fooled. In a blind rage, the devil slammed the bronze cathedral doors shut with such violence that the metal was bent out of shape and his thumb was ripped from his hand. The crack in the doors can still be seen to this day, and the "devil's thumb" still remains in one of the two (13th-century) lion-headed door handles. The chapel narthex (entrance area) contains two Roman era artefacts connected with this tale: a bronze she-wolf and a bronze pine cone, possibly once fountain decorations at the bath complex. The hole bored through the figure of the wolf is said to indicator the place where its soul was torn from its body, and the pinecone symbolizes the wolf's soul.

Historically, the cathedral originates with the construction of the Palace (Palatine) Chapel in 786, designed by Odo of Metz and completed in 805, originally as the chapel of Charlemagne's imperial palace. Charlemagne thought of himself as the rightful heir of the Western Roman Empire, and wanted his church to be a testament in stone to his dream of founding a new Rome. To this end, he had marble columns brought from Rome and Ravenna. As well as being a tangible expression of the link between the ancient world of Rome and the medieval West, the King envisaged the chapel as an image in stone, gold, and precious stones of St. John the Divine's heavenly Jerusalem as described by him in the Book of Revelations. The Palatine Chapel (also known as the "Octagon") was a domed structure modelled on the sixth-century Basilica of San Vitale in Ravenna, Italy, and the Chrysotriklinos (hall of state) built in the time of Justin II (565–578) in the Great Palace at Constantinople (Byzantium). The Chapel was built on an east-west axis, with a 2-story-high octagonal rotunda encircled by a 16-sided polygon. In the gallery of the chapel is the huge marble throne believed to have been used by Charlemagne and on which 32 Holy Roman Emperors were crowned.

When Charlemagne died in 814 at the age of 72, he was buried in the choir of the Palace Chapel, though the exact location of his original tomb is no longer known. In AD 1000, on the feast of Pentecost, despite Charlemagne's curse on anyone who should open his tomb, King Otto III had Charlemagne's vault opened and took a few relics from the body. According to a traditional story, Charlemagne was almost perfectly preserved, sceptre in hand, dressed in his imperial purple robes, with a crown on his head, sword by his side, an open Bible on his knees, and seated on his great marble throne. In 1165, the vault was again opened, this time by Emperor Frederick Barbarossa, who placed the remains in a sculptured marble sarcophagus, allegedly the same one in which Augustus Caesar was buried. In 1215, Frederick II had Charlemagne's bones put in a gold and silver casket, and they are now preserved in an ornate shrine in the Chapel.

During his life, Charlemagne collected a variety of religious relics, and the collection of sacred objects now contained in the late Romanesque silver shrine in the cathedral treasury is one of the most important ecclesiastical treasuries in Europe. The four most important of the sacred objects at Aachen Cathedral are the supposed swaddling clothes of Jesus, his crucifixion loincloth, the cloak of the Blessed Virgin, and the cloth on which the head of St. John the Baptist was placed after his beheading. These sacred objects attracted a vast amount of pilgrims to Aachen throughout the medieval period. In the mid-14th century, the custom began of exhibiting the four "Great Relics" only once every seven years, a tradition that is still observed today.

The grandeur and almost-mystical harmony of the architecture of the Palatine Chapel have inspired some questionable new theories about sacred geometry and hidden occult knowledge in stone. But the cathedral has also inspired some intriguing new lines of research into how sunlight may have been utilized by Emperors at Aachen. In the late 1970s, German photographer Hermann Weisweiler was in the Palatine Chapel waiting for the appropriate light to capture some shots of the interior, when he was startled by a sudden shaft of sunlight illuminating the church through one of the windows. Inspired by this occurrence Weisweiler decided to further investigate how sunlight entered the "Octagon." What he discovered was that at mid-day on the longest day of the year (June 21st), the sun shone through the windows and lit up the golden ball on the "Barbarossa chandelier" suspended from the center of the octagon's 105-foot-high dome. This bronze chandelier was presented by Frederick I Barbarossa in 1168 as a symbol of the heavenly Jerusalem.

But the most important of Weisweiler's discoveries was that, on June 21st, the top of Charlemagne's throne, located at the western end of the Palatine Chapel, would be bathed in sunlight streaming through the eastern octagon window. This would imply that the head of the emperor seated in his throne would be bathed in a resplendent glow by the sunlight entering the octagon on this particular date. Of course, we do not know if this effect is pure chance or if the original builders of the church engineered it this way.

Another of Weisweiler's ideas was that ancient knowledge from Britain had been utilized in the construction of the Palatine Chapel, perhaps via Alcuin of York, an English churchman and educator, at one time head of Charlemagne's Palace School at Aachen. Weisweiler's major discovery in this light came when he overlaid a plan of the inner horseshoe stone setting and its surrounding circle at Stonehenge on top of the ground plan of the Palace Chapel. He found an almost perfect fit; the two structures were of almost exactly the same dimensions. Despite the obvious difficulty of how Alcuin of York, or anyone for that matter, could have received "secret" architectural knowledge that had been handed down for around 3,000 years, there is no proof that Alcuin had anything to do with designing the Palatine Chapel. He was a teacher, not an architect, and his main contribution at Aachen was in the development of the "Carolingian minuscule," a clear and manageable script that significantly increased the uniformity, clarity, and legibility of handwriting.

In 1978, Aachen Cathedral, the oldest cathedral in northern Europe and one that took more than a millennium to achieve its present form, was one of the first 12 sites to be entered onto the UNESCO World Heritage List.

Chapter 15

The Mysterious Etruscans and the Labyrinth of Porsena (Italy)

The Etruscan Civilization flourished in modern Tuscany, Latium (modern Lazio), Campania, and part of the Po Valley, from roughly 800 BC until its complete assimilation into the Roman Republic around the fourth century BC. The origins and the language of the Etruscans are two of the most intriguing mysteries of ancient history. It was long thought by many scholars that the Etruscans were native to Italy and had developed from the preceding "Villanovan" culture. However, as far back as the fifth century BC, Greek historian Herodotus had in his *Histories* suggested a Near Eastern origin for the Etruscans (called by him "Tyrrhenians," a term used by Greek authors to refer to a non-Greek people):

Estrusca cippus (grave marker) in the shape of a warrior head, from the necropolis of Crocifisso del Tufo (Orvieto, Italy). Photograph by Nixdorf.

In the reign of Atys, the son of Manes, the whole of Lydia suffered from a severe famine...the King divided the population into two groups and determined by drawing lots which should emigrate and which should remain at home...The lots were drawn, and one section went down to the coast at Smyrna [modern Izmir in Turkey], where they built vessels, put aboard all their household effects and sailed in search of a livelihood elsewhere. They passed many countries and finally reached Umbria in the north of Italy, where they settled and still live to this day. (*Histories* 1:94)

Fascinatingly, DNA studies undertaken in 2004 by a team led by Guido Barbujani, professor of genetics at the University of Ferrara, lend some support to Herodotus's claim. Bone samples from 80 Etruscan bodies dated from the seventh to the third centuries BC were tested and proved to exhibit closer relationships to peoples from the Eastern Mediterranean than the modern Italian population. Further studies have been carried out by Dr. Antonio Torroni of the University of Pavia on the mitochondrial DNA of inhabitants from a small former Etruscan town in Tuscany called Murlo. Results from these tests showed that DNA from the residents of the town mapped closer to peoples of modern Palestine and Syria than modern Italians. A third study was developed by Marco Pellecchia and Paolo Ajmone-Marsan of the Catholic University of the Sacred Heart in Piacenza (northern Italy). The team examined the mitochondrial DNA from modern herds of *Bos Taurus* cattle in the north, south, and central regions of Italy. They found that the DNA of the Tuscan cattle differed from samples from the rest of Italy, genetically resembling Near Eastern cattle. Given the results of these three studies the best explanation would seem to be that, in the words of Dr. Ajmone-Marsan, "both humans and cattle reached Etruria from the Eastern Mediterranean by sea" (according to an April 3, 2007, *New York Times* online article).

The Etruscan language is a more of a mystery. We know that the Etruscans adopted the alphabet from Greek colonists in Pithekoussai (modern Ischia) in the first quarter of the eighth century BC, but the language died out completely and was eventually replaced by Latin. It has never been proved conclusively that Etruscan is related to any other language in the world; it certainly seems that it is not an Indo-European language. Though a rich Etruscan literature did exist, practically no works in the language survive. The evidence for the script comes in the form of around 13,000 inscriptions, mostly short epitaphs, from various parts of the Mediterranean dating to around 700 BC. Despite this fairly large corpus, the total vocabulary of Etruscan words known to us today is a meager 250 words or so. According to ancient sources, Roman emperor Claudius (10 BC–AD 54) was the last known person to be able to read Etruscan. Perhaps a copy of Claudius's famous lost work, *Tyrrenikà*—a history of the Etruscans in 20 books, which was based on Etruscan sources—will one day be discovered and shed much-needed light on this enigmatic people.

One of the lesser-known mysteries of the Etruscans is the legendary tomb and labyrinth of King Porsena. This monumental structure is said to have been located at the ancient Etruscan town of Clusium (modern Chiusi, in the province of Siena, Tuscany, north-central Italy). Known in the Etruscan language as "Clevsin," this city was one of the more powerful of the league of 12 Etruscan cities until it came under the control of Rome sometime in the third century BC. Towards the end of the sixth century BC, semi-legendary king of Clusium, Lars Porsena, is said to have attacked Rome and gained control of the city for a brief period. Before his death Lars Porsena had a magnificent tomb built, which was first described by Roman author Pliny the Elder in the first century AD, quoting from Roman scholar and writer Marcus Terentius Varro (116–27 BC):

> "Porsena was buried," says he [Varro], "beneath the city of Clusium; in the spot where he had had constructed a square monument, built of squared stone. Each side of this monument was three hundred feet in length and fifty in height, and beneath the base, which was also square, there was an inextricable labyrinth, into which if any one entered without a clew of thread, he could never find his way out. Above this square building there stand five pyramids, one at each corner, and one in the middle, seventy-five feet broad at the base, and one hundred and fifty

feet in height. These pyramids are so tapering in their form, that upon the summit of all of them united there rests a brazen globe, and upon that a petasus; from which there hang, suspended by chains, bells, which make a tinkling when agitated by the wind, like what was done at Dodona in former times. Upon this globe there are four other pyramids, each one hundred feet in height; and above them is a single platform, on which there are five more pyramids,"—the height of which Varro has evidently felt ashamed to add; but, according to the Etruscan fables, it was equal to that of the rest of the building. (*Natural History*, XXXVI, 19, 91ff.)

In the 18th century Father Angelo Cortenovis (1727–1801) proposed that the tomb of Lars Porsena could have been designed as a huge electrical generator, an idea also employed by Robert Scrutton in his 1978 book, *Secrets of Lost Atland*. However, not a trace of this vast edifice, popularly known as "The Labyrinth of Porsena," has ever been discovered by archaeologists, persuading most Roman historians that Varro's description is pure fantasy. If the tomb ever existed it must have been built in the late sixth/early fifth century BC, though it may well have been destroyed in 89 BC when Clusium was sacked by the Roman general Cornelius Sulla. Nevertheless, the Etruscan culture is well known for constructing elaborate sepulchers; the necropolis of 6,000 tombs at Tarquinia in the province of Viterbo (Latium, central Italy) is a particularly fine example. One interesting feature of Clusium that has persuaded some researchers that the Labyrinth of Porsena may have really existed, is its network of ancient tunnels, known as *cunuculi,* which still runs underneath the modern town. In his pioneering work, *The Cities and Cemeteries of Etruria* (1848), English author and explorer George Dennis wrote about his visit to Chiusi and a "so-called Labyrinthe" in the Paolozzi garden. Thinking he may have stumbled on remnants of the lost tomb of Lars Porsena, Dennis "eagerly rushed into the cavern" only to discover that it was merely a natural passage in the rock. He does, however, provide information about further examples in the town:

One entrance to these underground "streets" is near the church of San Francesco. Another is on the Piazza del Duomo. In 1830, in lowering this Piazza, four round holes, 2 feet in diameter, were discovered, and they were found to be for lighting a square chamber, vaulted over with great blocks of travertine, and divided by an arch. It was nearly full of earth, but in it were found a large flask of glass, fragments of swords, pieces of marble, broken columns. About 100 feet distant was another light-hole, giving admission to a second vault, about 27 feet deep, but so large that its extent could not be ascertained. (*Cities and Cemeteries of Etruria*, Vol. 2, p. 293)

Dennis found out from the local inhabitants that there were numerous underground passages running for long distances underneath Chiusi, but, because they were half-filled with water, they had never been fully explored. He adds that "the whole city, indeed, is supposed to be undermined by them, and by subterranean chambers, though what purpose they may have served is a mystery no one can fathom!"

The passageways located behind Piazza del Duomo are now open to the public. However, far from being the remains of the celebrated Labyrinth of Porsena, the complicated tunnel network at Chiusi served a far more mundane purpose, as Dennis realized almost two centuries ago when he expressed his opinion that the subterranean passages were "probably connected with the system of sewerage." In fact, the elaborate tunnel system was designed to provide drainage and drinking water for the inhabitants of the hilltop town. After the Roman occupation of Clusium, the Etruscan-built hydraulic system fell out of use, became blocked up with debris, and was soon forgotten. These subterranean passageways are not confined to the town of Chiusi; they run for hundreds of miles throughout central Italy, with particularly well designed examples at Viterbo, where the remains of Etruscan Surina lie. For the most part, these tunnel systems are attached to Etruscan towns and cities located on hills or plateaus, and attest to the remarkable engineering skills of their builders. It is now apparent from excavation that these cuniculi had multiple uses, such as irrigation, drainage, and the collection of clean water.

However, the mystery of the Labyrinth of Porsena still continues to exert its effect. In 2004, Giuseppe Centauro, a professor of urban restoration at Florence University, claimed that archaeologists have been looking in the wrong place for the celebrated tomb. His contention is that ancient

Clusium is not located in modern Chiusi at all, but closer to Florence at the archaeological site of Gonfienti. The remains of a hitherto unknown large Etruscan city are located on a plain near Prato, on the eastern side of the Arno River Valley, just more than 6 miles from Florence. From excavations at the site it has been determined that the ancient city, which covers an area of 12 hectares and boasts house foundations, avenues, tombs, and a sophisticated network of canals and artificial basins, was founded around 730 BC. For some reason, possibly severe flooding, the city was completely abandoned at the end of the fifth century BC. Centauro believes that the site at Gonfienti represents the remains of ancient Chamars (Clusium) and that, somewhere among the complex of tombs, the fabled monumental sepulcher of Lars Porsena may await discovery.

Chapter 16

The Hypogeum Funerary Complex of Malta (Malta)

"The Sleeping Lady," from the Museum of Archaoelogy,
Valetta, Malta.

The Maltese archipelago consists of five islands in the central Mediterranean Sea, 60 miles south of Sicily. Only three of these islands are inhabited: Malta Island, which is the largest, Gozo, and Comino. Malta has a history going back at least 7,000 years, with a wide range of archaeological remains, from the megalithic temples and underground chambers of prehistory to the baroque architecture of the medieval period. As the islands stood at the crossroads of the Mediterranean, a vast array of cultures have left a traces on Malta, including the Phoenicians, Greeks, Romans, Arabs, Normans, Knights Hospitaller, Ottomans, and British. But the most spectacular and enigmatic of the ancient remains on Malta are the Neolithic temples and tombs, built 1,000 years before the pyramids, and the oldest free-standing stone buildings in the world. One of the most fascinating and mysterious of these megalithic structures is known as the Hal Saflieni Hypogeum.

A "hypogeum" is the subterranean rock-cut chamber of an ancient building, and there are a number of this type of monument spread across the Mediterranean, in southern France, Sicily, Sardinia, and Crete. The Hal Saflieni Hypogeum is an underground tomb and temple complex, extending for around 5,380 square feet, and is located in the town of Paola, in the south of Malta Island. The site was discovered by accident in 1902 when workers digging cisterns for new houses above broke through the roof of one of the chambers. The first excavations at the site were performed by Father Emmanuel Magri of the Society of Jesus, and later continued by Temi Zammit, the first curator of Malta's Museums Department. Between 1905 and 1911 Zammit excavated a fascinating collection of archaeological material from the complex, including human remains, pottery, beads, amulets, and figurines, and wrote a series of reports of his work at the site that were published from 1910 onward. The Hypogeum was first opened to the public in 1908 while the excavations were still taking place.

The Hal Saflieni Hypogeum consists of a series of oval chambers, halls, and niches set on three levels, one underneath the other. The underground structures were all carved out of the solid rock in semi-darkness using stone mallets and antler picks, and later smoothed over using flint implements. The Upper Level of the complex consists of a hollow with a central passageway, with burial chambers cut into the natural caves on each side. This is the oldest level of the Hypogeum, in use from 3600 BC to 3300 BC, and is similar in plan to earlier rock-cut tombs found elsewhere on the Islands, such as the Xemxija Tombs, which date to around 4000 BC.

The Middle Level (3300–3000 BC), was cut into the sub-surface rock as an extension of the upper level of the structure. This level exhibits exquisite stoneworking skill in the elaborately carved trilithons (a construction with two upright posts with a horizontal one set on top) in imitation of the built masonry of the aboveground megalithic structures found elsewhere on Malta. This level also contains some of the most important features of the Hypogeum monument, such as the Main Chamber, the Oracle Room, and the "Holy of Holies." Most of the wall surfaces in the Main Chamber originally had a wash of red ochre, tracing out spiral and honey-comb designs, some of which are still visible today. The famous "Sleeping Lady," a 12-centimeter-long reclining terracotta figure with traces of red ochre, was recovered either from here or a nearby room known as the "Snake Pit." Believed to date from around 3000 BC, this corpulent ceramic figure is naked to the waist and wears a fringed skirt. She appears to be in a deep tranquil sleep on a bed with a rush mattress. Along with other similar figurines from Neolithic sites on Malta and elsewhere in the Mediterranean, the "Sleeping Lady" has been used as evidence for the theory of universal peace-loving mother-goddess (or "Great Goddess") worship in prehistory, proposed by researchers such as Dr. Marija Gimbutas. However, the absence of evidence, whether written or artifactural, aside from figurines to support such a widespread belief system, and finds of weapons and fortified sites dating to the period have considerably weakened this argument.

One interesting theory regarding the Sleeping Lady, whether goddess or not, is that, either in a trance or asleep, she may represent a place in the Hypogeum where dreams or trance visions were interpreted by priests or priestesses. Such a dark subterranean context would have been ideal for the stimulation of such states as would induce dreams and visions. Alternatively, because the area was used for burials, the statue may be a representation of eternal sleep. The enigmatic Sleeping Lady figurine is now on display at the National Museum of Archaeology in Valletta, capital city of Malta.

Also on the Middle Level, the roughly rectangular Oracle Room has an elaborately decorated ceiling of ochre painted spirals and a fascinating side chamber, which has the property to amplify and echo a deep human voice. Whether this intriguing effect was intentional or not is difficult to say, though the possibility that these strange acoustics were utilized in religious ceremonies performed in the chambers is an intriguing one. The "Holy of Holies" is perhaps the most elaborately decorated room in the whole complex, with its trilithon door frame and pierced stone ("porthole") entrance reflecting the architecture of Maltese free-standing Neolithic monuments. The ceiling of this room is also built in imitation of the corbelled roofing (a technique where each course of over-lapping stone projects farther out from the vertical of the wall than the course below) used on aboveground prehistoric temples on the island. This room did not contain any burials.

The third and lowest level at the Hypogeum is 35 feet below street level and has been dated to 3150–2500 BC. It consists of a maze of cham-bers, which were filled with water when discovered in the early 1900s. As there have been no finds of either bones or artifacts from this level, it has been suggested that the chambers here may have been designed as storage for water or grain. Water storage has also been put forward as the possible function of the hypogeum at Knossos, on Crete (dated be-tween 2150 and 2000 BC).

The primary function of the Hypogeum site was certainly as a cem-etery, as around seven thousand skeletons have been found in the cham-bers, ranging in date from 3600 to 2500 BC—in other words, spanning the life of the site itself. This amount of human remains is significantly higher than the tombs could have housed at any one period, indicating, along with the dates of the skeletons, that the complex was used for burials over several centuries. The fact that no human remains were discovered in some rooms, such as the "Holy of Holies," would suggest other functions for these parts of the site. Perhaps they were used for funerary rituals involving priests contacting the ancestors. An interest-ing clue to one of the original functions of the Hypogeum is the resem-blance of the site to natural caves. The near darkness of the original subterranean chambers and passageways is a little difficult to imagine nowadays, with the brightness of the artificial lighting at the site. But originally, whoever was allowed to venture down into the depths of the Hypogeum would only have had the dim light of animal fat lamps to help them through the maze of rooms, passageways, and niches. Perhaps what took place inside the Hypogeum involved some kind of procession or ritual initiation through the disorienting labyrinthine structure, which included passing through porthole entrances into particularly restricted shrines.

Such a mysterious subterranean structure as the Hypogeum is bound to generate its own legends and folklore. Indeed, there are a host of legendary tales associated with the Hypogeum, from disappearing parties of schoolchildren to subterranean monsters and underground alien bases. The majority of these stories can be traced back to an article by Richard Walter in the August 1940, edition of *National Geographic Magazine* entitled "Wanderers Awheel in Malta." This wartime piece discusses the various underground passageways on Malta being used as part of the fortifications and defense system of the island. It also states that at one time it was possible to traverse the island using these tunnels but "the Government closed the entrances to these tunnels after school children and their teachers became lost in the labyrinth while on a study tour and never returned." Apparently the parents of the children claimed they could hear the cries of the children for weeks afterward, coming from under the ground in several parts of the island. Shades of the Pied Piper of Hamelin folktale here, I think.

In this single article from the *National Geographic* lies the origin of a host of contemporary folklore about disappearances and secret tunnels underneath the Hypogeum, mostly built up on the Internet. The problem is that the original *National Geographic* article cites no sources for the tale, and no contemporary accounts of the tragedy have ever been discovered. The Hypogeum is not mentioned by name in the article, so we are not even sure if the alleged incident even occurred there. The story has the ring of local folklore, perhaps a tale concocted to keep children away from dangerous tunnels. It also brings to mind the mysterious disappearance of the Australian schoolgirls in Joan Lindsay's *Picnic at Hanging Rock* (1967), for many years believed to be a true incident, despite the protestations of the author of the novel.

Thanks to a number of stories published first in the 1960s and copied ad infinitum on the Internet over the past decade or so, the folklore of the alleged Hypogeum disappearance has taken on a life of its own. According to these stories, which conveniently don't cite any sources, 30 children vanished with their teachers while on a study tour of the

Hypogeum. New elements, with no foundation in fact whatsoever, were also added to the archaeology of the Hypogeum site itself to make the supposed disappearance more lurid. So we have 30,000 bodies discovered by archaeologists in the chambers—not 7,000—and the remains were all "human sacrifices to some underworld god."

In the best traditions of the modern folklore of underground archaeological sites, the tunnels underneath the Hypogeum are said to stretch for hundreds of miles—all the way to the catacombs underneath Rome. Improving on the original *National Geographic* article, we are told that a British embassy worker (or, in some accounts, an American tourist) called Miss Lois Jessup discovered a series of tunnels underneath the lower level of the Hypogeum, and, in an unexplored cavern, she encountered several large hairy creatures with strange powers. Apparently she later learned that this was the same cavern where the children and their teacher had disappeared, sometime in the 1940s, after which the entrance to the Hypogeum was sealed off, and nobody was allowed to investigate the site. From working at the British Embassy, Miss Lois Jessup went on to become secretary of the New York [Flying] Saucer Information Bureau (!). The sources for these bizarre stories include a 1960s printed lecture by onetime Director of Borderland Sciences Research Foundation, Riley Crabb (called "The Reality of the Cavern World") and a chapter ("Malta—Entrance to the Cavern World") in a 1966 book entitled *Enigma Fantastique* by W. Gordon Allen (essentially a reprint of the Crabb article).

There is one element of these bizarre legends about the Hypogeum that has some truth to it, however: The site was indeed closed for a number of years (between 1992 and 1996, to be exact), though not because of any mysterious disappearance in its tunnels. The reason was that major conservation work was being carried out due to the damage being done to the limestone walls by years of visitors exhaling carbon dioxide in the enclosed space. To protect against this damage, numbers are now restricted to 80 pre-booked visitors per day, and a micro-climate has been installed above the underground chambers to regulate air temperature and humidity. In 1980 the fascinating Hal Saflieni Hypogeum was added to UNESCO's World Heritage List.

Chapter 17

The Temple of Olympian Zeus (Greece)

Temple of Olympian Zeus showing the pillar
that collapsed in 1852.
Photograph by Chris Fleming.

The Temple of Olympian Zeus is the largest temple ever built in mainland Greece and is perhaps the most evocative ruin in Athens. Also known as the Olympieion, this huge monument lies in an ancient quarter of the city of Athens, about a third of a mile southeast of the Acropolis. As part

of the Unification of the Archaeological Sites of Athens Project, the current archaeological site of the Olympieion includes not only the Temple
of Olympian Zeus, but Roman baths, Classical houses, a Christian basilica, and part of the ancient fortification wall of the city.

In Greek mythology the Temple of Olympian Zeus is one of various
places associated with Deucalion and the Great Flood. This creation
story is recorded by a number of ancient Greek and Roman authors,
such as Ovid, in *The Metamorphoses* (AD 2–8) and "Pseudo Apollodorus"
in the *Library of Geek Mythology* (first–second centuries AD). Curiously,
there is no mention of a flood in the *Theogony* (c. 700 BC) of the early
Greek poet Hesiod, describing the origins and genealogies of the gods of
the ancient Greeks. In the myth, Deucalion (son of the Titan Prometheus
and his wife, Clymene) and Pyrrha are the sole survivors of a great flood
sent by Zeus to drown mankind because of their wickedness and impi-
ety. After nine days and nights being thrashed about by the waves inside
a great chest built for the purpose, the flood finally abates and the two
survivors come to rest on Mount Parnassos, in the area of the Delphic
Oracle.

In one version of the myth, after giving thanks to Zeus, the young
couple consult the Oracle about how to replenish the earth with people.
They are told to throw the bones of their mother behind them and a new
human race would appear. Deucalion and Pyrrha realized that "mother"
meant Gaia, the mother of all living things, and that her "bones" were
the rocks lying at their feet. When they threw the rocks over their shoulders they formed people, those thrown by Pyrrha becoming women, and
those thrown by Deucalion becoming men. These were the ancestors of
the Greeks.

The ancient Athenians, aware of the importance of this creation myth
to their own claims of having inhabited the area of Attica since remote
antiquity, reinvented the story. A summary of their version of the myth
was told to Greek travel writer Pausanias (second century AD), which he
adds to his description of the Olympieion:

> The whole enclosure is half a mile round, all full of statues.
> Every city dedicated a portrait of the emperor Hadrian...The
> antiquities of this enclosure are a bronze Zeus and a temple of

Kronos and Rea and some ground sacred to Olympian Earth. The ground here has split open about two feet; they say this is where the water ran away after Deukalion's flood. Once a year they throw in cakes of wheaten meal kneaded with honey...They say that Deukalion built the ancient sanctuary of Olympian Zeus, and for proof that he lived in Athens they point to a tumulus not far away from the modern temple..." (*Guide to Greece*, Volume 1: *Central Greece*, pp. 51–53)

The yearly ritual mentioned by Pausanias, was known as the *Hydrophoria* ("Water-Carrying"), a festival celebrated to propitiate the dead who had perished in Deucalion's Flood. This ritual, which seems to have been performed on the second day of the Dionysian spring festival of the *Anthesteria,* involved a procession of young girls carrying *hydriai* (water jugs) on their heads to the chasm in the ground near the temple of Olympian Zeus. Here the girls poured the water into the chasm as an offering to their ancestors who died in the flood and to celebrate the disappearance of the flood waters into the earth. As mentioned by Pausanias, a meal of honey cakes was also prepared for the dead, to satisfy the hunger of their ghosts in the nether world. This primitive meal was traditionally the first food cooked by Pyrrha and Deucalion after the flood. An intriguing discovery in the vicinity of the Temple, which may partly account for the traditional association of Deucalion with the site, was that of the scant remains of a small shrine with vaults beneath, which exited through a subterranean passageway to the nearby River Illisos.

The Temple of Olympian Zeus took an incredible 700 years to complete. The foundations and platform of the massive Temple were laid in the mid-sixth century BC by Greek statesman Peisistratos and his sons. Measuring around 328 by 100 feet, this vast edifice was designed to rival the huge temples of Ephesos and Miletus (in modern western Turkey), but work was abandoned when Pisistratus's son Hippias was overthrown in 510 BC. The Temple lay in this unfinished state for centuries, until 175 BC, when, under the patronage of the Hellenistic Antiochus IV Epiphanes (a divine title meaning "the shining one"), work began on the construction of a new temple of Pentelic marble (from nearby Mount Pendeli) on the old platform.

This work consisted of 104 Corinthian columns, each one 56 feet high, about 8-and-a-half feet in diameter, and weighing in the region of 802,363 pounds. Only 15 of these huge columns remain standing today; one was blown down during a gale in 1852 and still lies where it fell. However, in 164 BC, before the Temple was finished, Antiochus died, and work was again halted. In 86 BC, after sacking the city of Athens, Roman general Sulla removed two columns from the unfinished Temple and had them shipped to Rome to adorn the Temple of Jupiter on the Capitoline Hill. It was not until the second century AD that work on the Temple of Olympian Zeus resumed, this time under the Roman Emperor Hadrian, who finally completed it in AD 124/125. Hadrian also erected a huge gold and ivory statue of Zeus in the cella (the inner chamber) of the Temple and another next to it of himself, though not a trace remains of these colossal sculptures.

In the late fifth century AD, a Christian basilica was constructed in the Temple precinct from fragments of Classical buildings. Over the centuries, the Temple of Zeus, such as many large structures in Greece, was gradually brought down by earthquakes, and much of the stone was carted off for building material. Following the 1453 fall of Constantinople, which had been the capital of the Byzantine Empire from its beginnings in the sixth century AD, the Ottoman Turks went on to capture Athens in 1456, and so began Turkish rule in Greece. During this period most of Greece was part of the Ottoman Empire until its declaration of independence in 1821. Over these centuries many of the antiquities of Athens were destroyed or severely damaged. In 1759, in order to obtain building materials for a mosque that still bears his name (now a ceramics museum on Monastiraki Square), the Voivode (civil governor) Tzistarakis had one of the marble columns of the Temple of Olympian Zeus blown up by gunpowder to make high-quality lime for the stucco. English traveler and author of *A Classical and Topographical Tour through Greece* (1819), Edward Dodwell reports the incident as follows:

> It was undermined and blown down by gunpowder; but such was its massive strength, that the fourth explosion took place before it fell. The Pasha of Egripos inflicted upon the Voivode a fine of seventeen purses (8,500 Turkish piastres) for having destroyed those venerable remains.... The Athenians relate,

that, after this column was thrown down, the three nearest to it were heard at night to lament the loss of their sister! and that these nocturnal lamentations did not cease to terrify the inhabitants, till the sacrilegious Voivode, who had been appointed governor of Zetoun, was destroyed by poison." (*Tour Through Greece*, I, p. 390)

The people of Athens also blamed the outbreak of plague that year on the sacrilegious act of destroying the ancient column, which many believed released epidemics and catastrophes from underneath the Earth. In April 1841, Danish author and poet Hans Christian Anderson celebrated his birthday on the Acropolis, where he noted Ethiopian slaves owned by the Turks living in caves on its northern slope. He also visited the Temple of Olympian Zeus, where he saw these Ethiopians using the ruins of the Temple as a mosque. During the 18th century there was an Athenian tradition that a huge ghostly Moor (inhabitant of North Africa) guarded a vast treasure of gold coins beneath the ruins of the great Temple. Some even claimed to have seen this giant specter leaping from column to column on dark nights. At one time during the 19th century, an ascetic, known as "the Stylite," settled on top of one of the architraves (the lintel or beam resting on the capitals of the columns) of the ruined Temple and built a small hut to protect himself from the elements. Such religious ascetics had been known from the early days of the Byzantine Empire and were given the name "Stylites" after Saint Simeon Stylites, who spent 37 years on a small platform on top of a pillar in Syria during the mid-fifth century AD.

In 1809 John Galt, a Scottish novelist and friend of Byron, visited Athens during a severe drought and came upon both Turks and Greeks gathered among the ruins of the Temple of Olympian Zeus, desperately invoking their gods to send rain. Zeus was known to the ancient Greeks as the "cloud-gatherer" and was their God of rain. Galt mentions that the situation was so serious that the price of corn was skyrocketing and that public prayers for rain had been ordered for nine successive days at the Temple. He also adds, quoted in John L. Tompinson's book, *Athens,* the intriguing detail that the Temple of Zeus was "where they usually assemble for this purpose when the drought happens to continue long."

In an attempt to rekindle the ancient pre-Christian associations of the Temple of Zeus, a pagan group called *Ellinais* (known as "The Holy Association of Greek Ancient Religion Believers") recently held the first known pagan ceremony at Temple of Olympian Zeus since the ancient Greek religion was outlawed by the Christian Roman empire in the late fourth century. Despite a government ban, *Ellinais,* an Athens-based religious organization dedicated to reviving the worship of ancient Greek gods, staged the event on January 22, 2007, which included worshippers clad in tunics and flowing robes singing ancient hymns and chanting odes to Zeus, Hera, Aphrodite, and other ancient Greek gods. The purpose of this odd gathering, which also included the release of two white doves, and the pouring of water on the ground as an offering to the gods, was to pray for a peaceful hosting of the 2008 Olympics in Beijing. Although Ellinais is a legally recognized association, it has been forbidden from holding religious ceremonies, much to the relief of the all-powerful Orthodox Church, a violent critic of all pagan groups. Nevertheless, representatives of Ellinais have vowed to take the issue to the European Court of Human Rights, on the grounds of a "religious intolerance" that they claim dates back 1,700 years.

Chapter 18

The Oracle at Delphi (Greece)

Delphi in its stunning setting.
Photograph by Leonidtscetkov.

In this place I am minded to build a glorious temple to be an oracle for men, and here they will always bring perfect hecatombs [large-scale sacrifices], both they who dwell in rich

Peloponnesus and the men of Europe and from all the wave-washed isles, coming to question me. And I will deliver to them all counsel that cannot fail, answering them in my rich temple.
(*Homeric Hymn to Pythian Apollo*)

Located more than 1,800 feet up on the southwestern spur of Mount Parnassus, about 6 miles inland from the Corinthian Gulf, the ancient temple complex and oracle of Delphi is one of the most dramatically situated archaeological sites in Greece. The Pan-Hellenic sanctuary of Delphi is known throughout the world as the home of the celebrated oracle of Apollo and was regarded by the ancient Greeks as the centre of the world. There is a myth that tells how two eagles sent out by Zeus from the opposite ends of the earth to find the navel of the world met at Delphi. To mark the site as the center of the earth and the universe, an *omphalos* ("navel" in ancient Greek) stone was set up in the Temple of Apollo.

Also known as baetyli, there were many such sacred stones erected in the ancient world, and, though often claimed to be meteorites, this is not always the case. For example, a baetylus from the ancient city of Ephesus known as "The Diopet of Ephesus" was fashioned from a Neolithic (6000–4000 BC) greenstone artifact. The majority of baetyli were regarded as the abiding place of a particular god, or sometimes as the god himself. The omphalos stone currently in the museum at Delphi is an ornate domed marble pillar, carved with a knotted net covering its surface. This was probably made in the fourth century BC as a replacement for the original stone or group of stones. This stone was supposed to have been a meteorite, and is said to have been draped in a woven net, perhaps to represent a woven beehive.

The evidence for human occupation in the area of Delphi goes back to the Neolithic period at the Corycian Cave, said by ancient Greek travel writer Pausanias (second century AD) to be sacred to Pan. In 1969, French archaeologists excavated material from the Neolithic (c. 4000 BC), Mycenaean (c. 1600–c. 1100 BC) and Classical (c. 480–323 BC) periods at the cave. The finds from the site included bone flutes, iron and bronze rings, miniature bronze statues, 50,000 classical terra cotta figurines, and 24,000 astragoloi, or "knucklebones" (used for *astragolomancy—* "divination by knucklebones"). The earliest finds so far discovered at Delphi itself were the fragments of a Mycenaean settlement and cemetery, found on the site of the sanctuary of Athena Pronaia ("Athena before the temple"). The deposit of Mycenaean figurines discovered at this sanctuary may indicate cult activity at Delphi at this early date.

But it was not until the eighth century BC, when votive offerings began to appear and the cult of Apollo was established, that development of the sanctuary and oracle truly began. In 1891, the Greek government allowed the French School at Athens to undertake long-term excavations at Delphi. However, the village of Kastri, which had been built over the site in medieval times, had to be removed and relocated to allow the excavations to take place. "New Kastri," located half a mile from the archaeological site, is the modern village of Delphi. The French excavations uncovered a vast amount of spectacular archaeological remains, and today the French School, together with the Greek Archaeological Service, continue their research, conservation, and excavation of the two sanctuaries at Delphi: the Sanctuary of Apollo and the Sanctuary of Athena.

Apart from these sanctuaries, some of the most important buildings scattered over the hillside at Delphi are the ancient theater (where the Pythian Games took place), the stadium, the gymnasium, the Castalian Spring, and the various treasuries lining the Sacred Way, such as the impressive Athenian Treasury. These treasuries were commissioned by various cities or wealthy individuals, ostensibly for storing smaller votive objects and to express gratitude to the oracle for her advice, but most importantly for displaying the wealth and splendor of the city that built them.

The imposing Sanctuary of Apollo, situated on top of a large terrace, was undoubtedly the central part of ancient Delphi. According to legendary accounts, the first temple in the Sanctuary was made of laurel branches, the second of beeswax and feathers, the third of bronze, and the fourth was constructed by the legendary architects Trofonios and Agamedes, assisted by Apollo himself. Archaeologically, the earliest stone Temple of Apollo on the site was built at some time during the seventh century BC, but burned down the following century. Its replacement was completed around 510 BC by the Alkmaionid family of Athens, though this too had to be reconstructed after an earthquake in 373 BC. It is the remains of this structure that we see today. The famous Oracle of Delphi was located in an adyton or inner shrine, an underground chamber measuring just 9 by 12 feet. According to some accounts, access to this shrine was restricted to the priests interpreting the words of the Oracle priestess, called the *Pythia*.

There are various mythological explanations for the origin of the Delphic Oracle. In the earliest version, from the Homeric *Hymn to Apollo* (probably seventh century BC), Delphi was sacred to Gaia (the goddess personifying the Earth) and was guarded by her daughter, a ferocious dragoness called "Python" (also called "Delphyne" by later writers). The lair of this dragon was a cave by the Castalian Spring, where Apollo discovered her and slew her with his arrows. After killing the serpent, the new god of prophecy was given the name "Pythian Apollo." In *The Homeric Hymn to Pythian Apollo*, Delphi is described as "rocky Pytho." In order to populate his shrine, Apollo, in the form of a dolphin, leaped aboard a Cretan ship and forced the sailors, "strangers who once dwelt about wooded Cnossos," to be the keepers and priests of his temple. The great god told the Cretans to worship him as Apollo Delphinius (*delphís*; "dolphin" in Greek). A later tradition about the founding of the Oracle site comes from first century BC Greek writer and historian Diodorus Siculus. This story tells of a goat herder named Kouretas, who came upon a chasm in the earth and noticed that, whenever any of his goats approached the fissure, they would start leaping about and making strange sounds. Intrigued, the herdsman approached the chasm and peered down into it, only to discover that he too began to feel possessed, and also found he was able to foretell future events. After this event Diodorus Siculus (16.26.3–4) states:

> The report was bruited among the people of the vicinity concerning the experience of those who approached the chasm, an increasing number of persons visited the place and, as they all tested it because of its miraculous character, whosoever approached the spot became inspired. For these reasons the

oracle came to be regarded as a marvel and to be considered the prophecy-giving shrine of Earth…but later, since many were leaping down into the chasm under the influence of their frenzy and all disappeared, it seemed best to…station one woman there as a single prophetess for all and to have the oracles told through her. And for her a contrivance was devised which she could safely mount, then become inspired and give prophecies to those who so desired.

Similarly, Plutarch (AD 46–120), who served as a priest at the Temple of Apollo at Delphi, wrote that he believed the Pythia's oracular powers seemed to be linked to vapors from the Castalian Spring.

Originally, the Delphic Oracle only functioned on one day of the year, though this was subsequently extended to one day in each of the nine months between spring and autumn, when Apollo was said to be present at Delphi. In order to put a question to the Pythia the inquirer first had to purify himself with holy water from the Castalian Spring and pay a consultation fee, and then approach the temple uphill along the Sacred Way carrying laurel branches (the laurel tree was sacred to Apollo). An animal (usually a black ram) was then sacrificed in the forecourt of the temple, and, if the signs from examining the entrails of the sacrifice were favourable, the inquirer was allowed to enter the Temple. The Pythia was originally a virgin, but later a woman at least 50 years old and married. According to Diodorus Siculus (16.26.6) this change came about "in more recent times" due to Echecrates the Thessalian, who

> having arrived at the shrine and beheld the virgin who uttered the oracle, became enamoured of her because of her beauty, carried her away with him and violated her; and that the Delphians because of this deplorable occurrence passed a law that in future a virgin should no longer prophesy but that an elderly woman of fifty should declare the oracles and that she should be dressed in the costume of a virgin, as a sort of reminder of the prophetess of olden times.

After descending into the chamber, the Pythia, who wore a laurel wreath and carried a sprig of laurel leaves, sat on a great bronze tripod

while laurel leaves and barley meal burned on the altar. In some accounts, in order to achieve an altered state of consciousness, the Pythia
gazed into a bowl of water from the Castalian Spring (or drank from it);
in others she chewed laurel leaves or inhaled toxic vapours from a chasm
beneath the temple. According to later accounts, it was from her Apollo-
inspired mutterings that the male priests (*prophetai*) transcribed the oracular response to the enquiry.

One aspect of the Delphic Oracle that has fascinated scholars, scientists, and laymen alike, concerns the nature of Pythia's trance state
and what caused it. Was it the laurel leaves that she is supposed to have
chewed? The waters of the Castalian Spring? Or the vapors rising up
from an underground cavern? It is widely known that laurel leaves are
not hallucinogenic, and until recently it was thought that the Pythia's
supposed frenzied state could not have been induced by toxic gases
rising from cracks in the ground (because excavations had found no
traces of such fissures). However, in 200, an interdisciplinary research
team of scientists, led by geologist Jelle Z. de Boer of Wesleyan
University (in Middletown, Connecticut), discovered evidence of the
presence of ethylene, a potential hallucinogen, in the temple's local geology
and nearby springs. Thus the team have argued that ethylene intoxication
was probably the cause of the Pythia's divinatory trances.

Though this new research presents fascinating possibilities for the
origin of the Pythia's trance state it also leaves a few questions unan-
swered. The first problem is that if the inquirer and the Pythia were face
to face, as some researchers have suggested, then why was it only the
Priestess who was affected by these toxic gases? Another point is that
the quest to find what exactly put the Priestess of Apollo at Delphi into a
trance ignores the fact that her altered state may well have been self-
induced, perhaps to give the impression of objectivity when answering
enquiries. Another idea associated with the Pythia's supposed toxic high
is the misconception that the Pythia rambled incoherent gibberish when
in her trance, which had to be interpreted and reshaped into prophecies
by the priests.

In his book *The Delphic Oracle, Its Responses and Operations, with a
Catalogue of Responses* (1981), American classical scholar Joseph
Fontenrose (1903–1986) challenged this notion. Examining ancient

sources and separating literary artifice from the Pythia's genuine responses to inquiries, Fontenrose found that these answers were made in clear and precise prose, and the Priestess herself was represented in these texts as speaking lucidly and in her own voice. Indeed, as Ruth Padel has noted, Apollo-induced possession was the literary norm in Classical Greece. The most relevant example being Cassandra, daughter of Priam and Hecuba of Troy, who, similar to the Pythia, is described as being "possessed" by Apollo, while she uttered her oracles in a kind of frenzy. The only difference was that Cassandra's prophecies were destined never to be believed. Perhaps then, the only influence on the Pythia's state was the affect of the *pneuma* (the "soul" or "vital spirit," often associated in antiquity with a vapor), not as a toxic gas, but as the divine wisdom or breath of Apollo.

The sanctuary and the Oracle at Delphi were controlled by the local community until the early sixth century BC, when the Delphic *Amphicthyony* or *Amphictyonic League,* an association of 12 peoples from central Greece, Attica, Euboia, and the Peloponnese took control. Delphi gained an international reputation while at its peak between the sixth and fourth centuries BC, when its significance was such that it was consulted by Greek city-states on important policy issues, such as colonization. Many of these cities built treasuries at Delphi, and foreign rulers would also make dedications. The most famous of these was Croesus (595–546 BC), King of Lydia (a region of modern western Turkey). When Croesus asked the oracle whether his military campaign against Persia would be successful, he was apparently told by the Pythia that if he attacked the Persians, a great empire would be brought down. Encouraged by this response, Croesus therefore launched his campaign into Persia and was defeated. The great empire he had destroyed was his own.

There are parallels between Delphi and the other great oracle of the ancient Greek world at the sanctuary of Zeus at Dodona (in Epirus, northwest Greece). Both Dodona and Delphi were first inhabited in the Mycenaean period, and, according to ancient sources, similar enquiries were made at both Oracles. Excavations at the sanctuary of Dodona have yielded thousands of inscribed strips of lead, the oldest dating back to 500 BC, bearing questions put forth by both individuals and the state to the Oracle.

The Oracle at Delphi continued in use for a thousand years until AD 393, when its last recorded response was given. In this year Byzantine emperor Theodosius I (AD 347–395) ordered pagan temples to cease operation. With the advent of Christianity Delphi became an Episcopal see (a territory over which a bishop rules), and there is an impressive fifth century basilica on the site, but by the sixth and seventh centuries Delphi was abandoned, its place as the centre of the Greek World only a distant memory.

Chapter 19

The Mysteries of Davelis' Cave (Greece)

The entrance to Davelis' Cave.
Photograph by Y. Dondas.

Located just outside the throbbing metropolis of Athens, Profitis Ilias Cave, popularly known as "Davelis' Cave", has acquired a reputation within Greece for strange goings on, unexplained phenomena and clandestine military activity. Even today, this enigmatic ancient site is alleged by some to generate a form of magnetic energy that creates "paranormal activity."

Measuring 197 feet long, 131 feet wide, and 66 feet high, Davelis' Cave is situated high up on the southwestern slopes of Mount Penteli, just north of Athens, Attica. The cave is located within an ancient marble quarry, one of the sites that supplied the Acropolis with much of its marble.

Traces of fire, pottery vases, and abundant stone and bone tools show that Davelis' Cave was inhabited at least as early as the late Neolithic Period (c. 4000–3000 BC). It was later used as a "Panaipolion," a shrine to the god Pan, perhaps roughly contemporary with the Parthenon on the Acropolis, in the fifth century BC. Niches and pedestals still to be seen in the cave walls would once have contained statues and offerings connected with the Pan cult. On the eastern side of the entrance to the cave are two Byzantine chapels. The older of these two buildings, known as St. Spyridon, is carved entirely out of the natural rock, and contains engravings on its walls, probably carved by anchorites (religious hermits) as early as the seventh century AD—centuries before the construction of the church itself.

The other larger chapel, St. Nicholas, has the date 1234 or 1274 carved into its dome and once contained a mural showing Michael Akominatos, the last Greek archbishop of Athens before the city was overrun by the Crusaders in 1205. The wall painting is now in the Byzantine Museum in Athens. The two chapels were inhabited for much of their history by monks and hermits, and under the floor of St. Nicholas an ossuary was discovered, where their bones were buried. Behind the chapels is the vast chamber, which constitutes the cave itself. At the rear of this great natural hall is a narrow passage or tunnel that once led to a number of subterranean galleries, one of which contained a small lake and, according to some reports, an ancient temple dedicated to the god Pan.

Local legend has it that in the mid-19th century a famous Greek bandit called Christos Natsos, known popularly by the name "Davelis," used the cave as one of his various hideouts in Attica. According to local stories, this Hellenic Robin Hood robbed travelers and rich inhabitants of the nearby villages, and helped the poor of the area. Davelis also enjoyed romantic affairs with society ladies, one of whom was a French noble, the Duchess of Plaisance, who was staying at the Rododaphne (or

Plakentia) palace, lower down the slopes of Mount Penteli. It is said that underground passages in Davelis' Cave led to the Rododaphne palace, thus allowing Davelis to carry out his tryst with the Duchess undetected. Popular stories allege that these passages also lead to Pendelikon Monastery, caves in central Athens, Cape Sounion southeast of the city, and even the island of Salamis, to the west of the city.

Davelis acquired national fame when he kidnapped a French officer belonging to the Anglo-French force occupying the port of Piraeus. The outlaw demanded and received a large ransom from the French Minister for the safe return of the officer. But Davelis's career was cut short in the 1850s when he was captured and killed near Zemeno, a small town in Boioteia (far to the northwest of Athens). His head was subsequently taken to Athens and displayed on a pike in Syntagma Square.

Author John L. Tomkinson has argued that the name of Davelis' Cave does not derive from the 19th-century bandit at all, but is a Hellenised form of the word *diabolos* or *devil*. There are numerous Davelis' Caves in Central Greece, and Tomkinson believes that, as the Christian church always associated the Greek god Pan with the devil, these caves were probably locations for the ancient cult of Pan rather than the various hideouts of a single Greek outlaw. Another cave associated with Pan, the Cave of the Nymphs, lies just 328 feet above Davelis' Cave. Amongst the numerous finds from this cave, which date worship here from the fifth century BC to the second century AD, were a carved bowl, probably used for divination, and two ancient plaques. One of these plaques depicts Pan, the nymphs, and the Greek god Hermes. The finds from the Cave of the Nymphs are now in the National Archaeology Museum in Athens.

Davelis' Cave and Mount Penteli have long been associated with strange events, as folklore and local legend testify. Just after dusk on summer evenings in the 19th-century, resin collectors on Penteli would hear the sounds of ghostly musical instruments, laughter, and song drifting across the mountainside. One such resin collector was resting in the area of Katsoulerthi, when he claimed to see a tall naked being, wearing a huge mushroom-shaped hat. When the witness stood up, the being ran away screaming into the pine forest.

Woodcutters and shepherds reported strange lights dancing around in deserted areas, and giant bats and horned men were said by locals to

haunt the area. A more modern update of these folkloric stories is alleged to have occurred in May 1939, when a shepherd watching over his
flock claimed he saw a mushroom-shaped object with lighted windows
land on the mountain. The man described two entities resembling sponge-
divers emerge from a door in the craft and walk towards him. The creatures apparently communicated with the shepherd telepathically, inviting
him to leave with them. When he refused, they re-entered their craft and
took off. The man told his story in his village but was not believed.

Reports of strange phenomena in the area continued into the second
half of the 20th century, and in the late 1960s a group of paranormal
researchers, including George Balanos, author of the 1982 book *The
Riddle of Penteli*, decided to investigate. The group began their studies
by collecting and examining the folklore and legends of the area, examples of which have been stated, and which included unexplained
noises and lights, unnatural temperature changes, apparitions, and
sightings of strange creatures. The team measured the magnetic field
in and around the cave and apparently found strong anomalies. They
also noted a powerful ozone smell at the cave entrance and claimed to
experience problems when attempting to photograph certain parts of
the cave's interior.

The malfunctioning of electronic and other equipment in the area of
the cave was also noted by other visitors to the site. Misty shapes, often
covering people's faces, are alleged to have appeared on photographs taken
at the cave. Strange phenomena also reported by team members included
missing time, the bizarre behaviour of investigators, nausea, panic attacks,
and the temporary disappearance of both people and objects. Other witnesses have stated that on each visit to the Davelis' Cave, its physical
appearance had altered in some odd way, with features such as passageways being present on one occasion but not the next. One visitor
claimed to have witnessed hundreds of domestic cats running around
inside the cave, despite the fact that there are no houses in the vicinity.
Over the years, the remains of animal sacrifices have been found in
and around Davelis' Cave, and magic symbols discovered painted on
its walls, testifying to the attraction of the area for modern occult and
pagan group rituals.

On one occasion, a group of campers claimed they witnessed weird goings-on in the cave during the night involving humanoid creatures with long pointed ears. Another particularly strange event is recounted in George Balanos's *The Riddle of Penteli*. It was April 1977, and a Mr. L.X., his wife, and a friend, Miss V.M., were visiting Mount Penteli. While wandering around the area they noticed a car parked on a particularly inaccessible and dangerous rocky slope of the mountain. Over the next couple of weeks the three people revisited the spot many times to find the car still there. On one of these visits they decided to climb down to the hazardous position to get a closer look. When they arrived they noticed some unusual oval-shaped tracks in the snow, about 2 feet in length. The strangest thing about the tracks was that they were on a vertical rock face, where neither animal nor man could have climbed. Suddenly, Miss V.M., who was behind some bushes 10–15 feet away from the couple, started screaming. They ran to her, and when she had calmed down, she told them she had seen an oval-shaped "horrible white creature," about 5 feet tall and with "two huge luminous eyes." (See Thanassis Vembos's article "The Riddle of Pendeli's Cave," at *www.vembos.gr/indexen.htm.)* The couple did not see the creature but noticed that some nearby bushes were moving. Thinking the creature was perhaps still around, the group thought it better leave the area as quickly as possible.

Nevertheless, the couple returned to Penteli a few days later. On this occasion, Mr. L.X. was sitting in his car when he suddenly started trembling and began to scream. For a while the terrified man was unable to speak but when he calmed down he explained to his wife that he had been about to start the engine when an enormous rotating black sphere appeared just outside the car window. He described the weird contraption as a "hairy sphere" or "a sphere composed of thick black smoke." The man felt as if something was attempting to enter his mind and thought the sphere was attempting to get through the closed window of the car. This terrifying ordeal lasted for no more than a few seconds.

George Balanos and his team continued with their research, and in 1977 a documentary (which was never shown) was filmed at the site about the weird events there. Later that year, the military acquired Davelis' Cave, apparently for storage of unnamed materials. The area was cordoned off with barbed wire fencing, and military guards (presumably military, though some were said to be in plain clothes) were posted to keep away intruders. The military used bulldozers and dynamite to level the floor and create an open space within the cave, destroying large parts of the interior in the process. For some reason, the military also destroyed and blocked off the entrance passageway to the underground caverns, so now the passage, caverns, and underground pool are now choked with tons of rubble. During the intermittent work at the cave, the foundations of the chapels had to be strengthened with concrete.

The floor at the rear of the cave was excavated to a depth of 33 feet and, when human bones were discovered during work, the Greek Archaeological Service were alerted by an anonymous phone call. However, when the Service tried to intervene, they were told by the military that the cave now lay in a "forbidden zone." In the area in front of the entrance to the cave, the military built an unusual structure of concrete and iron, and various large tunnels were driven into the mountainside in the vicinity, probably with the purpose of reaching the cave from below. Rumors were that as well as the Greek military, NATO, the U.S. military (there is an abandoned U.S. Naval base at the foot of Mount Penteli at Nea Makri), various intelligence agencies and certain large companies were also involved in whatever was going on. But no one seemed to know exactly what the nature of the activity was, why it was being done, or who was responsible. The matter was even raised in Greek Parliament, but the then minister of National Defense Evangelos Averoff claimed that the work was a matter of "national security" and therefore not open to discussion.

During the military excavations at the cave, there were reports from those working at the site of unexplained phenomena including UFOs and the presence of a strange green glow in the cave at night. It was also rumored that the deaths from cancer of a number of workers a few years after being employed at the cave were highly suspicious. George Balanos, among others, discovered empty boxes that once contained cancer medicines inside the tunnels around the cave. In one of these tunnels, a set of footprints, about the size of a small child, was discovered in the concrete floor, made before the concrete had dried. Apparently these footprints stopped right in front of the wall at the end of the tunnel.

In 1990, the apparently purposeless activity at the cave ceased, the various structures were abandoned, and the half-completed work was never resumed. The Greek Ministry of Culture claimed that excavations were stopped because the chapels in the cave were being damaged, though it seems a little late for them to have expressed concern about the historical importance of the site. Apparently, the area was no longer top-secret; the guards left and investigators and curious sightseers were able to cut through the fence and enter the cave again.

What possible purpose could the military and whoever else was involved have had for this huge and apparently needless investment in time and money? Two explanations are often put forward for the construction work at Davelis' Cave: The first is that it was an underground storage facility for nuclear missiles, the second that it was to be a nuclear bunker for government members in nearby Athens. Researchers in favor of the latter theory point out that it is not a coincidence that the abandonment of the work coincided with the end of the Cold War. However, geologists and civil engineers who were asked about the choice of this particular location for a nuclear bunker/underground storage facility stated that the area was completely unsuitable for either of these functions. Another question is why the military and whoever else was involved chose an important archaeological site for their construction. Could the strange folklore and unexplained events occurring in the cave and its vicinity have any relevance to the choice of Davelis' Cave for the work? If the explanation of constructions connected with the Cold War is just a cover story, then the question remains of the purpose of the work at Davelis' Cave.

One highly imaginative hypothesis that has been put forward connects the work with the (now-decommissioned) nearby U.S. Naval base at Nea Makri. This theory goes that the naval base was sited at the foot of Mount Penteli due to a bizarre natural phenomenon that allegedly occurs near there. This phenomenon involves the presence of the end of a "magnetic tunnel" in the sea near to the base. Apparently the high level of magnetic activity present in this tunnel carries electromagnetic waves thousands of miles through the earth along this tunnel from one place on the surface of the earth to another. The other end of the tunnel is supposed to lie in Langley, Virginia, close to the CIA headquarters. The unusual daily current in the channel between the mainland of Attica and the island of Euboia is thought to have some connection with these electromagnetic waves.

This magnetic tunnel was allegedly used as a beltway along which electronic communications were sent from the base at Nea Makri to a receiving station in Virginia, without any chance of them being intercepted. There have even been suggestions that the 1943 Philadelphia Experiment, allegedly conducted by the U.S. Navy to make the naval destroyer *USS Eldridge* invisible, has connections with the area of Penteli, in the form of "electrogravity" experiments at the Nea Makri site. During one of the alleged experiments at Philadelphia, the *Eldridge* was supposed to have accidentally disappeared from the naval yards and reappeared at the Naval Base at Norfolk, Virginia. After several minutes the ship vanished again and reappeared at its original site in Philadelphia. The basis of the Greek connection is the fact that in January 1951, the *USS Eldridge* was transferred to the Greek Navy under the Mutual Defense Assistance program, in which she served as a destroyer escort known as *Leon* (Lion) until being decommissioned in 1991, though she was retained by the Greek Navy as a training hulk.

There seems to be no further concrete evidence for this connection, and the whole theory of a "magnetic tunnel" has the ring of modern folklore. Interestingly, however, gravitational and magnetic anomalies have been recorded on Penteli, and on a stretch of road linking Palaia Penteli with Nea Makri witnesses have told of their cars moving up the steep slope despite having the engines turned off. Some researchers, however, explain this apparently "negative gravity" as an optical illusion: The car is actually going downhill, as can be seen if witnesses look at the surrounding landscape rather than at the road in front of them. Such "gravity hills" occur elsewhere such as in Burlington, Ontario (Canada). Not everyone agrees with the visual illusion hypothesis, however; some maintain that the affects produced at these gravity hills vary over time, suggesting that the phenomena is caused by fluctuations of the magnetic field of the Earth. Indeed, these researchers have likened gravity hills to something akin to huge antigravity devices. It has been recorded that people visiting these spots have sometimes testified to strange feelings of dizziness and disorientation, as mentioned earlier regarding the area in and around Davelis' Cave.

Today Davelis' Cave is accessible to the public, though the previously attested eerie atmosphere of this part of Mount Penteli is rather dissipated by the presence of numerous climbers testing their skills on the rock faces in the vicinity. Perhaps the magnetic anomalies recorded in the area are the reason for the mysteries of the site, both in ancient times with its use in the Pan cult and in modern times with the military presence and the reports of unexplained phenomena. The main investigator of the site, George Balanos, is of the opinion that the cave acts as some sort of gateway, an entrance to another dimension. What is certain is that both the cave and Mount Penteli itself have been attracting strange stories and odd folklore for hundreds of years. Perhaps the ghostly music, mountain lights, demonic beings, and otherworldly laughing of the 19th century have become the UFOs and secret military experiments of the 20th and 21st centuries. There is certainly a strong folkloric element even to the modern reports of paranormal phenomena in the area, the evidence for which, as with folklore, is mainly anecdotal and based on very little hard evidence.

Obviously, a thorough investigation and archaeological excavation inside Davelis' Cave and its underground caverns would reveal much about the site, though, after the military destructions and blocking up of parts of the cave, this now seems highly unlikely. However, if the magnetic anomalies of Penteli have a bearing on the unexplained phenomena allegedly witnessed there, perhaps one day a thorough investigation (and publication) of these anomalies will reveal something about the mysteries of this ancient place.

Chapter 20

Axum:
The Ark of the Covenant
and the Queen of Sheba
(Ethiopia)

The Northern Stele Park in Axum.
Photograph by Jialiang Gao.

Known as Ethiopia's "Holy City," Axum (also "Aksum") is located on a plateau 7,200 feet above sea level in northeast Ethiopia on the horn of Africa. The ruins of the great ancient city that once stood here mark the site of what was once the heart of Ethiopia. Established around the fourth century BC, the political, economic, and cultural center of the powerful kingdom of Axum was situated on the caravan trade routes to Arabia, Nubia, and Egypt, and also had close contacts with the Red Sea port of Adulia. Consequently, Axum boasted trade links with places as far apart as India, Arabia, Egypt, Persia, Rome, and Greece. Its impressive archaeological remains, which generally date from the first to the 13th centuries AD, include tombs, palaces, monasteries, giant obelisks, and the ruins of ancient castles. It was from about AD 300 that enormous granite obelisks began to be erected at Axum, as funerary markers for tombs of the nobility.

The highest of these colossal monoliths reached 108 feet, one of the tallest stone monuments in the ancient world. The best-known obelisk, the 78-foot-tall, 160-ton "Obelisk of Axum," was looted from the ancient city by Italian troops in 1937. It was then taken to Rome and set up on the Piazza di Porta Capena, in front of the Ministry for Italian Africa, where it remained for 70 years, until it was returned to Ethiopia, amid much celebration, in 2005. The tallest obelisk still standing at Axum is the 70-foot-high "King Ezana's Stele." This obelisk, which, with its carvings of windows and a door, resembles nothing so much as a apartment building carved entirely from stone, was erected in the fourth century AD by King Ezana I (AD 320–350), the monarch credited as the first ruler of Axum to embrace Christianity.

Another building at Axum originally constructed during the reign of King Ezana I, and one surrounded by mystique, legend, and controversy, is the church of Our Lady Mary of Zion. Though the present structure was built in 1665 by Emperor Fasilidas, the original church on the site, which was destroyed and rebuilt at least twice during its lifetime, dated to the fourth century AD. Traditionally, all Ethiopian monarchs were crowned at the church of St. Mary of Zion. In 1955, to mark his Silver Jubilee, the Emperor Haile Selassie founded a new Church of St. Mary of Zion next to the old one. A decade later, a year after the new church had been completed, Selassie ordered the building of a small side chapel adjacent to the old church of Our Lady Mary of Zion to hold valuable church relics. Now known as the "Chapel of the Tablet," for many Ethiopian Orthodox Christians this is the building that is believed to house the true Ark of the Covenant.

According to the Bible, the Ark of the Covenant was a sacred container, inside of which polished stone tablets containing the Ten Commandments given by God to Moses on Mount Sinai were kept. The box itself was apparently constructed of acacia wood, and lined on the inside and out with pure gold. Set into the solid gold cover, or "mercy seat," were two cherubim facing each other, their outstretched wings meeting and forming the throne of God. Gold-plated carrying poles were inserted into the two gold rings on either side of the container so that the Ark could be carried. The Ark was said to be possessed of supernatural powers: It helped Joshua destroy the walls of Jericho, stopped the River Jordan so the Hebrews could cross, and would sometimes emanate light and fire, inflicting severe burns on the enemies of Israel. The Ark was sent to Jerusalem by King David and installed by King Solomon in a Holy of Holies in his magnificent Temple, built in the 10th century BC on Mount Moriah. When Jerusalem was destroyed by the Babylonians in 586 BC and the Temple sacked, most scholars believe the Ark was also destroyed, though many writers and researchers disagree with this.

The legend that connects the Ark with the city of Axum is found in the *Kebra Nagast,* or the *Book of the Glory of Kings,* a compilation of various history and traditions of the Ethiopian Orthodox faith, probably written in the 13th or 14th century AD. The book describes how the emperors of the country were allegedly descended from King Solomon and the Queen of Sheba, another semi-legendary figure who has links, real or imaginary, with the city of Axum. According to Ethiopian accounts, the Queen of Sheba (under the name "Makeda") ruled in Axum sometime in the 10th century BC, though no historical or archaeological evidence supports this, and the city of Axum was not founded until many centuries later. Local guides at Axum, however, claim the remains of the Queen of Sheba's palace lie in the city and point out a huge reservoir cut out of the solid rock known as the "Queen of Sheba's Bath."

The biblical Book of Kings refers to the Queen of Sheba as "The Queen of the East" and briefly describes a meeting between her and King Solomon at Jerusalem. The legend recounted in the *Kebra Nagast* goes much further. In this story Solomon and the great Queen Makeda had a son, who they named Ibn-al-Malik (known as Menelik; "the son of the king"). When Menelik was in his early 20s, he found out from his mother that his real father was King Solomon of Israel and decided to visit Jerusalem to meet him. Menelik was received by his father with great honor and stayed with him for three years, learning the Law of Moses (the Torah). One of Menelik's companions was Azariah, the son of the high priest of the temple of Jerusalem. Azariah had a dream that told him to smuggle the Ark of the Covenant out of Jerusalem and take it to Ethiopia, leaving a copy in its place. This he did and, though King Solomon discovered the theft, his army was unable to catch Menelik and Azariah. Solomon then had a vision that told him that his son was the rightful owner of the Ark, so he returned to Jerusalem and ordered his High Priests to keep the disappearance of the Ark a secret.

At Axum Menelik became the founder of the Ethiopian "Solomonic Dynasty," and the Axumites adopted Judaism and the Law of Moses. This legend is the cornerstone of the Ethiopian church, and many Ethiopian Christians today claim to be direct descendants of the "Solomonic Dynasty." The Ethiopian Jews, known as the "Falashas," claim descent from the Judean followers of Menelik, who escorted the Ark on its journey to Ethiopia.

In his popular 1992 book, *The Sign and the Seal: Quest for the Lost Ark of the Covenant,* English author and researcher Graham Hancock proposed that after the Ark left Jerusalem in the fifth century BC, it was transported to Elephantine Island at Aswan on the River Nile, where it was kept in a Jewish Temple. After this temple was destroyed, the Ark was taken to Tana Kirkos, an island in Lake Tana, the source of the Blue Nile, and the largest lake in Ethiopia. According to Hancock the relic was kept on this Island for 800 years before being brought to Axum around AD 350. Hancock also believes that the Ark was eventually taken out of Ethiopia by the ubiquitous Knights Templar, who believed it to be the Holy Grail. This is a fascinating series of events, though the vast majority of historians and archaeologists see Hancock's theory about the Ark as nothing more than unscholarly speculation.

Another researcher with his own theories on the Ark in Ethiopia was the late Dr. Stuart Christopher Munro-Hay, a specialist in Ethiopian archaeology and history, and author of the comprehensive 2006 book *The Quest for the Ark of the Covenant: The True History of the Tablets of Moses.* Munro-Hay believed that what is described in the *Kebra Nagast* as the Ark is in fact an altar stone, likely to be a replica of the original tablets of Moses. So, although there is indeed an ancient sacred artifact enshrined in the treasury next to the church of Our Lady Mary of Zion, it is probably not the Ark of the Covenant. Nevertheless, the Ark is firmly entrenched in Ethiopian religious tradition. Every Ethiopian Orthodox church and monastery now has a replica of the Ark of the Covenant, known as the "Tabot," secreted away within its holy of holies, and no church in the country is considered consecrated unless it possesses this sacred replica.

Despite these replicas, modern Ethiopian Christians firmly believe that the original Ark of the Covenant still exists today, kept at Axum under constant watch by a lone monk, "the Guardian of the Ark." The sacred object, described as a single polished stone tablet 2 1/2 feet long and 1 1/2 inches thick, was formerly paraded around the town of Axum once a year but is now concealed within its shrine in the Treasury building or Chapel of the Tablet, with only its specially selected guardian allowed to enter the building. It is said locally that if anyone other than the Guardian gets a glimpse of the Ark, he or she is either killed instantly, or goes blind and has his or her body badly burned. Understandably, this secrecy and lack of access to the sacred relic has convinced most scholars that the claims of the Ethiopian Orthodox Church are without foundation. But perhaps, when studying the Ark of the Covenant, it is not the object that is important, but the story itself. The tale of the Ark, representing the supreme power of the Israelite God, resonates through the centuries among a myriad of different cultures. Regardless of the existence or not of a physical object, the mystique surrounding the Ark of the Covenant shows no sign of decreasing in the 21st century. In fact, Ark lore now has a life of its own, only distantly related to the object's origin as the container of the Tablets of Moses.

Chapter 21

Mohenjo Daro
(Pakistan)

"The Priest King" sculpture from Mohenjo Daro, National Museum, Karachi, Pakistan. Photograph by Mamoon Mengal.

The remains of one of the first great cities of the world, Mohenjo Daro, lie on the bank of the Indus River in the Sindh Province of southern Pakistan. Mohenjo Daro was one of the major urban centers of the Indus Valley Civilization (also known as the "Harappan Civilization"), which originated around 3300 BC in the Indus and Ghaggar-Hakra river valleys in what is now Pakistan and western India. Around a thousand towns and settlement sites of the Indus Civilization have so far been discovered, with the main sites being the cities of Mohenjo Daro and Harappa (located 400 miles north of

Mohenjo Daro) and the coastal site of Lothal. Traces of the Indus Civilization have been discovered as far north as the Himalayas and northern Afghanistan and as far south as Mumbai (Bombay), in Maharashtra State, India. During its peak period, between 2600 and 1900 BC, it has been estimated that the Indus Civilization may have had a population of as much as five million.

Located on the lower Indus, surrounded by a fertile flood plain, Mohenjo Daro must have been an extremely prosperous city, controlling the trade routes based on the river network. This great urban center was rediscovered in 1922 by R.D. Banerji, of the Archaeological Survey of India, and, from this time until the late 1930s, the city was excavated by various officers and directors of the Survey, most notably English director general Sir John Hubert Marshall, who also excavated at the site of Harappa. Renowned English archaeologist Sir Mortimer Wheeler and Pakistani archaeologist Ahmad Hasan Dani began excavations at the site in 1946, and the last large-scale excavations were undertaken in 1964–65 by Professor G.F. Dales. After this date, because of the severe difficulties of preserving the exposed structures from the elements, all full-scale excavations at Mohenjo Daro were banned. However, there have been rescue (salvage) excavations, surface, surveys and conservations projects at the site, conducted by the Department of Archaeology and Museums, Government of Pakistan, in collaboration with several teams of international scholars.

The site of Mohenjo Daro was first occupied around 3500 BC but was at its peak during the time of the Indus Civilization (2600–1900 BC). The city covers an area of more than 250 hectares and, as with all the Indus Valley sites, was laid out on a grid pattern plan, with both wide and narrow parallel streets intersecting one another to divide the city into a grid filled with compact blocks of houses. Most Indus Valley towns also used the same size bricks and a standardized system of weights in the form of carefully worked colored cubes of stone. The majority of the buildings at Mohenjo-Daro and other Indus sites are made of baked brick, which gave greater durability than mud-brick construction, and is one of the reasons why so much survives at the site today.

One channel of the Indus River cuts through the site dividing it into the so-called "Citadel," situated on a huge artificial mound, and the "Lower

Town." The Citadel included an elaborate tank or bath constructed using fine-quality brickwork and drains, with steps down to the pool and a surrounding verandah. This building, referred to as the "Great Bath," is 39 feet long, 23 feet wide, and nearly 10 feet deep. Though its exact purpose remains unknown, it has been suggested that it was either a "ritual bath" used by priests or royalty, or a public bath akin to those built by the Romans more than two millennia later.

Also located in the Citadel was a huge structure with solid brick foundations known as "The Granary," which, despite its name, probably functioned as a public building, perhaps an assembly hall or a temple. Other buildings in this area include two aisled assembly halls and houses opening onto small internal courtyards, with bathing platforms, wells, and covered drains. The Lower Town was where most of the citizens of Mohenjo Daro lived and worked. This area consisted of numerous houses, many of which were two-storied, an extensive drainage system, potters' kilns, dyers' vats, and metalworking, bead making, and shell and ivory-working shops.

One unsolved mystery surrounding Mohenjo Daro and the Indus Civilization is its undeciphered language. In fact, we don't even know the original names of the cities of the Indus Valley. "Mohenjo Daro," for example, is Sindhi for "Mound of the Dead." The Indus script, used between 2600 and 1900 BC, consists of short texts written from right to left on flat stone tablets known as seals, and on pottery, copper tablets, bronze implements, and ivory and bone rods. Although there are around 4,000 objects inscribed with the Indus script, the texts are brief, the longest is only 26 characters, and there are numerous duplicate inscriptions. Sometimes the unidentified characters are accompanied by engravings of animals (elephants, tigers, rhinoceroses) and occasionally by anthropomorphic figures, which some scholars have identified with early versions of the Hindu deities first described two thousand years later in Sanskrit texts. There have been various claims to have deciphered the Indus script, but the general opinion of scholars is that, until a bilingual inscription is found, as with the ancient Egyptian Rosetta Stone, it is unlikely that we will discover the language of the inhabitants of Mohenjo Daro and the Indus Valley.

Signs of change at Mohenjo Daro began to appear after 1900 BC in the form of a new kind of pottery called "Jhukar" and seals inscribed with geometric designs rather than Indus writing. It has been suggested that contorted skeletons found scattered in the streets at Mohenjo Daro indicate that the city came to a violent end, perhaps at the hands of Aryan invaders from the north. For Sir Mortimer Wheeler, these remains brought to mind verses from the *Rig-Veda,* an ancient Indian collection of Vedic Sanskrit hymns dedicated to the gods, some verses from which tell of the destruction of cities by the terrible warlike god Indra. Wheeler stated his opinion of the skeletons at Mohenjo Daro in dramatic fashion: "men, women, and children were massacred in the streets and houses, and were left lying there or, at the best, crudely covered without last rites." However, no weapons or signs of such an attack have ever been found at the site. The 37 skeletons discovered were found in the Lower Town, the residential area of the settlement, rather than the fortified citadel, which also argues against any battle having taken place at Mohenjo Daro. Furthermore, when the skeletons from Indus cemeteries have been examined, tests have shown that the original inhabitants of the area were not supplanted by invaders with different physical characteristics.

Despite this evidence, some bizarre claims have been made surrounding the supposed destruction of Mohenjo Daro. Without doubt, the most extreme theory is that Mohenjo Daro and other cities of the Indus Civilization were destroyed by ancient atomic warfare. Cited as evidence for this are the "facts" that the skeletons found at the ancient city were highly radioactive, comparable with those from Nagasaki and Hiroshima, and that many of these skeletons were sprawled in the street some holding hands "as if some instant, horrible doom had taken place." The supposed discovery of "a heavy layer of radioactive ash in Rajasthan, India, [which] covers a three-square mile area" is also given in support of the claim of ancient atomic warfare.

What is the evidence for this amazing Hollywood version of prehistory? As usual with such sensationalist claims, non-existent "archaeologists" are quoted supporting the theory ("Francis Taylor"), as is a magazine that never existed ("*World Island Review*"). A writer who has published a popular article on the subject in a Russian magazine ("*The*

Sputnik Magazine") becomes an 'archaeologist', and also the author of a non-existent book (*"Riddles of Ancient History"*) by a publisher that never was ("Soviet Publishers, Moscow, 1966"). Furthermore, Rajasthan, the largest state of the Indian Republic, contains four working nuclear power plants, the oldest of which was established in December 1973, many years before any stories of radiation effected ancient skeletons were circulating. In 1992, there was an accident at one of the Rajasthan nuclear power plants, when 4 tons of heavy water were spilled; in fact most of India's nuclear power plants have had some accident or other over the years. Although the presence of these power plants would be more than enough to account for levels of radioactivity supposedly found in the skeletons of the Indus Civilization, one suspects that the main inspiration for the idea of ancient atomic warfare come from more familiar sources.

As is so often the case when talking about the origins of more extreme theories regarding advanced ancient technology, we need look no further than ancient astronaut theorist Erik von Däniken. In his 1970 book, *Gods From Outer Space,* von Däniken says that "the old Indian and Tibetan texts in particular…teem with science-fiction weapons. I am thinking of the divine lightning and ray weapons…and of the texts that seem to be referring to bacteriological weapons."

Another source that probably added to the myth is the *Vaimanika Shastra* ("Science of Aeronautics"), which first appeared in English in 1973, translated by G.R. Josyer. This supposedly ancient Sanskrit text discusses the construction of *vimânas*—mythical self-propelled aerial vehicles described in Sanskrit epics. Recent research into this text has, however, shown that the manuscript was actually written sometime between 1918 and 1922, though this has not prevented it having a significant influence on proponents of the theory that *vimânas* were real ancient flying machines, probably used for ancient aerial warfare. From here it is but a short step to ancient nuclear destruction. As was mentioned earlier, many of the structures at Mohenjo Daro were constructed of fired bricks, and it is partly for this reason that the site is one of the best-preserved ancient cities in the world. In fact, the walls of some of the structures still stand 10 feet or more high—pretty impressive after a nuclear destruction.

Anyway, getting back to reality. Rather than one catastrophic event overwhelming Mohenjo Daro, archaeologists now believe that various factors contributed to the decline of the city, and of the Indus Civilization in general. One of the main causes was almost certainly changes in the river flow pattern of the Indus. However, sudden catastrophic flooding of the city is less likely than periodic inundations that weakened the agricultural base of the Indus settlements. Because of these repeated floods people may have left the city over time, especially if the surrounding area was no longer able to produce the food they required. Today, the ruins of this once-great urban center face a similar problem. Threatened by erosion from the Indus River, a rising water table, and corrosion by salts, an international conservation campaign has been organized by UNESCO to save the site. In April 1997, UNESCO put $10 million into the 20 year long project, which will include extensive pumping and drainage of the site to lower the water table, and the cleaning of the walls to remove thousands of years of accumulated salts. So far, the project has successfully prevented the magnificent ruins at Mohenjo Daro from flooding.

Chapter 22

The Riddle of the
Chinese Pyramids
(China)

The mound of the Yangling Mausoleum, final resting place of
Han dynasty emperor Jingdi (second century BC).
Photographer unknown

For many years, the idea of the existence of huge pyramids or pyramidal structures in China to rival those of Egypt or Mexico was little
more than a legend. However, approximately 100 of these ancient structures have now been identified within a roughly 60-mile radius of the
ancient city of Xi'an, the capital of the north-central province of Shaanxi
(Shensi). These "pyramids" are in fact flat-topped earthen mounds, some

with small temples on top, and the majority range from 20 to 200 feet in height and 50 to 600 feet in width. All of the pyramids have their four sides aligned to the cardinal points and seem to have been used as mausoleums. The most spectacular example, and also among the oldest (work on it began in 246 BC), is the tomb of Qin shi Huangdi, first emperor of the Qin Dynasty, who had the famous Terracotta Army buried nearby (see Chapter 23).

The most enigmatic and written about of the Chinese pyramids is the legendary "White Pyramid," allegedly first glimpsed by Westerners in the 1940s, but bathed in mystery ever since. In fact, the first sighting of the White Pyramid has become almost as legendary as the structure itself, and is as much embroiled in folklore and myth. The story goes that, in the spring of 1945, U.S. Air Force pilot James Gaussman was flying back to Assam, India, from Chungking, China, when engine trouble forced him to descend. He found himself flying over a low-level valley where he suddenly noticed a huge white pyramid below him. In his report he described the structure as "shimmering white" as if made of metal, or some kind of stone, with a large, 200-foot-high capstone of gem-like material on top. The colossal pyramid towered up an estimated 1,000 feet, with a base of around 1,500 feet. Gaussman managed to photograph the structure, but when he arrived at Assam military duties forced him to forget about the sighting. Apparently his report and photographs were filed away in the military archive and forgotten about for the next 40 or so years, until one of the photographs was published by Australian writer Brian Crowley in his 1986 book, *The Face on Mars*.

Two years after Gaussman's sighting, in 1947, Colonel Maurice Sheahan, Far Eastern director of Trans World Airline, was flying over the Tsinling Mountains in Shaanxi Province, about 40 miles southwest of Xi'an, when he glimpsed a huge pyramid on the ground below. Sheahan's account of the sighting appeared in several U.S. newspapers, including the *New York Times* for March 28th of that year. Under the headline "U.S. Flier Reports Huge Chinese Pyramid in Isolated Mountains Southwest of Sian," the article quotes Colonel Sheahan stating that from the air "the pyramid seems to dwarf those of Egypt," and that it was located "at the far end of a long valley, in an inaccessible part." Sheahan estimated its height as 1,000 feet, with a width at the base of 1,500 feet, and also mentions another, much smaller pyramid, as well as "hundreds of burial mounds" at the near end of the structure. Though the *New York Times* did not include a photograph of the huge structure seen by Sheahan, a photograph did appear two days later in the *New York Sunday News* of March 30. Is it possible that Sheahan glimpsed a Chinese pyramid more than twice the height of the Great Pyramid in Egypt? And was it the same one seen two years earlier by James Gaussman?

Unfortunately, nowhere in Sheahan's description is there mention of the pyramid as being white, nor does he mention seeing a capstone of crystal. Complicating the issue further is the photograph. The pyramid that Sheahan claimed to have seen was located at the end of a valley, whereas the one in the existing photo of the "White Pyramid" shows an isolated structure in the middle of a plain. The building in the photo is also flat-topped, in contrast to Sheahan's description of a structure with a "perfect pyramidal form." But could there be two, or more, of these gigantic pyramids in China?

With no further sightings and no new information, the mysterious Chinese structure(s) gradually developed into the legend of the "Great White Pyramid of China." But it was not until 1983, with the publication of Bruce Cathie's book *The Bridge to Infinity*, that the subject was brought back to the public's attention. Cathie, a writer and ex-airline pilot from New Zealand, suggested that China's Great White Pyramid was one of many ancient monuments built at key points on an ancient energy grid that criss-crossed the planet, and was also used as a flight path by UFOs. Cathie was himself unable to locate the White Pyramid and was told by Chinese authorities in the late 1970s that the "pyramids" of China were actually the mausoleums of Western Han Dynasty emperors.

The subject of Chinese pyramids was given a further boost and entered new realms of mythology with the 1994 publication of *Die Weisse Pyramide*, later translated into English under the provocative new title *The Chinese Roswell: UFO Encounters in the Far East from Ancient Times to the Present* (1998). The author, German tour operator Hartwig Hausdorf, a friend of ancient astronaut theorist Erich von Däniken, shared von Däniken's belief in an extraterrestrial origin for various constructions and artifacts from ancient China, Japan, Tibet, and Mongolia, including the White Pyramid itself. He also attempted to explain ancient Chinese myths in terms of contacts with extraterrestrials. In his book, Hausdorf describes his travels to pyramids in "forbidden" parts of China, but as did Cathie before him, he failed to find the Great White Pyramid itself, though he did return with photographs of various pyramid-type structures from the country.

Hausdorf based his ideas about the White Pyramid partly on Bruce Cathie's research and also on the diaries of Australian traders Fred Meyer Schroder and Oscar Maman, who were in the area in 1912. After being impressed at the scale of the flat-topped pyramid-like structures in the province of Shaanxi, the traders asked their guide, a monk called Bogdo, about them. Bogdo told them he believed the structures were at least 5,000 years old, but that records kept at the monastery indicated that they dated back even further than that. The Australians were also apparently told that the pyramids were built at a time when the old emperors ruled China. Chinese myth speaks of these emperors as not of this earth, but descended from "sons of heaven, who roared down to this planet on their fiery metallic dragons." In Hausdorf's interpretation, extraterrestrials.

What is there to back up the extraordinary claims of ETs and alien-built pyramids? Sources are not quoted for the stories related to the White Pyramid in either Cathie's or Hausdorf's book, so it is difficult to verify their claims either way. But what is clear is that there seems to be no evidence for the existence of Air Force Pilot James Gaussman, originally mentioned by Bruce Cathie in *The Bridge to Infinity*. Writing in *Fortean Times 164* (November 2002), Steve Marshall proposed that the James Gaussman story may be a garbled fictional version of Colonel Maurice Sheahan's actual sighting, fairly widely published in the United States at the time. Another fact that has emerged is that Sheahan's size estimates for the huge pyramid quoted in the newspapers were inaccurate. In a letter written on January 31, 1961, to Mr. E. Leslie Carlson, Sheahan states, "The large pyramid is probably between 500 feet and 600 feet high and the reported 1,000 feet was exaggerated in several translations from the Chinese *li* to metric to feet."

There is another rather pertinent fact that may come as a surprise to many supporters of the more fantastical claims about Chinese pyramids: This is that Chinese archaeologists and historians have long known about the existence of huge pyramidal structures in the archaeologically rich area of the Wei River Valley of Shaanxi province, where the city of Xi'an is located. The difference is in the terminology: *Pyramid* is a far more romantic and evocative term than *earth-built mound*. But as early as 1908, Robert Sterling Clark, heir to the Singer sewing machine fortune, was in China with the U.S. Army carrying out zoological and ethnological research in the area of Xi'an. In his book, *Through Shên-kan: The Account of the Clark Expedition in North China, 1908-1909* (published in 1912), he mentions the "numerous mounds of unusual shape dotted about everywhere like immense molehills" and describes them as "the tombs of kings and emperors, and their wives, and of scholars and sages notable in their day." There is no mention of pyramids anywhere in his work.

Moreover, the tombs are not located in any "forbidden zone"; tours of the more famous ones are even advertised on Chinese travel Websites. Another theory—that the Chinese authorities had attempted to hide their pyramids from prying Western eyes by planting trees on them to make them blend into the landscape   is also a modern myth. The tombs were originally built with trees planted on them. In the case of the Maoling Tomb (25 miles northwest of Xi'an), and many others, yew trees have recently been planted to restore their original appearance, as well as to slow down soil erosion. In both Chinese and European folklore, the yew is seen as a symbol of immortality, as the tree lives to a considerable age, and also for its smell, believed to offer the dead protection from demons.

The mausoleums of 29 emperors and hundreds of other nobles rise up majestically from the fertile plains of the Wei River Valley. The majority of the larger tombs date from the Han (206 BC–AD 220) and Tang (AD 618–907) dynasties. Two of the best known of these structures are the Maoling Tomb and the Qianling Tomb. Located 50 miles northwest of Xi'an, the Qianling tomb is one of the best preserved in China, and holds the remains of Emperor Tang Gaozong (628–683) and his wife, China's only female ruler, Empress Tang Wu Zetian (624–705). Beginning with the second Tang Emperor Taizong (599–649) mausoleums were built on hills to allow easier construction, and the Maoling Tomb is a good example, located on the highest of three peaks on Liangshan Hill, 3435 feet above sea-level. The tomb has not been excavated and is unique in that it is the only imperial mausoleum untouched by tomb robbers. A "spirit path" or "Imperial Road" leads to the entrance to the tomb and is lined with statues, which include pairs of guardian generals, winged horses, and phoenixes, the latter creatures having power to exorcise evil spirits. There are also 17 subsidiary tombs of nobles and ranking officials in the area surrounding Qianling, five of which, including the tomb of Princess Yongtai, granddaughter of Gaozong and the Empress Wu Zetian, have been excavated. Set on top of the imposing Liangshan Hill the Quanling Tomb is a prominent feature in the landscape and one wonders if it is this structure that is the origin of the White Pyramid myth.

In December 2006, a new mystery arose at Qianling when it was reported that "crop circles" had been discovered during an aerial survey of the site of the mausoleum. Around 10 circles, mostly between 100 and 130 feet in diameter, but the largest with a diameter of 361 feet, were discovered during a survey by the Xi'an Preservation and Restoration Center of Cultural Relics. However, because the middle of the largest ring was found to be the site of one of the excavated satellite tombs of the Qianling Mausoleum, it is probable that most of the other crop circles are related to other Qianling tombs. Presumably, as there is a long history of human activity in the area, dating back at least 6,000 years to the middle of the Neolithic period, the other crop marks represent previously unknown buried prehistoric or historic remains.

Maoling is the mausoleum of Emperor Wu Di (also known as Liu Che) and, at 150 feet high, is one of the largest of all the mausoleums of Emperors built during the Western Han Dynasty (206 BC–24 AD). The tomb, which covers over 584,400 square feet, took 53 years to build and held an incredible array of rich burial goods. Maoling is surrounded by 20 or so satellite tombs of imperial wives, ministers, and nobles, as well as the houses of tomb-keepers and court attendants. Recently, author and science writer Walter Hain, and Chris Maier of *unexplainedearth.com* have used satellite photos to identify the pyramid-mound of the Maoling mausoleum as beyond doubt the "White Pyramid" of the celebrated black-and-white photo. What appears to have happened in the case of the White Pyramid is that modern folklore has built up around a single black-and-white photograph of the Maoling Mausoleum, probably taken in 1947 by Colonel Maurice Sheahan and later attributed to non-existent pilot James Gaussman.

Recently, in June 2006, there was news that Chinese archaeologists had discovered a group of pyramid-shaped tombs in the ancient city of Jiaohe, located in the Jilin Province in northeast China. The tombs, which may date as far back as 3,000 years ago, were exposed due to floodwater erosion on part of a mountain. The largest tomb was located on the south side of the mountain, and had been constructed of stone and earth dug out from the hillside. Its dimensions were roughly 164 feet by 98 feet, with an oval platform on top measuring around 49 by 32 feet, on which a stone coffin covered by a granite top had been placed. Finds from the site include a stone knife and axe, pottery, and bronze items. Discoveries such as this prove that there are probably still many Chinese "pyramids" that have gone unrecognized for millennia awaiting discovery, consequently certain aspects of the mystery of these structures are far from settled. Although archaeologists believe that these trapezoidal mounds were built and used as mausoleums, there will always be some writers and researchers inhabiting the wilder shores of alternative history who believe that the Chinese Pyramids had more exotic functions and origins.

Chapter 23

The Mausoleum of China's First Emperor (China)

Close-up of Terracotta warriors.

The monumental tomb of China's first emperor, Qin Shi Huang, is located 22 miles east of Xi'an, the capital of the Shensi province of modern China. The tomb itself, which, according to traditional Chinese geomancy, represented the eye of a huge dragon in the landscape, is underneath a huge vegetation-covered earthen mound, is 154 feet high, and measures 1,690 feet from north to south and 1,590 feet from east to west. The mound has eroded considerably in its 2,000-year history; it is believed that it once soared up to a height of 330 feet.

The emperor Qin Shi Huang (246–210 BC) is recorded to have ordered the building of his vast underground tomb complex at the age of 13. The emperor is known as the unifier of China, who brought warring tribes together, standardized the system of writing, and introduced a single currency. Qin Shi Huang also organized the construction of a vast system of roads and canals, and ordered the joining of the various walls on the borders of his kingdom into one long wall, the precursor to the Great Wall of China, to this day the longest man-made structure on earth. In 221 BC, Qin Shi Huang established the Qin dynastic empire and proclaimed himself the "First August Emperor of Qin": Qin Shi Huangdi. But although his reign was characterized by great advances in Chinese society, some ancient traditions record that the emperor also ruled with an iron hand, imposing large tax rates, oppressing the peasant population, and having all non-technical books burned (with the object of obliterating the ideas of Confucius).

In his later years, it is said that the emperor became deeply involved with mystics and alchemists, and increasingly unhinged. He was apparently obsessed with locating the elixir of eternal life, and sent out various expeditions to find the potion that would allow him to cheat death and make him an immortal emperor. One tradition states that the emperor sent an expedition of ships full of young men and women to Japan in search of the Penglai Mountains, home of the immortals, and supposed location of the fabled elixir. None of the expedition ever returned, as they knew that if they came back without the magical potion they would be executed on the spot. In 210 BC, while on a tour of Eastern China, Qin Shi Huang was given mercury pills by his court physicians, in a desperate attempt to transfer the supposed immortality-giving power of mercury to the emperor. The mercury proved lethal and the emperor met his death, to be buried inside his vast tomb complex at the age of 49.

Our sources for such stories of China's First Emperor come in the form of written records, oral traditions, art, and archaeological remains. But the majority of what we know of emperor Qin Shi Huang is from the Shi-Ji, or Records of the Historian: Biography of Qin Shi Huang, written by grand historian Sima Qian (c. 145–90 BC), an official at the Han imperial court. Written around 100 years after the death of the emperor, this semi-legendary work provides elaborate and, in the opinion of many scholars, entirely fanciful details about the life of the emperor and the construction of his great underground tomb. In the *Shi-Ji*, Sima Qian states that a vast army of 700,000 prisoners, slaves, and craftsmen were forced to work on the mausoleum for an incredible 36 years. When the work was complete, in order to preserve the secrets contained within, Qian says that the workers were all executed. According to this account, when the emperor died, he was entombed in a coffin built of bronze and jade, the latter supposed to prevent the corpse from decaying. This tomb was placed inside a bronze model of Qin Shi Huang's entire empire, which included mountains, rivers, lakes, and seas. The water flow was duplicated with mechanically circulated mercury, which, as long as it flowed, was meant to keep the emperor alive in his miniature enclosed world. According to the *Shi-Ji*, the ceiling was studded with pearls and other rare jewels to represent the sun, moon, and stars—in effect, a primitive planetarium. In the passageways leading to the tomb, a line of automatic crossbows were set up to fire poison arrows at any thieves who managed to break into the complex. And lastly, the vast earthen mound that was heaped over the mausoleum was supposedly covered in a layer of molten copper for protection.

For 2,000 years these seemingly fantastical descriptions were the basis of the stories surrounding Qin Shi Huang and his legendary mausoleum, and, as the tomb has never been excavated, one of the few sources for what the great tomb may contain. However, excavations around the area of the tomb have recovered some fascinating items, including ceramic human sculptures representing court officials and acrobats, bronze and ceramic sculptures of cranes, horses, and chariots, and stone carved armor designed for both humans and horses. Two bronze chariots, discovered in 1980 about 65 feet east of emperor Qin's mausoleum, are half-size scale-models and, when found, were encased in a wooden box buried 26 feet down. The chariots contained numerous gold and silver pieces and were perhaps created for the use of the Emperor in the afterlife.

There has recently been much controversy over whether or not to excavate the tomb of Qin Shi Huang at all. Archaeologists insist that such a vast undertaking should not be attempted until there is adequate provision for the preservation of the finds. However, until that time, there have been some fascinating results obtained from survey work by a team under Chinese archaeologist Dr. Duan Chingbo, using a combination of ground-penetrating radar, electrical resistance measurements, and core samples. These results have built up a three-dimensional picture of the entire underground tomb complex (actually more an underground city of the dead or necropolis), and have also lent support to some of the statements in Sima Qian's history about the vast treasures contained inside the tomb complex. A magnetic scan at the mausoleum revealed a large amount of coins scattered around in the unopened tomb of the emperor, which would indicate that Qin Shi Huang was buried with a considerable treasure. Around 4,000 soil samples were taken from the site that, amazingly, revealed high contents of mercury in the soil of the earthen mound, and in the tomb itself, indicating the truth of the descriptions in the *Shi-Ji*. Further survey work using remote sensing technology, in July 2007, revealed a mysterious 90-foot-tall building that had been constructed above the tomb, with four stepped walls, each with nine steps.

Although the findings from recent survey work at the mausoleum have in the main supported accounts in the *Shi-Ji*, there is one rather glaring omission in Sima Qian's work, whether intended or not. In 1974 while drilling a water well about three quarters of a mile from Qin Shi Huang's tomb, local farmers made a startling discovery: About 16 feet down they came upon a jumble of painted life-size clay figures, some of them clutching bronze weapons. After years of excavation at the site, which is still ongoing, archaeologists have excavated more than 1,000 of these soldiers, though they estimate there are as many as 7,000 magnificently crafted warriors, 130 chariots with horses, and 110 cavalry horses, buried to guard China's first emperor more than 2,000 years ago.

The soldiers, who all face east, are arranged in three huge subterranean pits supported by wooden frameworks, and are spread over an area measuring 135,630 square feet. Each pit is separated by a number of partitioning walls, which divide the army up into columns. The soldiers are all arranged in battle formation, with crouching crossbowmen, archers, infantry, chariots, and cavalry, all in their appropriate positions. Perhaps a tradition of the terracotta crossbowmen may have lingered on to become the legend that the Emperor's tomb was guarded against intruders by automatic cross bows? Every soldier in the Emperor's army is unique, with its individual face, hairstyle, height, uniform and weapons, all in accordance with his rank. The statues of the infantrymen vary in height from 5 foot 8 inches to 6 foot 2 inches, and the commanders tower over the ranks at six and a half feet tall.

It is recorded that after the Qin Dynasty was overthrown, rebel General Xiang Yu (232–202 BC) looted and then set fire to the vaults containing the terracotta warriors, causing them to collapse and bury the artifacts underneath. Ironically this is probably one of the main reasons why this vast army is generally so well preserved. Despite the looting and burning at the site, more than 10,000 bronze weapons have so far been excavated from the pits. These finely crafted pieces, which have remained free from rust over the centuries, include swords, daggers, billhooks, spears, axes, crossbow triggers, and arrowheads. The terracotta warriors represent a graphic illustration not only of the military prowess of the first emperor, but also of his ability to control the variety of resources contained in his newly unified China, and his elaborate attempts to replicate and continue his rule over that empire in the afterlife.

In 2006, the terracotta army was in the news when it received its first new recruit for more than 2,000 years. On September 16th, German art student and performance artist Pablo Wendel disguised himself as an ancient Chinese warrior, made his way into the museum that now contains the statues, and posed motionless among the soldiers. Wendel's disguise was so convincing that he was able to stand in the ranks of the frozen army for more than 20 minutes before being noticed. Police decided that the 26-year-old had no malicious intentions, and as he had caused no damage to the statues, he was let off with an official warning before being sent back to the eastern Chinese city of Hangzhou, where he was studying at the China National Academy of fine Arts.

Chapter 24

Angkor Wat (Cambodia)

The vast complex of temples that make up the area of Angkor are spread over about 40 miles around the village of Siem Reap (in northwestern Cambodia, just more than 190 miles from the Cambodian capital, Phnom Penh). Angkor was the capital of the Khmer (Cambodian) empire from the ninth to the 15th centuries AD, and at its height, in the early 12th century, the area contained more than a million people. The word *Angkor* is derived from the Sanskrit word *nagara,* meaning "holy city." The crowning achievement of Khmer architecture is the stunning 12th-century carved sandstone

Northwest corner tower of the first gallery of Angkor Wat. Photographer unknown

temple/mausoleum of Angkor Wat, the largest religious building in the world. The structure was built between AD 1113 and 1150 by King Suryavarman II, who dedicated the incredible structure to the Hindu god Vishnu. Angkor Wat is said to represent a microcosm of the Hindu universe, with its 4,921-by-4,265-foot moat representing the mythical oceans encircling the earth, and the five beehive-shaped towers of the Temple itself representing the five peaks of the sacred Mount Meru, the home of gods and center of the Hindu universe.

Angkor Wat was one of perhaps a thousand sacred structures in an area that also boasted a vast intricate network of reservoirs and canals on which the successful economy of the whole Khmer civilisation was based. Being able to control the water of the Mekong River for agriculture was the main reason why, at its height, the Khmer Empire was able to hold sway over an area including modern-day Cambodia and Laos, and considerable parts of Thailand and Vietnam. However, the heyday of the Khmer Empire was relatively short-lived, and, in 1177, Angkor was sacked by the Chams, from Central Vietnam, and Angkor Wat fell into ruins. The Empire was re-established by King Jayavarman VII (who ruled from 1181 to 1219), who established a capital at Angkor Thom and also made Mahayana Buddhism the state religion. After the death of Jayavarman VII, the Empire began to decline and various attacks by the Thai Empire led to the abandonment of Angkor in the 1430s.

Over the next few hundred years, Angkor Wat was visited by a number of western explorers and missionaries, but it was not until the arrival of French naturalist and explorer Henri Mouhot in 1860, and the subsequent publication of his book, *Travels in Siam, Cambodia, Laos and Annam* (1863), that the incredible structure was brought to the attention of the world. Unfortunately, Mouhot did not live to see his book in print; he died of malaria in the jungles of Laos while trying to discover a southern route into China by traveling north along the Mekong River. In 1992, the UNESCO World Heritage Committee declared the temple of Angkor Wat, and the whole city of Angkor, a World Heritage Site.

The walls of Angkor Wat are covered inside and out with beautiful bas-relief carvings, mainly illustrating scenes from Hindu mythology, but also the historical wars of Suryavarman II. Especially bewitching are around 2,000 "apsaras," gracefully dancing female divinities wearing pointed crowns. These figures are goddesses created solely for the entertainment of the Hindu gods. A fascinating god-creature from Hindu mythology that is found frequently in carvings at Angkor Wat is "Garuda," the king of birds, depicted as having the beak, wings, talons, and tail of an eagle, and the body and legs of a man. Garuda is associated with the rays of the sun and is frequently depicted carrying the supreme Hindu god, Vishnu, and his wife, Lakshmi, on his back across the sky.

In the great Sanskrit epic of ancient India, the *Mahabharata*, Garuda is the nemesis of the "Nagas" (serpents). This enmity arose because of an argument between Vinita, the mother of Garuda, and Kadru, the mother of the serpents, and, as a result, Garuda vowed to destroy all serpents he finds. Nagas (female—"Naginis"), are giant serpentine beings who usually reside under the earth in a beautiful city called Naga loka, Patala loka, or Bhogavati. In Tibetan Buddhism, water nagas are seen as keepers of secret books of wisdom, and they are also associated with springs, wells, and rivers, and can be guardians of treasure. These semi-divine beings are sometimes depicted in carvings at Angkor in fearsome fashion with seven or more heads and hood like crests, though they were only usually dangerous to those who committed evil deeds or mistreated the nagas. Nagas possessed various powers, one of which was an ability to take on human or wholly serpentine form at will. They also possessed deadly venom and were also associated with the elixir of immortality.

A fascinating phenomena allegedly connected with the Nagas occurs in the Mekong River in Thailand and in Laos, usually on the night of the full moon of the 11th lunar month. This is the "Bang Fai Phaya Nark" (Naga fireballs). Beginning around 6 p.m. and lasting for two or three hours, strange egg-sized reddish fireballs rise up silently from the river into the air as high as 65 or 100 feet, before disappearing without trace. There can be from around a dozen to tens of thousands of these eerie glowing spheres. Many Thai people living in the provinces along the Mekong River bank are of the belief that the River is the path of the Naga named "Pu Chao Sri Sutho." The glowing balls of light that float up from the River Mekong are said to be the eggs of the Naga rising from the water, or represent a gesture of homage by the huge serpent to the Lord Buddha.

Manas Kanoksin, a doctor from Nong Khai (in northeast Thailand), has devoted more than a decade to the study of the strange phenomenon of the Mekong River. His rather disappointingly mundane theory is that the fireballs are natural, and caused by the spontaneous combustion of methane gas formed by decaying riverbed sediment. Others believe the fireballs are caused by firework displays, and this is indeed what researcher Richard Freeman described seeing when he attended the Bang Fai Phaya Nark Festival in 2000. Whether the phenomena has been hoaxed to attract tourism since its beginning seems doubtful however, as there are consistent records of the event dating back more than a hundred years, and some descriptions of the phenomenon do not resemble fireworks. The still-unexplained mystery of the Naga fireballs is also said to occur in the ponds and rice fields close to the Mekong River.

The powerful monkey deity Hanuman is another of the Hindu pantheon depicted at Angkor Wat. Attempts have been made by some researchers to link the god Hanuman with sightings of an intriguing ape-like creature known as "Orang Dalam," a Malaysian version of the North American Bigfoot. Reports of hair-covered hominoids described as being from 10 to 13 feet tall, have been made for decades in the forests of Malaysia, particularly by the inhabitants of the jungle of Johor. However, though there may be something to these sightings, there seems to be no obvious connection between a possible cryptid (an unknown species of animal or one thought to be extinct, but that may still survived today) and the Hindu god Hanuman as depicted at Angkor Wat.

A far more controversial carving from the Angkor region, though not from the Angkor Wat temple itself, comes from the 12th-/early-13th-century Buddhist monastic complex of Ta Prohm. The carving is of a small creature with a short neck, four short legs, a small curving tail, and a humped back with plates running along its length. To many people, this enigmatic carving can only represent a stegosaurus, a creature that lived during the late Jurassic Period, about 156–140 million years ago. If this is the case, what is a carving of a dinosaur doing on the wall of a structure dating back a mere 800 or so years? The stegosaur depiction is sometimes offered as conclusive evidence that man and dinosaur co-existed until a few hundred years ago, or even that there are still dinosaurs alive today roaming the earth. To this end, the Angkor Stegosaur has been connected with another dinosaur-like cryptid known as the "mokele-mbembe," a large creature reported to inhabit the lakes and swamps of the Congo River basin of central Africa.

The fact is that much of this area remains unexplored and the numerous, consistent descriptions of the creature from locals as well as missionaries in the area have convinced many that there is an unknown animal out there somewhere. However, expeditions to the Congo have proven unsuccessful in terms of bringing back physical evidence of the creature, though they have recorded eyewitness testimonies of sightings. These negative results have persuaded scientists that the creature is a combination of misidentification, hoax, and folklore. Again, the connection between the unidentified carving at Ta Prohm and sightings of a dinosaur-like creature in central Africa are tentative to say the least, though that is not to say for certain that something extremely strange is not lurking in the swamps of central Africa.

The carving at Ta Prohm does not appear to be a hoax. One suggestion was that it was carved as recently as 2001, when the temple was being used as a location in the film *Tomb Raider*. But the depiction appears on examination to have been carved at the same time as the illustrations of stags and monkeys that surround it. So did the inhabitants of the area discover a complete fossilized skeleton of a stegosaurus 800 or so years ago and base their depiction on their discovery? Unlikely. The Khmer people would not have possessed the palaeontological knowledge to assemble a complete dinosaur skeleton correctly. Furthermore, there are no stegosaur fossils in the Cambodian dinosaur fossil record. Others have suggested that the creature depicted is a wild boar, perhaps standing in front of stylized leaves. This is perhaps the best explanation so far, though one curious factor in the mystery is that the "stegosaur" carving appears to be unique. Nothing similar has been found in the Angkor area, and it is this uniqueness that heightens its mystery. The "Angkor stegosaur" has now become the latest addition to the numerous legends associated with Angkor and its magnificent temple ruins.

Chapter 25

Ayers Rock:
Uluru and the Dreamtime
(Australia)

Uluru from the air.

Uluru is the Aboriginal name for Ayers Rock, an enormous isolated sandstone outcrop rising 1,140 feet above the Red Desert plain, in the Northern Territory of Central Australia, 208 miles southwest of Alice Springs. This huge rounded monolith has a perimeter of almost 6 miles, and extends underground for 1 1/2 miles. Due to the effects of the light, Uluru appears to change color from an intense pink-red glow at sunrise to a deep ocher at sunset. The Rock is a deeply sacred place to the Anangu ("human beings"), the Aboriginal peoples inhabiting the area, who consist of two different language groups: the Yankunytjatjara and Pitjantjatjara. In October 1872, the first non-indigenous person to see Ayers Rock, English explorer Ernest Giles, described it as "the remarkable pebble" in his book, *Australia Twice Traversed* (1889). The following year, surveyor William Gosse became the first European to climb the Rock, which he named "Ayers Rock," in honor of the then–Chief Secretary of South Australia, Sir Henry Ayers.

Although the smooth, bare rock of Uluru supports practically no vegetation, the rainwater runoff that collects at the base of the Rock has created a fertile area around the site that sustains a rich variety of plant and animal life. These favorable conditions have made the numerous caves and waterholes in and around the Rock a prime location for settlement, with the presence of Aboriginal groups in the area going as far back as 10,000 years ago, possibly as much as 20,000.

This Aboriginal "Holy Mountain" is currently part of the Uluru-Kata Tjuta National Park, and since 1985 has been jointly owned by the Pitjantjatjara people and Parks Australia, a division of the Australian Government Department of the Environment and Water Resources. In 1987 Uluru/Ayers Rock was added to UNESCO's World Heritage List. However, by 2000 the number of annual visitors to the site was topping 400,000, and maintaining the sacred nature of the place has now become a serious problem. Uluru's Aboriginal owners are part of the local indigenous community of Mutitjulu, who live in the shadow of the Rock and organize a series of guided tours for visiting tourists. But although the Anangu request that visitors do not climb the Rock because of its spiritual importance, climbing is allowed by the Australian government, which, mindful of tourist dollars, has established a hiking path to the top. Despite warning signs posted on Uluru, at least 40 people have died during ascents to the summit. Apart from safety concerns, one reason why the local Anangu population prefer people not to climb the Rock is that the hiking path crosses one of many traditional "dreaming tracks" (*iwara*), invisible paths or tracks that connect Aborigine sacred sites.

To the Aborigine, a dreaming track is a route taken by ancestral heroes in the "Dreamtime" (*Tjukurrpa*), in which all Aboriginal culture has its roots and before which, in their minds, the earth did not exist. In the Dreamtime, groups of ancestral beings (*Tjukaritja/Waparitja*) journeyed across the land, performing mighty deeds and creating the living species and features of the desert landscape. The adventures of these ancestors (often referred to as "totemic ancestors") are chronicled in sacred songs (*inma*), stories, and rituals. *Tjukurrpa* also established the rules of Aboriginal religion, law, moral systems, and social life. In the mind of the Aborigine, *Tjukurrpa* is a true record of how the landscape was formed—a landscape that is still inhabited by the spirits of their ancestor beings. By re-enacting the myths of the Dreamtime in song, story, and ceremony, the Anangu keep their ancestors' rules, beliefs, and relationship with the landscape alive. The massive rock-form of Uluru is seen by the Anangu as a living record of the Dreamtime activities of their ancestors, and the appearance and origin of every feature of the giant Rock is present on the mental map carried around by all Anangu people of the area.

Thus, a particular totemic ancestor has left a visible trace of his or her deeds at various locations on Uluru that Aborigines can identify. So although the Westerner sees caves, exposed rock strata, erosion gullies, cliffs, and scars, the Aborigine sees another, metaphysical reality. Rather than geological features, Uluru contains the marks of the Carpet Snakes, the camping places of the Marsupial Rats, and the ritual pole of the Hare-Wallaby men. There are various Dreamtime myths told of these totemic ancestors at Uluru, one of which explains the creation of most of the southern face of the Rock, which was formed during the battle between the Liru ("poisonous snake people") and the Kunia ("carpet snake people"). During this Dreamtime war, the Liru attacked the harmless Kunia, who were camped on the southern part of Uluru, with spears, spear throwers, stone knives, and wooden clubs.

The numerous desert oaks on the sand hills to the southwest of the Rock are testament to this encounter, being the metamorphosed bodies of the invading enemy. To end the battle, there was a single combat at Mutitjilda gorge between the Liru leader Kulikudjeri and a young Kunia warrior. These two enemies stood face to face, slashing each other's legs with stone knives, until both were severely wounded and the Kunia warrior crawled away, leaving a trail of blood, which is now the water-course flowing into the Mutitjilda water-hole. When Kunia Ingridi, the mother of the young Kunia warrior, found out that her son had been killed, she struck Kulikudjeri such a fierce blow with her digging stick that she cut off his nose. Liru leader's nose is now a huge 70-foot-tall pointed tower of rock that has split off from the main body of Uluru.

Another Creation myth involves two groups of ancestral spirits. The "Mala Wallabies" (also known as "Hare Wallabies") were performing an initiation dance on the western side of Uluru when they received an invitation to attend the ritual dances of the "Wintalka Men" (also known as the "Mulga Seed Men") at Docker River, 150 miles to the west. Deeply involved in their own ceremonies, the Mala Wallabies refused the invitation, invoking the wrath of the Wintalka Men, who sent an evil spirit (*mamu*) in the form of a ferocious spirit-dingo to punish the Mala. This terrible creature, called Kurrpanngu, attacked the Mala Wallabies on Uluru, causing great destruction, and forced them to abandon Ayers Rock and flee for their lives. Before they left, some Mala men managed to take their sacred *naldawata* pole from the middle of the ceremonial ground with them. The footprints made by the Mala men when they dragged the pole away are now great chasms on the northwestern corner of Uluru, and a huge column of rock towering up between them (known to non-indigenous peoples as "the Kangaroo Tail") is the transformed *naldawata* pole.

One final Dreamtime story involves the Red Lizard (*Tjati*), also known as *Kandju*, who traveled to Uluru in the creation period. When he arrived at Uluru, Tjati threw his curved throwing stick (*kali*, or boomerang), which embedded itself in the Rock's face. In his frantic but unsuccessful attempts to dislodge his *kali* with his bare hands, Red Lizard left a series of bowl-shaped hollows in the face of Uluru, which can still be seen today at Kandju gorge, as can his *kali*, in the form of one of the curving edges of a large pot-hole. On the northern side of Kantju gorge is a large cave where Red Lizard rested. At the mouth of this cave is a horizontal column of rock, which symbolizes the place where *Tjati* left his spear-thrower, and a long vertical fissure, which represents his spear.

Each of these stories of *Tjukurrpa* from Uluru has its own song-cycle as well as *churingas,* sacred objects comprising an oval or elongated slab of stone or wood. *Churingas* are created especially to act as memory-aid devices during ceremonies, and represent both the ancestral and the individual spirit of their owners. Just as each Aboriginal clan is divided into totems related to animals, plants, or objects, the spirit of which watches over the clan's affairs, the churinga records the myths and stories of each totemic group. Uluru remains sacred to several local Aboriginal tribes today, who still leave ritualistic paintings in its caves along the base of the Rock. The meanings of the Dreamtime stories are passed on to the Aboriginal youth in songs at initiation ceremonies that still take place in these caves. Indeed an Aborigine can, by touching parts of Uluru, invoke the ancestral spirits associated in *Tjukurrpa* with that particular feature.

Moving away from the Dreamtime very much into the modern physical world of Ayers Rock. In August 1980, Michael and Lindy Chamberlain took their three children on a camping trip to the Rock. On the night of August 17, 1980, the couple's 9-week-old daughter, Azaria, disappeared from the family's tent, apparently taken by a dingo. Lindy Chamberlain had reported seeing a large dingo skulking away from the tent that night, and a huge search was immediately launched, but the body of Azaria was never found. An initial coronial inquiry supported Lindy Chamberlain's account of Azaria's disappearance, but a week later a tourist from Victoria discovered her blood-stained jumpsuit at the base of Ayers Rock, near Maggie's Spring, 2 1/2 miles from the campsite. "Maggie's Spring" is the modern name for the Mutitjilda water-hole, where in the Dreamtime the single combat took place between the leader of the poisonous snakes and the young carpet-snake warrior.

According to media reports, the baby's jumpsuit had been "neatly folded" when found, which could only mean human involvement. This "evidence," as well as traces of what appeared to be blood discovered in the Chamberlains' car, and on Lindy's sleeping bag, was enough for Lindy Chamberlain to be tried and convicted of the murder of her child. The vital evidence of dingo tracks discovered by Aboriginal trackers from the Pitjantjatjara tribe at the campsite during the original search was completely ignored at the trial. On October 29, 1982, at the end of the most publicized trial in Australian history, Chamberlain was sentenced to life imprisonment. The Chamberlains made two unsuccessful appeals against the verdict, but it was to be a strange twist of fate that would bring the potential for reasonable doubt into the case.

On February 2, 1986, local police were searching among the rocks and brush below Ayers Rock for English tourist James Brett, who had disappeared eight days before. The police believed Brett had probably fallen to his death from the top of Ayers Rock during a night climb, and they eventually discovered the partially eaten remains of his body in an area full of dingo lairs. During the search, they also found Azaria's missing matinee jacket, partly buried in sand, about 500 feet away from where the jumpsuit had been found 5 1/2 years earlier. Five days later, the Northern Territory government released Lindy because she had "suffered enough" and, after a Royal Commission of Inquiry into the convictions, which included forensic tests that showed that there had in fact never been any blood in the Chamberlains' car, the conviction was finally overturned in September 1988.

Although many ill-informed people at the time found it impossible to believe a dingo could have carried off a 9-week-old baby, it emerged in the late 1990s that there had been at least 400 documented dingo attacks on Fraser Island, off the Queensland coast of Australia, alone, most of which were against children (though at least two were on adults). Due to the sensational and irresponsible nature of the media coverage of the trial, and the fact that the majority of the evidence initially presented in the case against Lindy Chamberlain was later rejected, the case is now used as an example of "trial by media." One important example of the grave mistakes made in the reporting and investigation of the case is that when the baby's jumpsuit was found it had not, as was reported, been neatly folded, but was "concertinaed," or scrunched up. (What seems to have started the rumor of the folded-up clothes is that a police constable rearranged the clothing for photographing after it had been discovered.)

The media also circulated a number of myths about the case, some of which are still believed today. The most widely circulated of these myths, quoted as truth for example in Dennis William Hauck's *International Directory of Haunted Places* (2000), is that the name "Azaria" means "sacrifice in the desert." The name in fact means "Blessed of God" or "Helped by God," and is a feminine form of the Old Testament name "Azariah." The erroneous interpretation of the name "Azaria" was also linked in the popular press with the fact that the Chamberlains were Seventh-Day Adventists, and allegations that this "strange cult" murdered babies as part of bizarre religious ceremonies. Further snippets of media falsehoods include that Lindy Chamberlain showed no emotion during the proceedings, interpreted as revealing a cold heart, and that the Chamberlains had always dressed Azaria in black. (In fact, she had a single black dress trimmed with red ribbon.) Interest in the Chamberlain case was briefly reignited in August 2005, when a 25-year-old woman named Erin Horsburgh came forward claiming to be Azaria Chamberlain. However, investigations by the authorities proved her story to be yet another untruth in a case rife with falsehoods. What this sad chapter in the history of Ayers Rock and its locale reveals is that what Lindy Chamberlain was really guilty of in the opinion of many Australians was that she was perceived as being "different," something the Aborigines of the country are entirely familiar with.

Chapter 26

Cahokia
(United States)

Monk's Mound.
Photograph by Derek Collins.

Located near Collinsville, Illinois, across the Mississippi River from St. Louis, Cahokia was a prehistoric Native American city at its peak from around AD 1050 to 1150. During this period it was among the largest metropolitan centers on earth, covering an area of 6 square miles, with a population of about 15,000 living in the city, and between 20,000 to 30,000 dwelling in surrounding houses and farms. A vast collection of temples, plazas, houses, and stockades, there was no city in North America comparable in size with Cahokia until late-18th-century Philadelphia. The remnants of this great metropolis consist of 80 surviving earthen mounds of an estimated total of around 120. In 1982, UNESCO designated Cahokia a World Heritage Site, and the Cahokia Mounds State Historic Site is now a park that protects 2,200 acres of the ancient city and is the focus of ongoing archaeological investigation.

Cahokia was the regional center of the prehistoric Mississippian culture of the eastern United States, and was surrounded by a number of satellite communities, a few of which were also multimound centers, as well as villages, farmsteads, and camps. From about AD 1200, the population of Cahokia began to decline and the site was abandoned by AD 1400, its population dispersed among the surrounding communities. The Osage, Omaha, Ponca, and Quapaw peoples are all believed to be direct descendents of the Native Americans who once lived at Cahokia.

The mystery of who the population of Cahokia actually were and how their society worked has intrigued archaeologists and historians for decades. Native American mythology and folklore are surprisingly silent on the subject of the great temple mound center, and the inhabitants themselves left no written records. Even the name "Cahokia" has no connection with the builders of the great city, being taken from a sub-tribe of the Illiniwek (or Illinois) group of tribes called the Cahokia—who moved into the area in the 1600s. The only clues we have about the city and its inhabitants are from archaeological investigations, including those at Mound 72 and Monks Mound, the latter structure being the most conspicuous feature of Cahokia, and the largest man-made earthen mound in North America. Monks Mound acquired its name from a community of French Trappist monks who lived at the site from 1809 to 1813 and planted fruit trees on its terraces. Standing 100 feet tall and covering 14 acres, Monks Mound is a flat-topped multiterraced platform mound, located within the central ceremonial area of the site. The mound was begun about AD 950 and is thought to have been completed by about 1150. The imposing focus of the city, Monks Mound was once topped by a large 50-foot-high building, perhaps a palace or temple from which Cahokia's elite ruled the area.

In March 1998, while five horizontal drains were being installed on the west side of Monks Mound to relieve internal water that was causing the structure to slump, the drilling rig hit stones 150 feet in—an unexpected find in what was supposed to be an entirely earth-built mound. The drill went through 32 feet of stone before the bit broke off, the stone being identified as either limestone or sandstone cobbles. Further investigation into the stones, which included hand coring with an auger and a magnetometer survey, has suggested that some represent groundwater drains, built into the mound when it was originally constructed, and others could represent walls or perhaps a ritual platform or a tomb. On the other hand, the stone layers may be of a purely ritual nature. Perhaps it was the *act* of transporting the stones from 10 to 15 miles distant, where the nearest outcrops are, and then adding them to the mound that carried most significance. Various investigations at Monks Mound over the last 40 or so years have revealed no stone layers in other parts of the structure, so it would appear that the stones are confined to the west side. Whatever the stones turn out to be, they are almost unique in sites of the Mississippian culture, which predominantly used wood as building material rather than stone.

One of the most spectacular finds from excavations at Cahokia, and one that sheds much-needed light on ritual and religious belief at the site, is the "Beaded Birdman Burial" from Mound 72, located half a mile to the south of Monks Mound. In total, there were 272 burials recovered from this mound, most of which were human sacrifices interred over a period of several years. Mound 72 is, in fact, a series of mounds built almost one on top of another, probably beginning around AD 1000. In one of these mounds, built over a large burial pit, archaeologists discovered the skeletons of 53 young women aged between 15 and 30, and four males with their heads and hands removed. The women had apparently been strangled as a human sacrifice, but who they were or where they came from remains a mystery, though the fact that they were all of child-bearing age has suggested to some researchers a rite connected with fertility.

The enigmatic Beaded Birdman Burial was that of a middle-aged man buried on top of a layer of 20,000 seashell beads arranged in the shape of a bird. Buried nearby were more than 800 flint arrowheads, a rolled-up sheet of copper, unprocessed mica flakes, and a cache of disc shaped stones known as "chunky stones." The beautifully worked arrowheads originate from places as far away as Arkansas, Oklahoma, Tennessee, and Wisconsin, and may have been sent as an offering for the deceased chief. It is hard to escape the conclusion that such elaborate burials were meant to demonstrate how the elite of Mississippian society disposed of retainers and raw materials in order to affirm their high status. However, a connection between the central male burial and the probable human sacrifices in mound 72 has not yet been established; they may not even have been interred at the same time. Because only a portion of the mound has been excavated, further work needs to be done before we can say for certain whether there is any direct relationship between the Beaded Birdman Burial and the other remains in mound 72.

The arrangement of the central male burial on shells in a shape of a bird, probably a falcon, with the bird's head turned to the side and visible beneath the man's head, and its wings and tail beneath his arms and legs, provides a link with the "birdman" motif common in Mississippian culture.

A further link with the birdman motif at Cahokia is the so-called "Birdman Tablet" discovered during excavation of the east side of Monks Mound in 1971. One side of this small sandstone tablet depicts a man with a beak-like nose, dressed in a falcon or eagle suit, with an outstretched right wing. He also wears an ear spool, many copper and stone examples of which have been found at the Cahokia site. The reverse side of the tablet is covered in cross-hatching, perhaps intended to represent the skin of a snake. Perhaps the tablet is meant to represents the sky and the earth, the upper or "spirit world" of the bird, and the lower "underworld" of the snake, indicating a dualistic aspect to the religion of the inhabitants of Cahokia. The illustration on the tablet could also be a depiction of the "thunderbird" of Native American mythology, which is thought to represent the shaman, with the power to invoke thunder, lightening, and rain. In Native American rock drawings the Thunderbird is always depicted with its head turned to the side and wings extended in the same manner as the Cahokia Birdman burial. The Cahokia Birdman now serves as the official logo of the Cahokia Mounds site.

The closest parallel to the birdman carving from Monks Mound is on a copper repoussé plate from Dunklin, Missouri, dated to between AD 1200 and 1400. Similar birdman motifs have also been found on artefacts discovered at the Spiro Mounds site in Eastern Oklahoma, near the modern town of Spiro, an important Mississippian site occupied from AD 850 to 1450.

Other examples of these engraved sandstone tablets have been found in the area of the Cahokia mounds, though the majority of them are simply engraved with diamond cross-hatching. One exception is the "Ramey Tablet," which displays two severed human heads wearing ear spools and two ivory-billed woodpeckers. It was found to the east of Monks Mound on Ramey Farm in the 19th century, and dates to around AD 1250. In November 2000, archaeologist Elizabeth Kassly was surface collecting on the farm of Vernon Schaefer near Valmeyer, Illinois, about 20 miles from Cahokia, when she picked up a playing card–sized piece of sandstone. Closer examination of the tablet revealed a carving of a Birdman of a similar type to that on the example from Monks Mound. Although this artefact, now known as the "Kassly-Schaefer Birdman Tablet," has a significant piece missing, it is clear that it depicts the dotted torso and outstretched right wing of the birdman, which appears to be wearing a fringed skirt, with a serpent-like figure across the top of the tablet. The back of the tablet is covered by crosshatching. There certainly seems to be a strong connection between the iconography on the two birdmen tablets, and some researchers believe the Kassly Tablet was actually made at Cahokia.

Generally, the execution of the designs on these birdman tablets is fairly haphazard, but this is not really much help in determining the function and meaning of these enigmatic carvings. Theories for their function include that they were visual aids in story-telling, played a part in shamanistic rituals, were used as folk magic amulets, or more prosaically functioned as stamps that were dipped in dye and used to decorate animal skins. Some writers on paranormal topics, such as John Keel, Gregory L. Little, and particularly Jim Brandon in his 1983 book, *The Birth of Pan,* have linked the birdman of Native American myth with modern sightings of strange creatures. Brandon believes that these strange sightings are the result of the affect of certain earth forces on the brain, producing archetypal images such as the birdman. Reports of these unusual creatures include what appear to be giant birds, or in the case of the "Mothman" sightings in West Virginia from 1966–67, a bird-man–type creature with huge glowing red eyes. According to photographer and documentary filmmaker Andy Colvin, producer of a documentary series called *The Mothman's Photographer,* the Mothman is fulfilling the age old role of crime-fighting archetype, sending visions, prophetic dreams, and messages to ordinary humans.

A particularly significant discovery at Cahokia has been that the mounds at the site seem to have been constructed at specific locations along certain important alignments. Central to the working out of these alignments have been the discoveries of five "woodhenges" at the site, dating from AD 900 to 1100. The name "woodhenge" is taken from the Late Neolithic (c. 2300 BC) henge and timber circle of that name located 2 miles northeast of Stonehenge (in Wiltshire, England). The five woodhenges at Cahokia, which stood just to the west of Monks Mound, were circles of evenly spaced wooden posts ranging in diameter from 240 feet to 480 feet. The circles probably functioned as celestial calendars to mark the seasonal solstices, equinoxes, and times of certain important religious festivals. Alternative theories for these circles suggest that some of the posts were aligned with certain bright stars or the moon, or were used in predicting eclipses. Perhaps the woodhenges were also used in sighting the placement of mounds on important alignments at Cahokia, as most are aligned with the cardinal directions. It is not difficult to imagine that the rulers of Cahokia used one or more of the woodhenge monuments to demonstrate their close connections with the sun. This connection would be dramatically illustrated at the spring and autumn equinoxes, when the sun would rise directly over the temple on the top of Monks Mound, as if to affirm the power of the ruling elite by shining its rays down onto the spiritual heart of their great city.

Chapter 27

Ohio Serpent Mound (United States)

Ohio Serpent Mound.
Photograph by Pollinator

Perhaps the most famous of North American effigy earthworks, Serpent Mound lies on a plateau overlooking the Miami River near Peebles (in Adams County, Ohio). An effigy mound is a raised pile of soil constructed by many Native American cultures, in the shape of mammals, birds, or reptiles; a typical example being those which make up the Effigy Mounds National Monument near Harpers Ferry, Iowa. Serpent Mound, which winds across the land for almost a quarter of a mile, has an average height of about 4 feet and is around 20 feet wide. The sinuous effigy is thought to represent an undulating snake with coiled tail and open jaws holding or eating a large hollow oval feature, variously interpreted as an egg, the sun, or an enlarged eye.

The Serpent earthwork was first measured and mapped in the mid-1840s by two early archaeologists from the Ohio town of Chillicothe: Ephraim G. Squier and Edwin H. Davis. Their landmark book on the ancient mound builders of North America, *Ancient Monuments of the Mississippi Valley: Comprising the Results of Extensive Original Surveys and Explorations,* was issued in 1848 and became the first publication of the Smithsonian Institution. From 1886 to 1889 the mound was again mapped and sections excavated, along with two nearby conical mounds, by F.W. Putnam, of Harvard's Peabody Museum. Unfortunately, Putnam found no artifacts inside the earthen mound with which to date its construction, though he thought it had been created by the same Native American culture that built the two nearby burial mounds he had excavated. These people are now known as the "Adena Culture" (800 BC–AD 100). Since that time the dating and origin of Serpent Mound have been surrounded by controversy and speculation, much of it connected with the myth of the so-called "Mound Builders."

Earth-built mounds in North America were first noticed by European settlers after the end of the Anglo-French War of 1756, when the fertile plains of the Ohio River Valley were filled with colonists hungry for land. The settlers found a wide variety of effigy mounds, some geometric in shape, and others in the form of birds, deer, alligators, lizards, bears, and felines. However, the colonists proceeded to plough a huge number of them out to use the land for agriculture. "Mound Builders" is now used as a rather general description of the Native North American cultures that created various styles of earthen mounds across the Great Lakes region, the Ohio River area, and the Mississippi River region. Among the earliest of the Mound Builders so far discovered are those of the Poverty Point Culture (named after a site near Floyd, Louisiana), whose massive earthworks were constructed between 1800 and 1000 BC. Another mound site, Watson Brake (near Monroe in northern Louisiana), has recently been dated to c. 3400 BC and is consequently the oldest Mound Builder site in America. However, the term "Mound Builders" once had quite a different meaning than that now used to describe Native American archaeological cultures.

Unable to believe Native Americans were sophisticated enough to erect huge, complex earthen monuments, and the majority never having witnessed the construction of the mounds for themselves, colonists came up with the Eurocentric idea that the structures must have been the work of a mysterious "Mound Builder" culture. Because metal artifacts and objects with inscriptions were discovered in some of the mounds, it was believed that the Native Americans, who were obviously too "primitive" to work metal and didn't seem to have a system of writing, could not have been the builders of the mounds. This ignorance of the separate cultures of Native American peoples, and the lack of understanding of how widely these cultures varied throughout the country, coupled with downright prejudice against the Native Americans, led to the myth of a "superior" race of mound builders, who were believed to have migrated to North America from the Old World at some unspecified date in the past. Consequently this mythical super-race were variously described as the Ten Lost Tribes of Ancient Israel, Egyptians, Phoenicians, Greeks, Chinese, Mongols, Vikings, Hindu colonists from India, or even refugees from Atlantis. In fact, just about any ancient Old World culture the colonists could think of.

However, there are a number of descriptions of the Native Americans constructing monumental earth-built mounds written from firsthand experience by Europeans. One of these accounts was written by

Spanish chronicler Garcilaso de la Vega (c. 1539–1616), also known as "El Inca" because of his Incan mother. De la Vega was record-keeper of the infamous De Soto expedition that landed in present-day Florida on May 31, 1538, and his *Historia de la Florida* (published in Lisbon in 1605, as *La Florida del Inca*) gives detailed descriptions of Native American Mound Cultures still practicing their traditional way of life. De la Vega's accounts include vital details about south-eastern Native American tribes' systems of government, tribal ter-ritories, and construction of mounds and temples.

Unfortunately, it would not be until 1894, when ethnologist Cyrus Thomas referred to De la Vega's writings in his report to the Bureau of American Ethnology, that people remembered that eye-witness reports about Mound Builder cultures existed. Thomas, as well as researchers before him, such as geologist and ethnologist Henry Schoolcraft (1793–1864) and third President of the United States Thomas Jefferson (1743–1826), discovered through excava-tion that the people buried inside the mounds were no different to modern Native Americans. Despite the work of Thomas and mod-ern excavations at mound sites such as Cahokia in Illinois (see Chapter 26), which show the mounds to be without doubt of Native Ameri-can origin, the mythical "mound-builder" super-race still has some currency amongst writers not too familiar with the facts of North American prehistory.

As mentioned, the Serpent Mound was thought by F.W. Putnam to belong to the Adena Culture. However, excavations of one sec-tion of the embankment of the structure in August 1991, uncovered pieces of wood charcoal that could be radiocarbon dated. The re-sult of these tests, which were performed in 1995, revealed Serpent Mound to be much younger than previously thought, dating the construction of the monument to c. AD 1070, and thus belonging to a Native American culture called the Fort Ancient Culture (AD 1000–1500). The Fort Ancient Culture were descended from the Hopewell culture (100 BC–AD 500), who were also a Mound Builder people. One of the main features of the Fort Ancient people was their earthen structures, and they are believed to have created hundreds of effigy burial mounds throughout Wisconsin, Minnesota, Ohio, and Iowa. One example is the "Alligator Mound" in Granville (in Licking County, Ohio), which is 200 feet long, is 5 to 6 feet high, and, despite its name, resembles a panther or an opossum rather than an alligator. During small-scale excavations of part of the Alligator Mound in 1999, charcoal fragments were recovered from near the base of the structure, which yielded radiocarbon dates averaging between AD 1170 and 1270, which gives the structure a similar date to Serpent Mound.

Excavations of numerous Native American mounds have often revealed elaborate burial practices, artifacts, and raw materials accessible only through wide-ranging trade networks. But although excavations in the vicinity of Serpent Mound have shown that the area was inhabited from at least as far back as 1000 BC, its function, similar to that of the many other mounds that did not include burials when excavated, has puzzled archaeologists for years. One interesting fact about Serpent Mound that has been known since the early 1900s is that it is located on a plateau with a unique cryptovolcanic structure. In 2003, geologists from the Ohio Department of Natural Resources Division of Geological Survey, and from the University of Glasgow (Scotland), concluded after studying deep rock and mineral core samples from the site, and geophysical surveys and remote satellite imagery for the area, that a meteor had struck the area during the Permian Period, about 248 to 286 million years ago. Whether the unique nature of the area's geology was a factor in the establishment of Serpent Mound in this particular location is an intriguing, though as yet unproven, theory.

The simplest explanation for the designs of effigy mounds is that they represent tribal or family totems. English researcher Paul Devereux has suggested that Serpent Mound and other effigy mounds may have been created to represent the "power animals" of shamans, the helping spirits that give wisdom and power to the shamans during their trance rituals. True, we don't know that those Native Americans of the Fort Ancient Culture practiced a shamanic religion, but shaman-like figures in Native American rock art roughly contemporary in date with Serpent Mound suggest that this idea is not entirely without merit.

Other explanations for the structure center around a plumed or horned snake god, known from depictions on Native American artifacts and rock carvings, especially along the Mississippi Valley and in Native American mythology. The connection with water is felt by some researchers to be significant, as the majority of effigy mounds are located in river valleys. The great horned water snake *Uktena,* of the Cherokee, a tribe whose homeland was the southern Appalachian Mountains, was said to be as large around as a tree trunk with a blazing crystal-like crest on its forehead. One Cheyenne myth, recounted to researchers Alice Marriott and Carole K. Rachlin, concerns a "water monster" living in the Mississippi River. This story describes a young warrior who eats two giant eggs that he finds lying on the ground, only to find himself slowly changing into a giant horned snake. The snake-man travels to the Mississippi River in which he makes his home. Since that time, the Cheyenne never fail to offer food and tobacco to the water snake when crossing any large body of water. The earliest-known official record of the Cheyenne is not until the mid-1600s in the Great Lakes area, and there is no evidence to suggest they were in any way connected with the Fort Ancient culture, though the huge snake and giant eggs of this tale certainly bring to mind Serpent Mound.

The radiocarbon date for the construction of Serpent Mound of c. AD 1070, has suggested to some researchers a link with the appearance of Halley's Comet in AD 1066, the brightest ever recorded for the comet. Some contemporary chroniclers stated the brightness of the comet to be equal to a quarter of that of the full moon. Although it is of course possible that Serpent Mound was created in response to this cosmic event, the actual form the monument takes does not really resemble the long straight form of Halley's Comet. Another astronomical theory is that Serpent Mound was laid out on the ground to reflect the positions of the stars in the constellation

Draconis (Draco), the word *Draco* ("dragon") being linked in this theory to a snake and thus Serpent Mound. However, though it is known that some Native American tribes laid out structures to mirror heavenly constellations—the Pawnee of the Western Plains, for example—there is no evidence that the Native Americans who created Serpent Mound knew this particular constellation under the name "Draco" (the name being of Middle Eastern derivation) or connected it in any way with a dragon/serpent. Incidentally, the temple of Angkor Wat in Cambodia (discussed in Chapter 24) has also been "revealed" to be a representation of the constellation of Draco on earth (at the time of Spring Equinox in 10,500 BC), by author Graham Hancock in his 1998 book, *Heaven's Mirror.*

When contemplating the reason why Native Americans constructed Serpent Mound, and effigy mounds in general, perhaps we should shift our thinking away from the end product and think, as suggested by Dr. Joe W. Saunders, excavator of the Watson Break mounds site, that there was something significant in the act of mound creation itself. Perhaps it was the construction of these enigmatic effigy monuments that was the purpose, the sacrifice of time and labor it involved, the organization, and dedication. But until a great many more un-looted effigy mounds are properly examined by careful remote sensing or if necessary limited excavation, then we will never really know why Native American cultures undertook such huge complicated tasks. And perhaps not even then.

Chapter 28

The Bighorn
Medicine Wheel
(United States)

Bighorn Medicine Wheel.
Photographer unknown

There are between 70 and 150 Native American stone structures known as "medicine wheels" spread over the northern United States and southern Canada. They are found in Alberta, Saskatchewan, South

Dakota, Montana, and northern Wyoming. But what are these enigmatic structures and who built them? Were they ancient observatories, locations for Native American vision quests, or perhaps burial places for long-forgotten warriors?

Though each individual structure is unique, the shape of the most common type of medicine wheel resembles that of a wagon wheel lying on its side, with a central cairn from which lines of cobblestone radiate outwards to a surrounding ring of stones. The diameter of medicine wheels, as well as the number and length of their "spokes," varies. The largest so far discovered has a diameter of around 80 feet. Occasionally there will be a break in the outer stone circle to allow a stone pathway or "entrance" into the center of the structure, and sometimes one of the spokes can be considerably longer than the others, perhaps signifying the importance of the direction in which it is pointing. The dates of these medicine wheels also vary considerably, but it is acknowledged that the oldest so far investigated is the Majorville Cairn (south of Bassano, Alberta), which was started around 5,500 years ago.

The term *medicine wheel* was first recorded in the 1895 by ethnologists visiting the Bighorn Mountain range in northern Wyoming, where they heard local Native Americans use the words to describe a loose stone circle on top of Medicine Mountain. This irregular circle, the Bighorn Medicine Wheel, is located more than 9,600 feet up, near the summit of Medicine Mountain in the Bighorn Mountains, 30 miles east of Lovell and in an area now designated the "Bighorn National Forest." Because of snow, the Wheel is only accessible from around mid-June to late August each year. The central cairn of the structure measures about 12 feet across and 2 feet high, and has 28 spokes radiating out from it to a rim of stones about 80 feet in diameter. This rim has five smaller cairns spaced along it, with another outside the circle linked to the center by one of the spokes. The Medicine Wheel is not an isolated monument; it stands within a vast complex of historic and prehistoric Native American sites stretching back 7,000 years. In the surrounding area archaeologists have discovered tipi rings, scatters of

Palaeolithic stone tools and weapons, buried archaeological sites, and a system of relict prehistoric Native American trails.

Excavations at the site have revealed that the Medicine Wheel on Bighorn is a composite feature, probably constructed over the past 300 to 800 years (archaeologically speaking, the second half of the Late Prehistoric Period), and has been maintained by various tribes since that time. Pottery found inside the Medicine Wheel has been identified as Crow and Shoshone; indeed there is ceramic evidence for the presence of the Crow tribe on the western slopes of the Bighorn Mountains beginning in the 1500s to 1600s.

Due to the relatively long life span of the medicine wheel, archaeologists are doubtful whether its function and meaning have remained unchanged over time, and believe that its original purpose may now be now lost forever. Consequently, we can only speculate as to who actually constructed the Wheel, whether it functioned as a sacred site for its entire lifetime, and if it was the center of the local ritual/ceremonial area. Although archaeology can tell us very little about the function and use of this enigmatic structure, recent ethnological research in the area can add something to our knowledge. This ethnological evidence reveals that the Medicine Wheel and its surrounding area constitutes an important ceremonial and traditional landscape for many tribes, including the Arapaho, Bannock, Blackfeet, Cheyenne, Crow, Kootenai-Salish, Plains Cree, Shoshone, and Sioux. Chief Joseph (1840–1904) of the Nez Perce tribe was known to fast at the Wheel, and Chief Washakie (c1804–1900), a chief of the Eastern Shoshone of Wyoming, claimed to have received his medicine there. The Crow (*Apsáalooke*—"Children of the Large-Beaked Bird") call the summit of the Big Horn Mountains *Awaxaawakússawishe* ("Extended Mountain"), and it is considered the most sacred place of their world.

The area of the Medicine Wheel contains contemporary Native American sites such as ceremonial staging areas, medicinal and ceremonial plant gathering areas, sweat lodge sites, altars, offering locales, and fasting (vision quest) enclosures. Native American tribes travel to the Medicine Wheel to pray and hold religious ceremonies, and re-gard the Wheel as a piece of living religious architecture, a part of the wider spiritual landscape of the alpine forests and peaks of the Bighorn Mountains, rather than merely as an "archaeological site" or an "ancient monument."

Native American tribes relied almost solely on oral traditions, handed down from generation to generation within a tribe, to pass on important knowledge and information. But because a great deal of this oral tradition has been lost, there are only fragments of tra-dition relating to the Bighorn Medicine Wheel. When questioning members of the Crow tribe about the Wheel in the early 1900s, ethnologist S.C. Simms was told by one Crow elder that Medicine Wheel was built "by people who had no iron" (reported in "A Wheel-Shaped Stone Monument in Wyoming," in a 1903 issue of *American Anthoropologist*). Another Crow chief stated that the structure was built "before the light came." Other visitors around the same time were told by local tribes that it was built before they had arrived in the area, or that it was built by the sun as a guide from the heavens for constructing the first tepees. A late-19th-century report quoted by ethnologist George Bird Grinnell, in 1922, states that during re-ligious ceremonies medicine men of various tribes would occupy the cairns of the Medicine Wheel, and the larger cairn in the center "was supposed to be the abode of Manitou."

One Crow oral tradition ascribes the creation of the Medicine Wheel to a boy named Burnt Face. According to the legend, when very young, the boy fell into the fire and severely scarred his face. When he grew into a teenager, Burnt Face went on a vision quest in the Bighorn Mountains, where he fasted and built the Medicine Wheel as a gift to the Sun. During the quest, Burnt Face drove away a huge otter that had been attacking baby eaglets and was rewarded by the Great Eagle, who made his face smooth again.

One of the most widespread of traditions among Native American tribes, such as the Crow, Shoshone, Cherokee, Choctaw, and Comanche, is that of "Little People." In relation to the Bighorn Medicine Wheel, the stories of the Little People of the Crow are especially relevant.

Some of these stories are centered on the area of the Pryor Mountains just to the west of the Bighorns, and known to the Crow as the Arrowhead Mountains, as there is an abundance of flint found there with which to make projectile points.

One traditional story the Crow tell involves a place on Pryor Creek, known as the "Baby Place," where more traditional members of the tribe would leave offerings to the Little People and say a prayer to have children. If they wanted to know the sex of their child, they would leave boy or girl gifts as offerings and return the following day to see which offering had been accepted by the Little People. A common offering at another sacred site in the Pryors, called Arrow Rock, was to shoot arrows into the cliff face. Another revered place in the area is known as "Little People's Cave." Chief Plenty Coups (c. 1848–1932), the last of the traditional Crow chiefs, had a number of prophetic visions at the sacred area of Castle Rocks in the Pryor Mountains involving the Little People and accepted them as his personal spiritual guides.

A story told about Crow Chief Long Hair (also known as "Red Plume"; c. 1750–1836) involved him meeting the Little People when he was on a vision quest at the Bighorn Medicine Wheel. The vision quest was one of the main rites of the Sun Dance religion, and usually lasted from three to four days. The quest involved going up into the hills to a quiet, remote place, where the young person would fast and pray in the hope of acquiring "medicine power," or perhaps the answer to an important question. If the young man was successful, he was rewarded with a dream or vision as a sign from a guiding spirit. The messenger in the vision usually took the form of a bird or an animal. When he returned to the camp, the young man would visit a medicine man who would interpret his vision and give any further instruction, such as making a medicine bundle to preserve the medicine power he had acquired on his quest.

According to the legend, while at the Bighorn Medicine Wheel, Chief Long Hair, who had apparently passed four days without food or water, was visited by Little People who lived inside the passage of the Wheel. The people led him down to where they lived inside the earth and told him he must always wear a red eagle feather, because from that time onward it would be powerful medicine for him, which is how he received the name Red Plume. When he was dying, Long Hair told his people that if they wanted to talk to him after he had passed on, they would find his spirit at the Wheel.

Although for most people these Little People of tradition are entirely imaginary, there is no doubt that many Native Americans firmly believed in their existence. In this light, there was an intriguing discovery made in 1932 by two men prospecting for gold in the San Pedro Mountains, about 60 miles southwest of Casper, Wyoming. Known as the "Pedro Mountains Mummy," this 14-inch mummified corpse was put on public display for several years before being examined by Dr. Harry Shapiro, from the American Museum of Natural History, who concluded that it was indeed human. Some speculated that the body was the remains of one of the Little People referred to in Crow and Shoshone myth. In 1979, the X-rays were examined by George Gill, an anthropology professor at the University of Wyoming, who concluded that the mummy was the remains of an infant suffering from anencephaly, a disease where the child is born without a major portion of the brain, skull, and scalp. In 1994 a second (female) mummy, which had also been discovered in a central Wyoming cave, was examined by Gill and also by physicians at Denver's Children's Hospital. After DNA, and radiocarbon and radiographic analysis, the researchers concluded that it was the remains of a malformed infant. The body was carbon dated to around 300 years old, and DNA analysis revealed that it was Native American.

Gill later proposed that the discovery of such diseased infants by Native Americans who believed they were the remains of miniature adults could have inspired the Little People myths, though this seems unlikely, as only three such mummies have ever been found.

Although some tribes, such as the Blackfeet and Blood Indians, created medicine wheels to mark either the grave or the position of the last tipi occupied by a great warrior chief, it is unclear if the

Bighorn Medicine Wheel was ever used in this way. In 1922 George Bird Grinnell noted that the plan of the Bighorn Medicine Wheel exhibited many similarities to that of a Cheyenne medicine lodge or Sun Dance Lodge, and that the structure could be a symbolic replica in stone of the Medicine Lodge. It was at the Medicine Lodge that the Sun Dance ceremony, a profoundly sacred ritual performed during the full moon in June or July, was held. According to Oglala Lakota (Sioux) Medicine Man, Black Elk (1863–1950), the Sun Dance Lodge originally had an entrance at the east and 28 rafters representing the days in the lunar cycle, which does echo the ground plan of the Bighorn Medicine Wheel.

In his 1987 book, *The Wolves of Heaven: Cheyenne Shamanism, Ceremonies, & Prehistoric Origins,* author Karl H. Schlesier links the Bighorn Medicine Wheel with the 56-day-long Cheyenne Massaum ("Crazy Buffalo Dance") ceremony. Schlesier sees the Wheel as a depiction, on a horizontal plane, of the Cheyenne Massaum lodge, a closed tipi with a frame based on 28 poles, where the secret part of the ceremony was held. Cheyenne mythology says the ceremony originated at the sacred site of Bear Butte, in South Dakota. It was to this place that Cheyenne Shaman Sweet Medicine and a female companion were sent when the tribe were desperate and close to starvation. The couple were taken inside the mountain where the Keepers of the Animal Spirits taught them the rites of the Massaum ceremony, a ritual impersonation and hunting of animals, which would bring enough game to feed the people.

One theory for the function of medicine wheels, and one that links in with aspects of the Cheyenne Massaum Ceremony, was put forward in 1974 by astrophysicist John Eddy. After studying a number of medicine wheels, and the Bighorn Medicine Wheel in particular, Eddy concluded that the structures could have functioned as observatories to identify the rising or setting of celestial bodies important to local Native American tribes. The significant alignments that Eddy measured at the Bighorn Medicine Wheel were marked by the five cairns on the rim of the Wheel and the one outside, and denoted the Summer Solstice sunrise and sunset, and the bright stars Aldebaran, Rigel, and Sirius—all important stars associated with the Solstice. Thus the Wheel could have been used to mark certain important days of the year, perhaps for the accurate timing of important religious ceremonies and to forecast events such as the return of the buffalo. The stars Aldebaran, Rigel, and Sirius play symbolic roles in the ancient Cheyenne Massaum ceremony, which lasted for two moons every year from the Summer Solstice to the midsummer rising of these three stars. However, some researchers are far from convinced about the observatory theory, believing that Native Americans' knowledge of the landscape and the night sky would have been enough for predicting the positions of rising stars and the sun, and thus timing ceremonies accurately.

A number of researchers have drawn parallels between the astronomical function of the Bighorn Medicine Wheel and the Neolithic stone circle of Stonehenge (in Wiltshire, England), where the first stones were erected on an older monument around 2600 BC. However, there is no proof that Stonehenge was designed predominantly as an observatory, though it is probable that religious ceremonies celebrating the Winter Solstice were held there. Perhaps this could also be said of the Bighorn Medicine Wheel. There is no doubt that the Wheel may have served some astronomical function, but it is more probable that this would have been part of wider ritual use, perhaps involving hunting magic or buffalo fertility. This is not to say that Native Americans were not sophisticated enough to build observatories, but in one sense to state that the Bighorn Medicine Wheel was built only to make complex astronomical calculations is to apply modern Western ideas from a 21st-century technology-dominated era back into the past. This explanation reflects *our own* concerns with time-keeping, calendars, computers, and space, not necessarily those of the Native Americans who built and used the Bighorn Medicine Wheel.

Chapter 29

Mount Shasta: Creator of Legends (United States)

Mount Shasta.
Photograph by Shasta Pix

Rising majestically to 14,179 feet above sea level and dominating the surrounding forests and plains, Mount Shasta is a double peaked mountain, the second-highest volcano in the United States. Visible on clear days from more than a hundred miles distant, Shasta is part of the

Cascade Mountain Range (in Siskiyou County in Northern California), and has long been a sacred place for Native American populations in the area. In the 20th and 21st centuries Shasta has also become home to a booming new age tourist industry, and reports of refugees from ancient Lemuria, UFOs, and Bigfoot are rife. But what lies behind these reports? Does the mountain itself possess certain energies that attract or create strange phenomena? Or are we dealing with urban legends and modern folklore?

Mount Shasta was probably named after a local Indian tribe, the Shasta, and, perhaps because of its prominence in the landscape, it has acquired an important place in the legends and religious practices of a number of Native American tribes. The Shasta Indians themselves presently occupy an area to the northwest of the Mountain, but their territory once included sections of southern Jackson County, Oregon, and Siskiyou County. The Shasta people believed that Chareya, Old Man Above, created Mount Shasta when the earth was new and the land flat. Chareya bored a large hole in the sky through which he pushed down masses of snow and ice until a huge mountain was formed that rose up to the clouds. He then climbed down from the clouds through the hole he had made and onto the peak of Shasta. The sun shone through the hole and melted the ice and snow so Chareya was able to plant the first trees. He created birds by blowing on the leaves that fell from the trees, and from small twigs broken off from his great walking stick he made fish, which he placed in the mountain streams. From the rest of his walking stick he created the other animals, including the beaver, the otter, and the grizzly bear. The grizzly bear Chareya created could walk on its hind legs and talk, and was so ferocious that he made it live at the bottom of the mountain.

Another Shasta legend explains the eruption of Mount Shasta. Known as "Coyote and the Yellow-jackets" this myth describes how Coyote, a trickster/culture hero character present in many Native American myths, has his packs of salmon repeatedly stolen by yellow jackets (wasps). Finally, he enlists the help of the Shasta Indians and together they chase the yellow jackets to the top of Mount Shasta, where they disappear into a hole. Coyote and the Shasta start a fire on the top of the mountain and try to smoke out the yellow jackets. When that fails, Grandfather Turtle sits on top of the hole until the mountain begins to rumble. Sensing danger, Grandfather Turtle climbs down, when suddenly there is a huge explosion throwing rocks, fire, and Coyote's salmon high into the air. Coyote, the Shasta Indians, and Grandfather Turtle then sit down and enjoy a delicious meal of smoked salmon. The Shasta Indians today conclude this story by saying, "This is how volcanic eruptions began long, long ago on Mount Shasta."

The Achumawi, also known as the "Pit River Indians," were located in northeastern California between the Pit River basin near Montgomery Creek in Shasta County and Goose Lake on the California–Oregon border. They have a number of myths involving Mount Shasta, many of which were recorded in the 1920s by zoologist, ornithologist, and ethnographer C. Hart Merriam, and published under the title *Annikadel,* the name of the chief spiritual being of the Achumawi. In one story recorded by Merriam, Edechewe (the "Fisher-Man"), the older brother of Yahtch ("Weasel-Man"), assembles a group of various legendary beings, including Spider and Coyote, on Mount Shasta in order to find his brother who has been kidnapped. In another tale Jamul (Coyote) and Kwahn ("Silver Fox-man") were arguing about summer and winter. Kwahn maintained that winter should have four moons and no more, and summer eight. But Jamul disagreed and was adamant that winter should have 10 moons, and summer just two. So Kwahn told Jamul to go up to the summit of Mount Shasta and see what it was like to have 10 moons of winter.

Mount Shasta is known as "Bohem Puyuik" ("big rise") or "Waydal Buli" ("north mountain") to the Wintu people, who today inhabit parts of Trinity, Tehama, Shasta, and Siskiyou counties. The Wintu have a number of legends in which Mount Shasta plays a prominent role, including "Mole and Mount Shasta," where Mole tries to make Mt. Shasta the highest of all mountains, but twists his wrist while attempting it, which is the reason why, to this day, Mole has a broken wrist. In a Wintu story entitled "Norwanchakas and His Brother Keriha Traveling Upward," Norwanchakas smokes out the monster Supchet from his tunnel in Mount Shasta using his shield of hardened elk skin to fan the flames, and then kills him when he emerges from the hole. Later in the tale the brothers meet an Indian on the McCloud River, south of Mount Shasta, who tells them about a race of bad people ("Bedits") living on the eastern side of Mount Shasta. The two men decide to visit the sweat lodge of the bad people and set it on fire, burning the Bedits to death. The brothers then wait for the souls of the bad people to escape from the smoke hole of the lodge and strike them so they can't escape and reform somewhere else. One Bedit soul does escape, however, but the brothers pursue it to the top of the mountain, where they imprison it in a fissure in the rock. Even today you can still hear the cries of the Bedit as he tries to escape from his rock prison. On the eastern side of Mt. Shasta, there is a blackened area marking the spot where the sweat lodge of the Bedits was burned down.

These legends, similar in some respects to the Aboriginal tales centered on Ayers Rock (see Chapter 25), show that for the Native Americans around Mount Shasta, the Mountain was, and still is, a place of power and a sacred location in many different ways. This is especially true for the Winneman ("middle river people"), a small group belonging to the Wintu tribe, who have important sacred sites on Mount Shasta. Up until her death in 2003, at age 95, the formidable shaman Florence Curl Jones led this band. This remarkable woman was born into a family of healers, along the banks of the McCloud River. When she was 10 years old, Florence was sent by her tribe on an 80-mile, weeklong coming-of-age journey, alone through the Mt. Shasta area in order to find her power as a spiritual healer. For her shamanic training Florence was taken to a sacred place called Panther Meadow, a peaceful wildflower-covered area on the southern side of Mount Shasta just below the snow line. Her renown as a traditional healer or "top doctor" for the tribe, and also as someone who preserved the traditional Wintu ways, spread well beyond the confines of her own tribe. Jones was also tireless in her fight for the protection of sacred Indian land from development, and in her attempts to get the Winnemem group returned to the Bureau of Indian Affairs' list of officially recognized tribes.

Throughout her life, Florence Jones led ceremonies at the Winnemem Wintu's sacred sites on and around Mt. Shasta, and conducted the annual Circle at Coonrod, a four-day Wintu healing ceremony that has been held by the tribe each summer for centuries. The ceremony, which takes place at a sacred spring in Panther Meadow, was featured in Christopher "Toby" McLeod's PBS documentary *In the Light of Reverence,* a film dealing with Lakota, Hopi, and Wintu efforts to preserve and worship at their sacred sites, first shown nationally in the United States in 2001.

Mount Shasta has also inspired a considerable amount of legend and folklore of a non–Native American type. In the 1880s, Frederick Spencer Oliver, a teenage resident of Yreka, just to the north of Mount Shasta, wrote a fantasy novel called *A Dweller on Two Planets: or, The Dividing of the Way* (first published in 1905). The book, which Spencer Oliver maintained was dictated to him by a "spirit" named "Phylos the Thibetan," is the origin of much of the esoteric and new age lore that surrounds Mount Shasta. The "I AM" movement, an organization founded in the 1930s that believes they are receiving instructions for humanity from the Ascended Masters, took the idea of a mystic brotherhood on Mount Shasta from Oliver's book. The founder of the cult, American mining engineer Guy Warren Ballard, wrote (using the pseudonym Godfré Ray King) in his 1934 book *Unveiled Mysteries* that, while hiking on the slopes of Mount Shasta in 1930, he met the Ascended Master Saint Germain who asked him to become the messenger for the Ascended Masters of the Great White Brotherhood who lived on Mount Shasta.

The basis for the popular legend of the secret Lemurian city inside Mount Shasta also comes from *A Dweller on Two Planets*. In Spencer Oliver's book, Lemurians journey to Mount Shasta after their continent sinks beneath the Pacific Ocean, and make their home inside the Mountain in a network of jewel-encrusted tunnels. Further writings perpetuated the Lemuria-Shasta connection, one of which was a two-page magazine article by "Selvius" entitled "Descendants of Lemuria: A Description of an Ancient Cult in California," published in 1925. In 1931, a book by Wishar Spenle Cerve called *Lemuria: The Lost Continent of the Pacific* appeared. Chapter 11 of this book, "Present-Day Mystic Lemurians in California," drew heavily on the 1925 article by Selvius and brought new fame to the Lemurians-living-in-caverns-beneath-Mount-Shasta legend. The book also added a new piece of folklore to the tale when it mentioned "tall, graceful, and agile" Lemurians visiting one of the smaller towns in the Shasta area to "trade nuggets and gold dust for some modern commodities." The author of this work was actually Harvey Spencer Lewis (of which "Wishar Spenle Cerve" is an anagram), an occultist, mystic, and founder of the Rosicrucian Order, also known as the Ancient Mystical Order Rosæ Crucis (AMORC).

Legend and folklore have progressed a little since the Lemurians and Ascended Masters first appeared on Mount Shasta, though the stories are still basically the same. Once the property of the Lemurians, the network of tunnels beneath Mt. Shasta now belong to aliens and lead to a UFO base there, and perhaps even form part of a world-wide tunnel network. There have been, however, genuine reports of unexplained light phenomena on or near Mount Shasta on occasion. As English researcher and writer Paul Devereux notes in his book, *Earth Lights Revelation*, the Cascade Mountain Range, of which Mount Shasta is a part, is located on a tectonic plate margin (where the majority of earthquakes and volcanoes occur), as graphically illustrated by the catastrophic 1980 eruption of Mount St. Helens.

Before Mount St. Helens erupted, there were reports of luminous displays, including "eerie blue lightening" in the area. It was over another part of the Cascades, Mount Rainier, only 60 miles from Mount St. Helens, in 1947, that Kenneth Arnold saw the flashing objects that were to become the archetypal "flying saucers." Now known as "earthquake lights", this phenomenon has been reported accompanying seismic activity on numerous occasions—for example, before the 1976 Tangshan earthquake in China, and before and after the Saguenay, Quebec, earthquakes of 1988–1989, where there were around 46 well-documented reports of globular light forms, tongues of fire, and seismic lightning. Perhaps such anomalous light forms could explain some of the unexplained lights reported at Mount Shasta, and perhaps a few of the legends connected with the Mountain may have been inspired by such displays.

Another legend associated with Mount Shasta is that of Bigfoot or Sasquatch. Some researchers believe that Native American mythology contains references supporting the existence of Bigfoot, but there are no ape-like hominids in the canon of Native American mythology. However, as in the legends and folklore of most cultures, there are man-like giants, though these creatures cannot be linked directly to sightings of Bigfoot in the modern era. Nevertheless, sightings of a Bigfoot-type creature on Mount Shasta do occur.

One 19th-century Sasquatch report first appeared in *Many Smokes*, a national Native American magazine, in the fall of 1968, under the title "Encounters with the Matah Kagmi," and was reprinted in the magazine *INFO Journal* (Vol. 2, No. 2, Spring 1970). The article was apparently written by the grandson of the witness. The first meeting with the Sasquatch (there are a number of encounters described in the article) is supposed to have occurred between the grandfather of the writer (a Modoc Indian) and a Sasquatch just to the north of Mount Shasta, near Tule Lake, in the summer of 1897. On other occasions, the Saquatch, given the name *Matah Kagmi* in the article, left fresh deerskins, wood for fuel, wild berries, and fruits for the grandfather. In a further encounter a few years later, the Modoc man was bitten by a rattlesnake on Mount Shasta and fainted. When he recovered, he saw three 8- to 10-foot-tall creatures standing around him, one of which had made a small cut, and removed the venom from his wound and covered the bite with cool moss. One of the *Matah Kagmi* then carried the man down the mountainside and put him down under a tree and left. It is difficult to know what to make of these stories, if genuine, except that the name used to refer to the creature, "Matah Kagmi," is strikingly similar to the Tibetan term *metoh-kangmi* (*Metoh* means "man-bear," and *Kang-mi* translates as "snowman") used to de-scribe the Abominable Snowman or Yeti. If this similarity of names is not a hoax, which it certainly sounds to be, then there is a considerable mys-tery here to be solved.

There are a number of 20th-century reports of a Bigfoot/Sasquatch-type creature on the Mountain, though details are often sketchy. In the summer of 1962, a woman named Bonnie Feldman stared in astonishment from the porch of her trailer on the east side of Mount Shasta, while a female Bigfoot gave birth next to the base of an upturned pine tree. An undated report describes an incident at an altitude of around 8,000 feet, where two men drinking beer saw Bigfoot emerge from the forest and hand them a crystal, before disappearing back into the woods. In 1980, hunters on the mountain caught a Bigfoot in the crosshairs of their rifles as he made his way across a field and entered some woods. They estimated the creature as being about 8 feet tall and weighing around 800 pounds. In 1986, a report from a team of naturalists described a Bigfoot walking across a field of berries at dawn. Although these reports are certainly intriguing, descriptions and details of the incidents are vague, and there is nothing to suggest the sightings are not hoaxes or misidentifications. That is not to say that all cases are explainable, but such anecdotal evidence as we have supports a folkloric explanation rather than the reality of ape-like creatures inhabiting Mount Shasta.

   In August 1987, the reputation of Mount Shasta as a world-renowned spiritual power center was sealed when the "Harmonic Convergence," a new age spiritual event held at various sacred and 'mystical' places all over the world, came to the slopes of the Mountain. The event, which was attended by between 3,000 to 5,000 people, was intended to herald a new phase of universal peace and harmony in the world. It also inspired the creation of new piece of folklore when, during the event, a Ms. Boettcher of Mount Shasta City claimed to see a flaming white angel on her TV. The story spread quickly and soon hordes of people were lining up at the door to get a glimpse of Ms. Boettcher's "holy TV." Some who saw the splodge of white light on the screen did indeed see an angel; others saw Jesus, and some a "light being." However, when the technicians at Shiloh Electronics in town examined the TV they found that the problem was a faulty capacitor in the low-voltage power supply. The technicians even set up a TV at their store showing an identical "angel" on the screen and offered to install an angel on everyone's TV for $99.99 per set. Surprisingly, there were no takers.

Chapter 30

Legends of the San Luis Valley (United States)

Great Sand Dunes National Park, with the
Sange de Cristo Mountains in the background.
Photograph by Wayne L. Bart

Located in the Rio Grande Basin of south-central Colorado and north-central New Mexico, the San Luis Valley is the world's largest Alpine Valley, covering approximately 8,000 square miles, with an average altitude of 7,500 feet. Important features of the Valley include the Great Sand Dunes

National Park, the tallest sand dunes in North America, rising to about 750 feet above the Valley floor; the Sangre de Cristo Mountains, one of the longest mountain chains on Earth, containing 10 peaks more than 14,000 feet high; and Mount Blanca, an important sacred place to Native Americans of the Southwest for hundreds if not thousands of years. The Navajos regard this peak as one of the four sacred mountains of their ancestral land.

The prehistoric archaeology of the San Luis Valley is imperfectly understood, with few extensive excavations having taken place in the area. However, from the research and excavation that has been undertaken, mainly by the Smithsonian Institution in Washington, D.C., we do have a general framework within which to work. The first known inhabitants of the San Luis Valley were the early Paleo-Indian Clovis culture, around 11,000 years ago, who have been identified by their characteristic stone (usually flint) projectile points. The later Folsom Culture (8900 to 8200 BC), identified by their chipped flint points known as Folsom points, used the valley as the Clovis did for the seasonal hunting of game and the gathering of native plants, as indicated by the lack of permanent structures and the scattering of finds. One prehistoric kill site in the Valley used by the Folsom people is known as the "Stewart's Cattle Guard" site, and is located in Alamosa County, Colorado. Excavations at this important site by Pegi Jodry, field director of the Paleoindian/Paleoecology Program for the Smithsonian, yielded 3,500 bison bones and fragments, more than a thousand tools, and more than 38,000 pieces of flaking debris from tool/weapon manufacture. Another roughly contemporary site, excavated by Jodry and her husband, Dennis Stanford, curator of North American Archaeology for the Smithsonian, is known as the Black Mountain Folsom site. An important feature of this site is the remains of a campfire location, from which charcoal samples yielded a carbon-14 date of 8500 BC.

These early Paleo-Indian peoples were followed by cultures of the Archaic era (c. 6000 BC–AD 500), who were also nomadic hunter-gatherers. The next stage of development in the San Luis Valley is marked by the emergence of the Ancestral Pueblo People, also known as the "Anasazi"— an anglicized Navajo word meaning "ancient ones" or "enemy ancestor," from around AD 800 to 1300. The Anasazi were characterised by their skilled agriculture, refined ceramics, and distinctive building techniques, the latter including multi-storied cliff dwellings. From the 1400s onwards, the remains of summer villages, temporary food-processing sites, and military fortifications show that the Valley was regularly visited by the Ute, Jicarilla Apache, Navajo, and Comanche peoples, and occasionally by the Cheyenne, Arapaho, Kiowa, and Kiowa Apache. In 1895 the Utes were removed from the Valley, and confined to the Southern Ute and Ute Mountain Indian reservations.

The San Luis Valley was once a northern frontier of the Spanish Empire, and the first non–Native Americans to visit the Valley were Spanish explorers in the early 1500s. In 1708, Juan de Ulaterri claimed the area for the king of Spain, but it was not until after the Valley had been purchased by the United States in 1848 (as part of the Treaty of Guadalupe Hidalgo) that the area became extensively settled, mainly by Hispanic farmers and ranchers from New Mexico. The oldest surviving settlement in Colorado, San Luis was founded in the Valley in 1851. The population of the San Luis Valley escalated in the late 1870s and early 1880s with the arrival of Mormon settlers from the southern United States and Utah, who founded the towns of Manassa, Sanford, and Richfield. With the discovery of gold and silver near Summitville in the San Juan Mountains in 1870, there was a huge influx of miners and adventurers into the area, with numerous mines, mining camps, and eventually permanent towns following.

It is hardly surprising for an area with such a varied and colourful history that the San Luis Valley is rife with folklore and legends. One particular motif that occurs frequently in tales of the Valley is that of the Devil. In the 1940s, William Jones Wallrich collected various tales of *El Diablo* from the Spanish-speaking inhabitants of the smaller communities of the Valley, some of which were subsequently published in the journal *Western Folklore.* In the light of the relatively recent reputation of the Valley as a paranormal hotspot, a few of these folktales are particularly intriguing. As with many stories of the paranormal, the majority of tales of *El Diablo* from the area are told as having actually happened, either to a close friend or relative of the narrator. One concerns a biplane that, shortly after World War I, was being delivered to a Dr. H.C.

Myers of Antonito, Colorado. It was obviously the first airplane to be witnessed in the area, as when the pilot flew low over the Myers' residence the family washwoman at work in the backyard "threw her apron up over her head...and ran inside where she hid under a table, all the time shouting, '*Diablo, Diablo!*' at the top of her healthy lungs," according to William Jones Wallrich's article in *Western Folklore* (April 1950).

Another type of tale concerning *El Diablo* from the San Luis Valley is that of the young girl who danced with the devil (called by Wallrich "Demon Dancer'" stories). The most common version of this story involves a beautiful young girl who loved to dance so much that she refused to stop even during Lent, when all her friends were giving up what they enjoyed most. The girl's mother begged her to make the sacrifice or there would be terrible consequences, but the girl refused, as she had been invited to go to a big dance. At the dance, the girl stood out from the crowd as the most beautiful girl and best dancer, and after a while a handsome stranger asked her to dance with him. She agreed and the couple danced and danced until a few minutes before midnight, when the orchestra began playing a fast piece of music. The couple were now alone on the dance floor, but soon a hush came over those present as, unbeknownst to the girl, the stranger began to change. Bumps started to appear on his forehead, and the toes of his boots grew out into points and curled up. The orchestra carried on playing as if in a trance, and in the distance a bell rang out the hour of midnight. At this, Wallrich reported, the "the girl who loved to dance so much and her strange dancing partner disappeared in a huge cloud of dark, acrid smoke." Everyone present realized that because, the girl had not given up dancing for Lent, she had the last dance of her life with the devil himself.

Also connected to the devil motif in the area are tales of witches (*brujas* in Spanish) and their malevolent influences, which were common throughout the Spanish Southwest in the 1940s when Wallrich was collecting his material. One of these, called "The Balls of Fire," is particularly relevant in light of recent reports of unexplained lights and various other UFO-related phenomena in the Valley.

In this tale, that William Jones Wallrich wrote about in the October 1950 issue of *Western Folklore,* Juan Ascendro, a young man from Costilla County in south-central Colorado, was returning home from a friend's house when, at a bridge at the edge of town, he encountered "four balls of fire dancing back and forth and up and down in the brush just across the water." Apparently well-versed in local lore, Ascedro quickly removed his clothes, turned them inside out, and put them back on again. He then scratched a circle in the soil with the toe of his boot, at which the balls of fire became still and lay on the ground. Juan used his willpower to control the balls, which glowed "balefully" as they remained on the ground, until about one o'clock when balls of fire "gave up," and Juan saw, standing on the river bank opposite him, four women from his town. Meanwhile the balls of fire had vanished. The four women screamed at Juan and begged him to erase the circle, but he refused. They then "advanced toward him with strange, terrible looks upon their faces" and he noticed to his horror that their legs were cut off at the knees. As the terrible women moved ominously toward him on stumps, Juan still refused to break the circle, until they finally gave up and pleaded with him for mercy. Juan made the witches promise never again to travel around at night as balls of fire, after which he made an opening in the circle, and the four women's legs were restored. They then thanked Juan and hurried off into the darkness.

Beginning in 1989, due mainly to the research of local journalist and author Christopher O'Brien, the San Luis Valley has developed a reputation as a center of intense paranormal activity. There have been a wide range of reports of strange phenomena in the area, including UFOs, humanoids, ghosts, Bigfoot, cattle mutilations, witches, appearances of the devil, secret underground bases, and covert military activity. In fact, the Valley has just about anything "weird' you can imagine, even its own "UFO Watchtower." Is the area a "portal" to another dimension, as has been suggested in the case of the Skinwalker Ranch in Utah? Though O'Brien christened the San Luis Valley a "paranormal Disneyland" in his book, *Secrets of the Mysterious Valley,* skeptics believe there is no evidence that area is any more paranormal than anywhere else, and that O'Brien has simply exaggerated local tales and used them as factual accounts of UFOs, humanoids, and so forth. Indeed, if genuine paranormal activity has been occurring in the Valley on a large scale for 25 years or more, then there should be some solid physical evidence by now.

Some of the "sightings" of unusual objects and "humanoids" are certainly no more than folktales, and others are explicable in terms of natural phenomena. For example, the San Luis Valley is particularly prone to a phenomenon known as "ice fog" (in the Shoshone language, *pogonip*—"white death"). This ice fog forms on cold, clear nights when the temperature drops below 0° C. If the temperature is low enough (it needs to be at "dew point," the temperature at which condensation occurs) moisture in the air forms tiny floating ice crystals. Because these ice crystals reflect light, they are highly visible, and make take on the appearance of a shaft of light ("light pillar") or a shimmering glow. The form that these ice crystals take is due to bright light passing from the sun, moon, or an artificial light source (such as street lights) through the part of the sky containing the ice crystals. The result can be extraordinary, but quite natural, apparitions. Furthermore, if the light source itself is many miles distant from the observer, the person is not able to observe the relationship between the reflected image in the sky and the light on the ground, thus making the phenomenon seem all the more inexplicable. Ice crystals cannot, of course explain every UFO reported in the San Luis Valley, but if conditions are right, ice fog and its effects should be considered before jumping to conclusions about alien spacecraft.

One mystery from the Valley that has now been explained is that of the "San Luis Valley Skull," supposed to be akin to the famous "Mitchell-Hedges" skull, a carved quartz crystal model of a human skull, possibly of Aztec origin. The artifact from the San Luis Valley was discovered on the border of the property of a female rancher in 1994, and was said to be the cause of various strange and unexplained events, such as a spare tire exploding, a video camera malfunctioning, strange smells, and various accidents around the house. The story received a large amount of media coverage at the time, and one newspaper account (the November 10, 1996, edition of the *Rocky Mountain News*) was seen by neighbors of the rancher, the Chadez family. They informed the rancher that their son, a glass-blower, had made a series of these skulls to sell at Day of the Dead festivities at Santa Fe. Mr. and Mrs. Chadez had placed this particular skull, a defect, on a fence as a property line marker.

The most famous of the San Luis Valley mysteries and the one that started the entire "animal mutilation" mystery is that of "Snippy" the horse. On September 8, 1967, a horse named Lady (later nicknamed "Snippy" by the press), a 3-year-old mare, was found dead on the King Ranch 20 miles northeast of Alamosa, Colorado. It was reported that the horse's skin and flesh had been cleanly removed from the shoulders to the ears, and that crushed vegetation and strange depressions in the ground had been found nearby. Duane Martin, a forest ranger, claimed to have measured a high level of radioactivity on a Geiger counter near the strange marks, although, when later questioned by an investigator (the incident was investigated by Robert Low, coordinator of the Condon Committee, the University of Colorado's UFO Project), he admitted that his meter had registered only a slight level of activity two weeks after the discovery of the body. The horse's owner, Nellie Lewis, was convinced that flying saucers were responsible for Snippy's death and later reported that her boots were radioactive. Nellie was a correspondent for a local newspaper, the *Pueblo Chieftain,* and wrote an account of the strange incident for the paper that was picked up by the Associated Press. (Christopher O'Brien states in *Secrets of the Mysterious Valley* that the story was actually spread by Nellie's neighbour Pearl Mellon Nicholas, society editor of the *Valley Courier.*) By early October, most of the United States knew the story of Snippy's death, and reports of UFOs and eventually "animal mutilations" began to flood in.

Later that year, Dr. Robert Adams, head of Colorado State University's Veterinary and Biomedical Science School, was asked by Robert Low to examine the carcass of the horse. Adams found that it had a severe infection in its right flank and postulated that someone had found the suffering horse and cut its throat to put it out of its misery. Dr. Adams believed that after the throat had been cut predators could have stripped away the flesh from head and neck and removed the organs. The brain and spinal fluid would have evaporated in the heat of the day. In December, Dr. Wallace Leary, operator of a local veterinary clinic, examined the corpse and found two bullet holes in the left pelvis and right thighbones. He believed the horse was probably shot by a couple of kids. Two years after the horse's death, it was reported by local residents that no grass would grow on the site where Snippy's carcass was found, a common folklore motif attached to tragic deaths.

In March 2007, Snippy's bones appeared on the eBay auction site, with a reserve price of $50, 000, but the bidding stalled at $1,825. Snippy now even has his own Website and blog, where you can buy "Exclusive Snippy Merchandise." It is unfortunate that the question of whether or not there is convincing evidence for unexplained phenomena in the San Luis Valley, which requires serious investigation and publication, comes a distant second to maintaining the reputation of the area as a "paranormal hotspot" for new age tourists.

Chapter 31

The Mysteries of Cuzco: Navel of the Incan World (Peru)

The Coricancha.
Photograph by Gabriel Lovato

The Inca capital, Cuzco, was began around AD 1100, and was once a lavish city of temples, palaces, gardens, and gold-covered walls. This city, located 11,000 feet up in the Andes Mountains, was to become both the physical and spiritual center of the Inca world. Cuzco lies within what is known as the Sacred Valley, part of the Urubamba River watershed, an area that contains a string of notable Inca remains including the fortress-temple sites of Pisac and Ollantaytambo.

There are two main origin myths for the Inca, both similar in content. In one version of the myth, Ticci Viracocha, the creator of civilization, sends his four sons, including the semi-legendary Manco Capac, and four daughters up from a cave in Pacaritambo (15 miles south of Cuzco) to conquer the tribes of the Cuzco Valley and take control of Cuzco itself. There Manco becomes their leader, the first lord of the Kingdom of Cuzco, and the founder of the Inca dynasty. According to the other legend, after seeing the desperate state of the world, Tayta Inti ("Father Sun") sends his two children, Manco Capac and Mama Ocllo, to bring back order and peace. The children emerge from Lake Titicaca (or through a cave in another version) with a golden staff and are told by their father to settle permanently wherever the staff should sink into the earth. At a hill overlooking the valley of the present city of Cuzco, the staff sinks into the ground, revealing the fertility of the soil. It was in this place that the brother and sister and their followers founded the Inca city of Cuzco, where they taught the people how to live proper lives and set up a Temple of the Sun for the worship of Tayta Inti.

By the mid-1400s, the Incas ruling from the city of Cuzco were lords over the largest state in the prehistoric Americas, with at least eight million people under their control in an empire that stretched 2,500 miles (from modern-day Colombia to Chile). Cuzco was not really a city in the modern Western sense; it was more akin to an enormous sacred organism. This is reflected in the plan of Cuzco, laid out in the form of a giant puma, a sacred animal to the Incas and one that symbolized their empire, illustrating that, for the Inca—as with many ancient cultures—there was no real difference between their physical and spiritual worlds. The belly of the great puma was formed by Cuzco's main plaza, the river Tullumayo was its spine, and the great head of this gigantic beast was formed by the 15th-century walled complex of Sacsayhuaman, just outside the city. Ancient Cuzco was closely linked to the sun, and at its center was the Coricancha ("golden enclosure"), the Incas' most important temple, dedicated to the Sun God, Inti. This building, whose walls and floors were once covered with solid gold, was not only the focus area for major rituals, but also functioned as an observatory marking solstices, equinoxes, and eclipses, the accurate tracking of which was vital to the timing of Inca religious and secular activities. After the Spanish sacked the city in 1533, the church and monastery of Santo Domingo was built on the ruined foundations of the site, though some fine Inca stonework was preserved and incorporated into the structure.

The Coricancha occupied a position representing the genitals of the puma, and from here 42 lines or *ceques* radiated outwards towards the mountains. Along these lines were placed a system of 328 religious shrines or *huacas*. The *ceques* had multiple functions: They could be used as astronomical sight lines, to organize sacred space, and as ritual pathways. This complex system of mostly imaginary lines was maintained by ayllus (kin groups) who made offerings at the *huacas* in their district. *Huacas* could be any location or feature thought to contain spiritual power, such as a prominent rock, waterfall or spring, or man-made objects such as temples, shrines, or tombs. Offerings made at these shrines included textiles, guinea pigs, baskets of coca leaf, marine shells, llamas, and, on occasion, Capacocha, or child sacrifice.

One story of a child sacrifice concerns a 10-year-old Incan girl called Tanta Carhua, described by one Spanish chronicler in Liesl Clark's article "Ice Mummies of the Inca" (on the Nova Online Website) as "beautiful beyond exaggeration." She was given by her father, a local lord, to the Emperor as a Capacocha sacrifice, and taken by priests to meet the Inca Emperor at Cuzco, where celebrations and processions were held in her honor. On Tanta Carhua's journey from Cuzco to the mountain where she was to be sacrificed, the entourage passed through her village, where, according to the legends, she told the villagers: "You can finish with me now because I could not be more honored than by the feasts which they celebrated for me in Cuzco." Tanta Carhua was then taken high up into the Andes, where she was given a drink of Chicha, a maize alcohol, and then placed inside a shaft tomb surrounded by sacred artifacts and sealed in alive. After her death, Tanta Carhua was honored as a goddess. Although there is no evidence that this particular story is literally true, it does contain a fairly accurate record of Inca Capacocha. It is known that child sacrifices were usually killed at a *huaca* connected with their homeland in times of famine, disease, or military defeat, or on the

Summer and Winter Solstices. The Capacocha served to form an unbreakable tie between the chief whose daughter (or son) was sacrificed and the Inca Emperor, and through the observance of the ritual the sacred city of Cuzco was linked to the farthest corners of its empire.

As the Inca Empire was so vast, some of the children chosen for sacrifice would have to travel a thousand miles or more from distant villages to come to the great Inca center. When leaving Cuzco, the children would not be taken on normal roads but follow the appropriate *ceque* lines leading out of the city. Over the last few years, archaeologists have discovered the sad evidence for the Inca practice of Capacocha in the form of often-frozen mummies sealed up in snow-covered tombs, high up in the Andes.

When the Spanish conquered Cuzco, much of the elaborate gold decoration from its buildings and gardens was either melted down and shipped back to Spain, or transformed into decoration for Christian churches in the city, such as Cuzco Cathedral, the Church of La Merced, and the Church of the Society of Jesus. But there were stories circulating that some of the gold had been smuggled out to jungle hideaways or even tunnels and caves underneath the Cuzco Valley, close to the impressive ceremonial center-cum-fortress of Sacsayhuaman on a hill to the north of Cuzco. One 16th-century Spanish chronicler, Garcilaso de la Vega, wrote of underground tunnels connecting the towers of this complex. The walls at the Sacsayhuaman complex are excellent examples of Inca architecture; the massive cut stone blocks fitted together so tightly that mortar was not needed. Some of the blocks used at Sacsayhuaman weigh a staggering 70 tons, and it is still a mystery how the Incas moved such boulders and how they were able to fit them together so precisely.

The series of underground passageways close to Sacsayhuaman are known as *chincanas,* and are the result of underground water erosion and later modification by the Incas. These labyrinthine tunnels have been surrounded by myth and folklore since the time of the Spanish chroniclers more than 470 years ago. One legend says that, when Francisco Pizarro had Atahuallpa, the 13th and last emperor of the Incas, executed, the Incas hid as much of their treasures as they could in these underground passageways, which were afterward blocked up. In 1600, a Jesuit Friar told of these tunnels being built to allow the Inca royalty and their armies to pass unnoticed during times of war from Sacsayhuaman to worship at the Temple of the Sun in Cuzco.

There have been various attempts over the centuries to locate this hidden treasure, one of which is supposed to have occurred sometime in the 17th century, when three Spanish explorers entered an opening at Sacsayhuaman and ventured deep inside the tunnels, never to be heard from again. Another incident apparently took place in the mid-18th century when two students entered the same opening, and again nothing was heard from them. But this time there was a survivor of the ill-fated underground expedition, as some days later one of the young men managed to grope his way out from a passageway under the main altar of the church of Santo Domingo, built over the site of the Inca Temple of the Sun. When he emerged half-insane from his nightmarish ordeal, he was clutching a golden ear of maize. Before he could reveal the secrets of the Inca tunnel system, he collapsed and died on the spot.

Another version of what appears to be the same story again describes a lost treasure hunter in the maze of tunnels under Cuzco. Around a week after his disappearance, during a mass at the church of Santo Domingo, the sound of loud tapping sounds echoed through the church. The shocked congregation turned to the priest who quickly had a large stone slab taken up from the floor. To the astonishment of both priest and congregation, the treasure hunter emerged from the underground passageways carrying a gold bar in each hand.

There is also a modern variant on this story. This incident is said to have occurred "a few years ago" and involved students from a foreign university. In this version of the tale, the students had only a day's supply of food and water when they went into the tunnels and disappeared. Weeks after the students had vanished into the passageways, a janitor at the cathedral in the Plaza de Armas was working late one night when he heard a digging sound coming from behind one of the walls, so he removed a stone slab and, to his horror, thought he saw a monster moving around in the dark. He immediately put the slab back and sealed up the hole. But his curiosity got the better of him, and he returned a few days later and slowly removed the slab again. Inside he was shocked to discover the emaciated body of a boy clutching a stalk of maize made of solid gold. The janitor took the golden object and sealed the body back up behind the wall, telling no one. According to the tale the janitor started living it up after his find but soon became ill, and lost his son in a car accident and his wife to influenza. He soon died of his illness, and his secret was lost with him.

In 1814, Brigadier Mateo Garcia Pumacahua, leader of the 1814–15 rebellion against the Spanish, is alleged to have taken an officer blindfolded down a secret stone stairway hidden behind some rocks somewhere in Cuzco. The stairs led to the underground tunnel system of Cuzco, and, when the blindfold was removed, the officer saw a huge silver puma with emerald eyes, gold and silver "bricks," and other treasures. While down in the tunnels, the officer could hear the clock of Cuzco cathedral chiming above him. Whether this story is true or not, in March of the following year, Brigadier Mateo Garcia Pumacahua was executed by the Spanish. Writing in her 1877 book, *Isis Unveiled,* occultist and founder of the Theosophical Society Madame H.P. Blavatsky describes her travels in South America and states "along the entire length of the corridor, from Bolivia to Lima and Cuzco, are smaller hiding places filled with treasures of gold and precious stone." She also claimed to possess an accurate plan of this vast tunnel obtained from an "old Peruvian."

Perhaps taking the idea from Blavatsky, author Eric Von Däniken maintained in his 1972 book, *Gold of the Gods,* that there was "a gigantic system of tunnels, thousands of miles in length" running under South America, constructed, he believed, with technology not of this world. According to modern Spanish author and journalist Javier Sierra, several precious items disappeared at the time of the Spanish conquest, including a solar disc known as the "Treasure of Inca King Atahualpa." The disappearance of these objects has been linked with the supposed passageway from Cuzco up to Sacsayhuaman. During his research, Javier Sierra noticed that the Coricancha, the convent of Santa Catalina, the church of San Cristobal, and Sacsayhuaman were aligned. Sierra believed that this alignment meant that the tunnel ran in a straight line, and thought there must be an opening under the main altar of Santo Domingo, as indicated in the stories. A Spanish treasure hunter called Anselm Pi Rambla (often wrongly described on the Web as an archaeologist), who had once traveled to Cuzco with von Däniken, claimed that he had entered the Cuzco tunnels in 1982 and later, in August 2000, sponsored by Texan financier Michael Galvis, used ground-penetrating radar to attempt to map out the passageways. Under the title of the "Coricancha Project," these investigations revealed a 6 1/2-foot-wide cavity underneath the altar of Santo Domingo, which Pi Rambla believed could be "the entrance to a great tunnel" (according to Philip Coppens's article "The Gold of Gran Paititi").

According to the Spanish EFE news agency for March 2003, the same team, now called the "Wiracocha Project," would, in May of that year, explore the tunnels under the church. However, in August 2003, the EFE news agency announced that the project was being cancelled by order of the National Institute of Culture and the authorities of the Convent of Santo Domingo due to lack of results. In April 2006, Pi Rambla and his company, Bohic Ruz, were being investigated for financial irregularities and damage done to the church of Santo Domingo during their investigations. Apparently after having had enough of archaeological investigation, the intrepid explorer reinvented himself. In June 2004, the *New York Times* reported that a company called Kokka Royal Food & Drink was producing a new soft drink called KDrink, the most important ingredient of which was coca, the green leaf used to make cocaine. The "Spanish investor" spearheading the project was none other than Anselm Pi Rambla.

But where does all this leave the secret tunnels of Cuzco? The various stories of groups of investigators getting lost for days in the underground maze, only to emerge alive with tantalising evidence of Inca treasure, are almost certainly folkloric variants of a single legend, possibly dating back to the time of the Spanish chronicles. The folklore of the Cuzco tunnel system is still being added to today. Not only do we have Anselm Pi Rambla's mythical 1.2 miles of tunnel being touted as fact on the Internet, but also that the tunnels may have been constructed by people from the lost continent of Atlantis (echoing James Churchward in his 1932 book, *The Children of Mu*), and that one of the passageways leads to an underground alien base. In fact, UFOs are seen from time to time in the Cuzco valley, and in 1965, during a wave of alleged sightings of strange dwarf-like creatures associated with unidentified aerial objects in Peru, there was a strange report from Sacsayhuaman. According to the newspaper account in *La Prensa*, just before noon on August 20, 1965, a group of people, including an engineer, Señor Alberto Ugarte, and his wife, and a Señor Elwin Voter, claimed to see what they described as a tiny disc land on a terrace of the Sacsayhuaman complex. The miniature craft was only around 5 feet wide, and of a bright silvery color. As the astounded group watched, two "small beings of strange shape and dazzling brightness" emerged from the disc, only to disappear back inside when they realized they were being watched. The craft then rapidly ascended into the sky and disappeared into the west. There is no more information on this intriguing incident, so it is difficult to tell whether it is a newspaper hoax, a misidentification, or a genuine sighting of something extremely odd.

So does a system of passageways exist underneath *Sacsay*huaman? It may well do. The tunnels could even hold Inca treasures, and conceivably connect with the center of Cuzco. But to probe the reality of such claims, professional archaeological investigation needs to be carried out, with knowledge, not treasure, as the goal of the operation.

Chapter 32

Lake Titicaca (Peru)

Lake Titicaca.

Lake Titicaca is a sacred lake 12,500 feet up on the plateau of Collao in the Southern highlands of Peru, on the border with Bolivia. The highest commercially navigable lake in the world, Titicaca covers an area of 3,200 square miles and has an average depth of 350 feet (though in places it can be as deep as 1,000 feet). The lake has 41 islands dotted over its surface; the three most important are the Isla Del Sol (the Island of the Sun), the Isla de la Luna (the Island of the Moon), and Isla Amantani (Amantani Island). The Lake is also home to the Uros Islands or Floating Islands (Islas Flotantes), a group of artificial islands made of floating reeds. The origin of the name "Titicaca," a Spanish corruption of the local Aymaran "Titi Karka," is obscure, but it has been variously translated as either "Rock Puma," "Gray Puma," or "Stone-Colored Puma." The lake is also known as "Mama Kocha," which means "the Mother Lake."

According to a creation legend of the local Aymaran people, the mountain gods (apus) of the area around Titicaca became angry at the arrogance of humans and so sent a plague of pumas against them. Seeing the chaos that resulted from the violent attack, other spirits began to cry. Their tears filled the empty basin and drowned both the humans and animals. As with many flood legends from all over the world, only two people survived, Mama Occla and Manco Capac, who, when they looked around them after the terrible deluge, saw the vast lake of tears with hundreds of dead pumas floating on its surface with their bellies turned upward. "Titi Karka," they said.

A variation of this legend tells that in the remote past when terrible floods were ravaging the earth and mankind was nearly annihilated, the creator god, Viracocha, arose from the depths of Titicaca and traveled across the lake to the Isla de la Luna, the Isla del Sol, and the island of Amantani. Viracocha ordered the sun (Inti), the moon (Mama-Kilya) and the stars to rise. He then created a new man and a new woman, Mallku Kapac and Mama Ocllo, from stones, and sent them out to repopulate the world. It was, traditionally, these two flood survivors, the Incan Adam and Eve, who went on to found the Inca Empire.

The three main islands in Titicaca are scattered with Incan and pre-Incan ruins. The Islands of the Sun and the Moon were two of the most sacred places in the Incan Empire, possessing important shrines to which Incas from throughout the Empire made pilgrimages. In the northern part of the Island of the Sun, the largest island in Lake Titicaca, at the town of Challapampa, is El Labarinto ("The Labyrinth"), a vast maze-like complex of stone walls belonging to an Inca Temple complex. Inside this Incan labyrinth is a small well, once visited by Inca pilgrims and believed by them to contain sacred water, which they used to purify themselves. Also in this part of the island are two natural marks in the bedrock that have become known as "Huellas Del Sol" ("Footprints of the Sun"), said to have been created by the Sun after its birth on Titicaca Rock.

During a survey of pre-Hispanic archaeological sites on the Island of the Sun, University of Illinois at Chicago archaeologist Brian Bauer and his team discovered fascinating evidence that indicates how Incan rituals were performed. The team excavated the remnants of two substantial stone pillars, as well as a large platform area just outside the walls of one of the sanctuaries on the island. These pillars are similar to those around Cuzco, described by several 16th-century Spanish chroniclers, and were used to record the location of the horizon of the sun at the June and December Solstices. The research undertaken by Bauer and his team suggests that at the June Solstice, close to the time of the Sun Festival (*Inti Raymi*), the Inca king and his high priests would have gathered at a small plaza next to the sacred rock of Inca mythology. The worshipers assembled there to witness the setting sun framed between the two stone pillars. On a second platform, located outside the sanctuary wall, the event was observed by a lower class of pilgrims. Watching from the secondary position with these pilgrims, one would have seen the sun setting between the solar markers, directly above the ruling Inca elite, who were known as "the children of the sun." Bauer believes that this elaborate and impressive Solstice ritual was organized in such a way to reinforce the authority of the Inca ruling class in dramatic fashion.

One of the popular legends associated with Lake Titicaca is that of lost Inca treasure, hidden when the Spanish conquistadors, led by Francisco Pizarro, arrived in Peru in 1532. Allegedly, much of this vast store of Inca treasure was kept in the "Coricancha," the Inca Temple of the Sun at their capital Cuzco (see Chapter 31), subdued by the Spanish in 1533. The fantastic treasures this temple was said to contain included a huge, 4,400-pound gold chain belonging to the Inca emperor Huascar; the "Garden of the Sun," a life-sized replica in gold of a country garden; the mummies of 13 Inca emperors coated in gold, studded with jewels, and seated on golden chairs; and a huge sun-disc, an image of the sun and its rays fashioned from pure gold. To prevent these treasures from falling into the hands of the Spanish, the Incas hid them away in caves or threw them into lakes, such as Lake Titicaca. In 1968 Jacques Cousteau mounted an expedition to explore Lake Titicaca to a depth of 220 feet for submerged Inca treasure using a mini-submarine, but found nothing.

As well as lost Inca treasure, local legends speak of a lost city called Wanaku, supposedly submerged beneath the waters of Lake Titicaca. In 2000, a fascinating discovery was made in the lake by an Italian team of divers called Akakor Geographical Exploring. Submerged in the depths of the lake, the expedition found evidence for pre-Columbian constructions in the form of a huge temple, 660 feet long and 130 feet wide, traces of a paved road, a 2,300-foot-long retaining wall, a terrace for crops, and ceramic artifacts. Although the Bolivian government has agreed to provide financial backing for further study of these intriguing underwater ruins, the investigations at the sacred lake have caused controversy with the local people. The locals are frightened that the investigations in the lake are disrespectful and will bring bad luck to the communities living in the vicinity.

However, some people are dubious about the grand claims of the Akakor team. Researchers who have been working in the area of Lake Titicaca for years, such as distinguished Bolivian archaeologist Dr. Carlos Ponce, and Johan G. Reinhard of the National Geographic Society, believe the Akakor findings to be as mythical as the treasure supposed to be at the bottom of the Lake. Dr. Ponce is skeptical of how 12 previous expeditions to Lake Titicaca, including that of Cousteau with his mini-sub, could have failed to locate any sign of the submerged structures supposedly discovered by Akakor. Many researchers also believe that the 20-day investigation at Lake Titicaca by Akakor was insufficient for a thorough archaeological investigation, and have also criticized the team for calling a press conference to announce its results rather than publish them in a peer-reviewed journal. Another archaeologist, Charles S. Stanish, from the University of California, Los Angeles, has excavated a variety of ancient sites on the Island of the Sun in Titicaca, and believes that the structures described by Akakor could never have been missed by the many investigations of the lake, especially as the supposed location of the new discoveries is in a part of the lake with frequent boat traffic.

Akakor plan further work at Titicaca, so perhaps some of these criticisms are premature, though there are a number of things about the group's methods that do not inspire confidence. One is the fact that the Akakor investigation team of 24 members only included one archaeologist. In addition, the descriptions of Akakor's activities on their Website makes unsubstantiated claims of "underwater ruins from 6000 years ago," and describes finds such as that of a "gold idol about 35 kilos in weight," which "opens up the possibility of the existence of a fabulous treasure a mitical (sic) pirate's dream"—hardly the language of serious researchers into the archaeology of Lake Titicaca. The group also claim to have discovered the remains of a cave used for child sacrifice by the Incas, as well as "the remains of the little children." Nowhere on their website are there photos or drawings of the finds from the investigations, nor have Akakor published anything to substantiate their claims, so it is difficult to be entirely confident about the existence of buried structures at the bottom of Lake Titicaca.

In the summer of 2000, Alexei Vranich, an archaeologist from the University of Pennsylvania, and his team had a total budget of $9,300 for three months of excavation at a pyramid in the important pre-Incan city of Tiwanaku, 12 miles from the shore of Lake Titicaca. In sharp contrast, Akakor's budget for their three weeks at Titicaca in 2000, including equipment provided by numerous sponsors, was well in excess of $100,000. Eight years on from Akakor's initial investigations, the lack of physical proof for the structures claimed by the group and the absence of a published report of their findings makes one wonder if money for research at Titicaca is going to the right people.

What is certain is that the investigations and sensational claims of Akakor have added a 21st-century element to legends of a sunken city and buried Inca gold at the bottom of Lake Titicaca.

Bibliography

"Aachen—Historical Information." Aachen City Tourism Website. *www.aachen.de/ EN/ts/160_about_aachen/20_aachen_history/index.html* (accessed April 19, 2008).

Abbott, G. *Ghosts of the Tower of London.* Nelson, Lancashire, UK: Hendon Publishing Co. Ltd., 1989.

———. *Mysteries of the Tower of London.* Nelson, Lancashire, UK: Hendon Publishing Co. Ltd., 1998.

Adam, Karla. "Terracotta Army May Be Guarding Buried Treasure." *The Independent* Website. *news.independent.co.uk/world/asia/article321132.ece* (accessed April 19, 2008).

Adams, Henry. *Mont-Saint-Michel and Chartres.* Boston: Houghton Mittlin, 1913.

"Ancient Temple Found Under Lake Titicaca." BBC News Website. *news.bbc.co.uk/ 2/hi/americas/892616.stm* (accessed May 2, 2008).
 Andrews, C., and P. Delgado. *Circular Evidence: A Detailed Investigation of the Flattened Swirled Crops Phenomenon.* London: Bloomsbury Publishing Ltd., 1990.

"Angkorian and Pre-Angkorian Temple Ruins." Visiting Cambodia. Canby Publications Co., Ltd. Website. *www.canbypublications.com/siemreap/ srtemples.htm* (accessed April 19, 2008).

"Arqueologías Fantásticas." Laicacota Weblog. *laicacota.blogspot.com/2007/04/ arqueologas-fantsticas.html* (accessed April 19, 2008).

Ashe, Geoffrey. *King Arthur's Avalon.* London: Collins, 1958.

Atkinson, R.J.C. *Stonehenge: Archaeology and Interpretation.* London: Penguin Books, 1990.

"Avebury—A Present from the Past." Avebury Website. *www.avebury-web.co.uk/ index.html* (accessed April 19, 2008).

Barker, Graham, and Tom Rasmussen. *The Etruscans (Peoples of Europe).* Oxford: Blackwell Publishing, 2000.

Bauer, Brian S. *Ancient Cuzco: Heartland of the Inca.* Austin, Tex.: University of Texas Press, 2004.

Bauer, Brian S., and Charles Stanish. *Ritual and Pilgrimage in the Ancient Andes: The Islands of the Sun and the Moon.* Austin, Tex.: University of Texas Press, 2001.

Blavatsky, H.P. *Isis Unveiled, Vol. 1—Science.* Pasadena, Calif.: Theosophical University Press, 1988 (1877).

Bord, Janet, and Colin Bord. *Alien Animals.* London: Panther Books, 1985.

Briard, Jacques. *The Bronze Age in Barbarian Europe. From the Megaliths to the Celts.* London: Book Club Associates, 1979.

Broad, William J. *The Oracle: Ancient Delphi and the Science Behind its Lost Secrets.* New York: Penguin (Non-Classics), 2007.

Brockman, Norbert C. *Encyclopedia of Sacred Places.* New York: Oxford University Press, 1998.

Brooks, J.A. *Ghosts of London.* Norwich, UK: Jarrold Publishing, 1991.

Brown, Theo. "The Dartmoor Legend of Mr. Childe." *Folklore,* Vol. 65, No. 2 (September 1954): 103–109.

———. *Devon Ghosts.* Norwich: Jarrold Publishing, 1982.

Burl, Aubrey. *From Carnac To Callanish: The Prehistoric Stone Rows of Britain, Ireland, and Brittany.* New Haven, Conn., and London: Yale University Press, 1993.

Burl, Aubrey. *A Guide to the Stone Circles of Britain, Ireland and Brittany.* New Haven, Conn., and London: Yale University Press, 2005.

———. *Prehistoric Avebury.* London: Book Club Associates, 1979.

———. *Rites of the Gods.* London: J.M. Dent & Sons, 1981.

Cahokia Mounds State Historical Site Website. *www.cahokiamounds.com/ cahokia.html* (accessed April 19, 2008).

Camp, John M. *The Archaeology of Athens.* New Haven, Conn.: Yale University Press, 2001.

Carley, James P. *Glastonbury Abbey: The Holy House at the Head of the Moors Adventurous.* Glastonbury, Somerset, UK: Gothic Image Publications, 1992.

Chapman, Fred. "The Bighorn Medicine Wheel 1988–1999." *Cultural Resource Management* 22, No. 3: 5–10.

Charpentier, Louis. *The Mysteries of Chartres Cathedral.* Northamptonshire, UK: Thorsons, 1975.

Chartres Tourist Office Official Website. *www.chartres-tourisme.com/pages/en/ page.php* (accessed April 19, 2008).

Children, George, and George Nash. *Neolithic Sites of Cardiganshire, Carmarthenshire & Pembrokeshire (Monuments in the Landscape).* Woonton, Herefordshire, UK: Logaston Press, 1997.

———. "Rites of Passage and the Cultural Life of the Doorway: An Expression in Metaphor and Social Statementing," *3rd Stone,* No.29 (January–March 1998): 29–33.

Chippindale, Christopher. *Stonehenge Complete.* London: Thames & Hudson Ltd., 2004.

"Circlemakers: Home of England's crop circle makers." Circlemakers Website. *www.circlemakers.org* (accessed April 19, 2008).

Clapp, Nicholas. *Sheba: Through the Desert in Search of the Legendary Queen.* New York: Mariner Books, 2001.

Coe, Michael D. *Angkor and the Khmer Civilization.* London: Thames & Hudson Ltd., 2003.

Coppens, Philip. "Ancient Atomic Wars—Best Evidence?" Philip Coppens Website. *www.philipcoppens.com/bestevidence.html* (accessed April 19, 2008).

———. "The Gold of Grand Paititi." Philip Coppens Website. *www.philipcoppens.com/granpaititi.html* (accessed April 19, 2008).

Cowan, James. *Mysteries of the Dream-Time. The Spiritual Life of Australian Aborigines.* Dorset, UK: Prism Press, 1992.

"Crop Circles Appear at Tomb of Chinese Empress." China.org.cn Website. *www.china.org.cn/english/MATERIAL/193401.htm* (accessed April 19, 2008).

Darvill, Timothy. *Stonehenge: The Biography of a Landscape.* Stroud, Gloucestershire, UK: Tempus, 2007.

Davies, Sioned (translator). *The Mabinogion.* Oxford: Oxford University Press, 2007.

"Delphi." Hellenic Ministry of Culture Website. *odysseus.culture.gr/h/3/ eh351.jsp?obj_id = 2507* (accessed April 19, 2008).

Dennis, George. *Cities and Cemeteries of Etruria.* London: J.M. Dent, 1907 (1848).

Devereux, Paul. "The Dragon Project." Paul Devereux Website. *www.pauldevereux.co.uk/new/body_dragonproject.html* (accessed April 19, 2008).

———. *Earth Lights Revelation.* London: Blandford, 1989.

———. *Haunted Land: Investigations into Ancient Mysteries and Modern Day Phenomena.* London: Piatkus, 2001.

———. *The Sacred Place.* London: Cassell & Co., 2000.

———. *Secrets of Ancient and Sacred Places.* London: Blandford, 1992.

———. *Stone Age Soundtracks.* London: Vega, 2001.

Diodorus Siculus. *Diodorus of Sicily in Twelve Volumes with an English Translation by C. H. Oldfather. Vol. 4–8.* Cambridge, Mass.: Harvard University Press, 1989.

The Discovery Programme Website. *www.discoveryprogramme.ie* (accessed April 19, 2008).

Doan, James. "The Legend of the Sunken City in Welsh and Breton Tradition." *Folklore, Vol. 92, No. 1 (1981)*: 77–83.

Dyfed Archaeological Trust Website. *www.acadat.com/main.htm* (accessed April 19, 2008).

Eddy, John, "Probing the Mystery of the Medicine Wheels." *National Geographic 151 (January 1977)*: 1, 140–46.

Edmonds, Margot, and Ella E. Clark. *Voices of the Winds: Native American Legends.* New York: Facts on File Inc., 1989.

Emerson, Thomas E. *Cahokia and the Archaeology of Power.* Tuscaloosa, Ala.: University of Alabama Press, 1997.

Eogan, George. *Knowth and the Passage Tombs of Ireland.* London: Thames & Hudson Ltd., 1986.

"Etruscan City and Burial Site of Lars Porsena Discovered." Athena Review: Archaeology in the News Website. *www.athenapub.com/archnew2.htm* (accessed April 19, 2008).

Evans, Arthur J. "The Rollright Stones and Their Folk-Lore." *Folklore,* Vol. 6, No. 1 (March 1895): 6–53.

Evans-Wentz, W.Y. *The Fairy Faith in Celtic Countries.* Secaucus, N.J.: Citadel Press Secaucus, 1990 (1911).

Evelyn-White, Hugh G. (ed.). *The Homeric Hymns and Homerica.* London: William Heinemann Ltd., 1914.

"Experts Look for 'Watery Kingdom'." BBC News online Website. *news.bbc.co.uk/2/hi/uk_news/wales/mid_/5016240.stm* (accessed April 19, 2008).

Fagan, Brian (ed.). *The Seventy Great Mysteries of the Ancient World.* London: Thames & Hudson Ltd., 2001.

First People of America and Canada Website. *www.firstpeople.us* (accessed April 19, 2008).

Fontenrose, Joseph Eddy. *Python; a Study of Delphic Myth and its Origins.* Berkeley, Calif.: University of California Press, 1959.

Forero, Juan. "New Peruvian Soft Drink Packs a Punch." *New York Times* Online, June 10, 2004. *query.nytimes.com/gst/fullpage.html?res = 9E02E2DA1730F933 A25755C0A9629C8B63* (accessed May 2, 2008).

"Foundations of Aksumite Civilization and Its Christian Legacy (1st–7th century A.D.)". Metropolitan Museum of Art Website. Time Line of Art History. *www.metmuseum.org/toah/hd/aksu/hd_aksu_1.htm#* (accessed April 19, 2008).

Freeman, Richard. "In the Coils of the Naga." *Fortean Times* 166, January 2003: 30–35.

Gathercole, Clare. "English Heritage Extensive Urban Survey. An Archaeological Assessment of Glastonbury." Somerset County Council Website. *www.somerset.gov.uk/media/1B25C/EUS_GlastonburyText.pdf* (accessed April 19, 2008).

Giese, Paula. "Aboriginal Star Knowledge—Native American Astronomy." Beaded Lizard Web Designs Website: Native American Indian: Art, Culture, Education, History, Science. *www.kstrom.net/isk/stars/starkno5.html* (accessed April 19, 2008).

Grinnell, George Bird. "The Medicine Wheel." *American Anthropologist, New Series,* Vol. 24, No. 3 (July–September 1922): 299–310.

Grinsell, L.V. "Barrow Treasure, in Fact, Tradition, and Legislation." *Folklore,* Vol. 78, No. 1 (Spring 1967): 1–38.

———. *The Folklore of Prehistoric Sites in Britain.* Newton Abbot, Devon, UK: David & Charles, 1976.

———. "The Legendary History and Folklore of Stonehenge." *Folklore,* Vol. 87, No. 1 (1976): 5–20.

Hadingham, Evan. *Lines to the Mountain Gods.* London: Harrap, 1987.

Hancock, Graham. *The Sign and the Seal: Quest for the Lost Ark of the Covenant.* London: Arrow Books Ltd., 1993.

Hare, John Bruno. Preface to *The Vaimanika-Shaastra. Internet Sacred Text Archive. www.sacred-texts.com/ufo/vs/vspref.htm* (accessed April 19, 2008).

Hatcher Childress, David. *Technology of the Gods: The Incredible Sciences of the Ancients.* Kempton, Ill.: Adventures Unlimited Press, 2000.

Hausdorf, Hartwig. *The Chinese Roswell: UFO Encounters in the Far East from Ancient Times to the Present.* Boca Raton, Fl.: New Paradigm Books, 1998.

Heritage Malta. Heritage Malta Website. *www.heritagemalta.org/index.html* (accessed April 19, 2008).

Herodotus. *The Histories.* Translated by Aubrey de Sëlincourt. Harmondsworth, UK: Penguin, 1972.

Houlder, Christopher. *Wales: An Archaeological Guide.* London and Boston: Faber and Faber, 1974.

Howard, Michael. "The Womb of Ceridwen." *New Age Journal* Website. *www.newage-journal.com/wombofceridwen.htm* (accessed April 19, 2008).

Hugot, Leo. *Aachen Cathedral A Guide.* City unknown, Germany: Einhard, 1993.

"Is This an Angel on a TV?" College of the Siskiyous Website. *www.siskiyous.edu/class/engl12/angel.htm* (accessed April 19, 2008).

James, Peter, and Nick Thorpe. *Ancient Inventions.* London: Michael O'Mara Books Ltd., 1995.

———. *Ancient Mysteries.* New York: Ballantine Books, 1999.

Kaisar, David. "Sacred Preseli." *3rd Stone,* No. 46 (Spring and Summer 2003): 34–37.

Kennedy, Maev. "Tower's Raven Mythology May Be a Victorian Flight of Fantasy." *The Guardian* Website. *www.guardian.co.uk/monarchy/story/0,2763, 1351402,00.html* (accessed April 19, 2008).

Keno. "Ice Fog and Fata Morgana." *The Crestone Eagle* Website. *crestoneeagle.com/archives2004/jan04_b1.html* (accessed April 19, 2008).

Kenoyer, Jonathan Mark. *Ancient Cities of the Indus Valley Civilization.* New Delhi: Oxford University Press, 2005.

———. "Mohenjo-Daro!" Mohenjo Daro Website. *www.mohenjodaro.net* (accessed April 19, 2008).

Kerenyi, C. *The Gods of the Greeks.* London: Thames & Hudson Ltd., 1951.

Kitt Chappell, Sally A. *Cahokia: Mirror of the Cosmos.* Chicago: University of Chicago Press, 2005.

Laber, Emily. "Archaeological Frauds?" *The Sciences,* January/February 2001. Published by the New York Academy of Sciences. *www.nyas.org/publications/sciences/pdf/ts_01_01.pdf* (accessed May 2, 2008).

Lambrick, George. *The Rollright Stones.* Oxford: Oxford Archaeological Unit, 1983.

Layton, Robert. *Uluru: An Aboriginal History of Ayers Rock.* Canberra, Australia: Aboriginal Studies Press, 2001.

Legendary Dartmoor Website. *www.legendarydartmoor.co.uk* (accessed April 19, 2008).

Lepie, Herta. "The Stones of Aachen Cathedral." *UNESCO Courier, November 1991.*

Lewallen, Judy R. "The San Luis Valley Crystal Skull: A Transparent Mystery." *Skeptical Inquirer, September/October 1997.*

Lindesay, William, and Guo Baofu. *The Terracotta Army of Qin Shi Huangdi —First Emperor of China.* Hong Kong: Odyssey Publications. 2002.

Lindy Chamberlain-Creighton Website. *www.lindychamberlain.com/content/home* (accessed April 19, 2008).

Little, Gregory L. *People of the Web.* Memphis, Tenn.: White Buffalo Books, 1990.

MacGown, Kenneth. *Wonders of the Boyne Valley.* Dublin, Ireland: Kamac Publications, 1984.

Maier, Chris. "China's Lost Pyramids." Unexplained Earth Website. *www.unexplainedearth.com/xian.php* (accessed April 19, 2008).

———. "The Fantastic Creatures of Angkor." Unexplained Earth Website. *www.unexplainedearth.com/angkor.php* (accessed April 19, 2008).

Mann, Nicholas R. *The Isle of Avalon Sacred Mysteries of Arthur and Glastonbury Tor.* St. Paul, Minn.: Llewellyn Publications, 1996.

Manning, Percy. "Stray Notes on Oxfordshire Folklore." *Folklore, Vol. 13, No. 3 (September 29, 1902)*: 288–95.

Markale, Jean. *Cathedral of the Black Madonna: The Druids and the Mysteries of Chartres.* Rochester, Vt.: Inner Traditions, 2004.

Marriott, Alice, and Carole K. Rachlin. *American Indian Mythology.* New York: Mentor, 1968.

Marshall, Steve. "The White Pyramid." *Fortean Times 164, November 2002*: 28–36.

McIntosh, Jane. *A Peaceful Realm: The Rise And Fall of the Indus Civilization.* Boulder, Colo.: Westview Press, 2001.

Meaden, Terence. *The Secrets of the Avebury Stones.* Londom, Souvenir Press. 1999.

Mee, Christopher, and Antony Spawforth. *Greece (Oxford Archaeological Guides).* Oxford: Oxford University Press, 2001.

Métraux, Alfred. *The History of the Incas.* Translated from the French by George Ordish. New York: Pantheon Books, 1969.

Michell, John. *Megalithomania: Artists, Antiquarians and Archaeologists at the Old Stone Monuments.* London: Thames & Hudson Ltd., 1982.

Miller, Malcolm. *Chartres Cathedral.* New York: Riverside Book Company, 1997.

"Mount Shasta Companion." College of the Siskiyous Website. *www.siskiyous.edu/Shasta* (accessed April 19, 2008).

Mountford, Charles P. *Ayers Rock. Its People, Their Beliefs, and Their Art.* Sydney, Australia: Pacific Books, 1971.

———. *Brown Men and Red Sand.* Melbourne, Australia: Sun Books. 1967.

Muecke, Stephen, and Adam Shoemaker. *Aboriginal Australians: First Nations of an Ancient Continent.* London: Thames & Hudson Ltd., 2004.

Munro-Hay, Stuart. *The Quest for the Ark of the Covenant: The True History of the Tablets of Moses.* London: I. B. Tauris, 2006.

"The Mystery of the Hypogeum." *The Malta Independent* Online. *www.independent.com.mt/news.asp?newsitemid = 5084* (accessed April 19, 2008).

"Mythical Ireland—Tara." Mythical Ireland Website. *www.mythicalireland.com/ancientsites/tara* (accessed April 19 2008).

Nabokov, Peter. *Where the Lightning Strikes: The Lives of American Indian Sacred Places.* New York: Viking, 2006.

"The Negotiating Avebury Project." Department of Archaeology, University of Southampton Website. *www.arch.soton.ac.uk/Research/Avebury* (accessed April 19, 2008).

"New Archaeological Evidence Illuminates Inca Sun-Worship Ritual." Science Daily website. *www.sciencedaily.com/releases/1998/09/980930081949.htm* (accessed May 2, 2008).

"New Recruit Joins Terracotta Army." BBC News Website. *news.bbc.co.uk/1/hi/world/asia-pacific/5355546.stm* (accessed April 19, 2008).

North, F.J. *Sunken Cities: Some Legends of the Coast and Lakes of Wales.* Cardiff, Wales: University of Wales Press, 1957.

"Nuclear Power Plants in Operation." Nuclear Power Corporation of India Limited Website. *www.npcil.nic.in/PlantsInOperation.asp* (accessed April 19, 2008).

O'Brien, Christopher. *Secrets of the Mysterious Valley.* Kempton, Ill.: Adventures Unlimited Press, 2007.

O'Connor, J.J., and E.F. Robertson. "Alcuin of York." The MacTutor History of Mathematics Archive Website. *www-history.mcs.st-Andrews.ac.uk/history//Biographies/Alcuin.html* (accessed April 19, 2008).

O'Kelly, Claire. *Concise Guide to Newgrange.* Cork, Ireland: Claire O'Kelly, 1990.

O'Kelly, Michael J. *Early Ireland: An Introduction to Irish Prehistory.* Cambridge, UK: Cambridge University Press, 1989.

———. *Newgrange. Archaeology, Art and Legend.* London: Thames & Hudson Ltd., 1998.

"Orkneyjar—The Heritage of the Orkney Islands." Orkneyjar Website. *www.orkneyjar.com/index.html* (accessed April 19, 2008).

O'Sullivan, Muiris. *Tara: The Mound of the Hostages.* Dublin, Ireland: Wordwell Books, 2005.

Padel, Ruth. "Women: Model for Possession by Greek Daemons." In Camerron, Averil, and Amélie Kuhrt (eds.). *Images of Women in Antiquity.* London: Routledge, 1993.

Parnell, Geoffrey. *The Tower of London: A 2000 Year History (Osprey Landmarks in History).* Oxford, UK: Osprey Publishing, 2000.

Pausanias. *Guide to Greece. (Volume 1:Central Greece).* London: Penguin Books, 1979.

Pearson, Mike Parker. "Stonehenge Riverside Project." University of Sheffield Website. *www.shef.ac.uk/archaeology/research/Stonehenge* (accessed April 19, 2008).

Pennick, Nigel. *Lost Lands and Sunken Cities.* London: Fortean Tomes, 1987.

Pettit, Paul. *Prehistoric Dartmoor.* Newton Abbot, Devon, UK: David and Charles, 1974.

Pitts, Mike. *Hengeworld.* London: Arrow Books, 2001.

Pliny. *Natural History, Volume X, Books 36–37 (Loeb Classical Library No. 419).* Cambridge, Mass.: Harvard University Press, 1962.

Pollard, J., and A. Reynolds. *Avebury: The Biography of a Landscape.* Stroud, Gloucestershire, UK: Tempus Publishing Ltd., 2002.

La Prensa. Lima, Peru. August 23, 1965.

Pryor, Francis. *Britain B.C.* London: Harper Perennial, 2004.

"The Pyramids of China." Trilobia Central Website. *www.trilobia.com/pyramids.htm* (accessed April 19, 2008).

Rahtz, Philip. *Glastonbury: Myth & Archaeology.* Stroud, Gloucestershire, UK: Tempus Publishing, 2003.

Ravelli, Franco, and Paula J. Howarth. "Etruscan Cuniculi: Tunnels for the Collection of Pure Water." Franco Ravelli Website. *www.francoravelli.it/cunicoli/english/cuniculi%201984/1988-0.htm* (accessed April 19, 2008).

Renfrew, Colin (ed.). *The Megalithic Monuments of Western Europe.* London: Thames & Hudson Ltd., 1983.

"The Rollright Stones—a Mystical Ancient Site." The Rollright Stones Website. *www.rollrightstones.co.uk* (accessed April 19, 2008).

San Luis Valley Archaeological Network Website. *www.slvarchnet.org/Index.html* (accessed April 19, 2008).

San Luis Valley Dweller Website. *www.slvdweller.com* (accessed April 19, 2008).

Saraceni, Jessica E. "Redating Serpent Mound." *Archaeology Magazine* Website. *www.archaeology.org/9611/newsbriefs/serpentmound.html* (accessed April 19, 2008).

Service, Alastair, and Jean Bradbury. *The Standing Stones of Europe. A Guide to the Great Megalithic Monuments.* London: J.M. Dent, 1993.

Sheaffer, Robert. "UFOs Hot and Cold—San Luis Valley, Colorado." *Skeptical Inquirer,* September–October 2003.

Silva, Freddy. *The Secrets of the Fields. The Science and Mysticism of Crop Circles.* Charlottesville, Va.: Hampton Roads Publishing Company, Inc., 2002.

Silverberg, Robert. *Mound Builders.* Columbus, Ohio: Ohio University Press, 1986.

Slavin, Michael. *The Book of Tara.* Dublin, Ireland: Wolfhound Press, 1996.

Smith, A.W., and William Blake. "And Did Those Feet...?: The 'Legend' of Christ's Visit to Britain." *Folklore,* Vol. 100, No. 1 (1989): 63–83.

Smith, Helena. "By Zeus!" *The Guardian* Website. *www.guardian.co.uk/g2/story/ 0,,2003096,00.html* (accessed April 19, 2008).

Spencer, John, and Anne Spencer. *The Encyclopedia of Ghosts and Spirits.* London: Book Club Associates, 1992.

Spooner, B.C. "The Stone Circles of Cornwall." *Folklore,* Vol. 64, No. 4 (December 1953): 484–87.

St. Leger-Gordon, Ruth E. *Witchcraft and Folklore of Dartmoor.* New York: Bell Publishing Company, 1972.

"Stonehenge Quarry Site 'Revealed.'" BBC News Website. *news.bbc.co.uk/2/hi/ uk_news/wales/south_west/4123764.stm* (accessed April 19, 2008).

Stout, Geraldine. *Newgrange and the Bend in the Boyne.* Cork, Ireland: Cork University Press, 2003.

Sullivan, Danny. "Going Underground. Malta's Hypogeum." *3rd Stone,* Issue 40, Summer/Autumn 2001.

Sweat, John. "The Pyramids of Xi'an." The Anthropogene Website. *webpages.charter.net/anthropogene/arc_vol3_is1.html* (accessed April 19, 2008).

"3000-Year-Old 'Pyramid' Discovered in NE China." China View Website. *news.xinhuanet.com/english/2006-06/21/content_4727356.htm* (accessed April 19, 2008).

Tilley, Christopher. *A Phenomenology of Landscape: Places, Paths and Monuments.* Oxford: Berg Publishers, 1997.

"Tiny Mummies Are Not the Prehistoric Little People." University of Wyoming Website. *www.uwyo.edu/news/show.asp?id = 12502* (accessed April 19, 2008).

"Tiwanaku 2004 Expedition—Summary." Akakor Geographical Exploring Website. *www.akakor.com/english/tiwabrief-uk.html* (accessed May 2, 2008).

Tomkinson, John L. *Athens (Greece Beyond the Guidebooks).* Athens, Greece: Anagnosis Publications, 2006.

———. *Attica (Greece Beyond the Guidebooks).* Athens, Greece: Anagnosis Publications, 2002.

"The Tower of London." Historical Royal Palaces Website. *www.hrp.org.uk/ TowerOfLondon* (accessed April 19, 2008).

"Uluru-Kata Tjuta National Park." Australian Government Department of the Environment, Water, Heritage and the Arts. Australian Government Website. *www.environment.gov.au/parks/uluru/index.html* (accessed April 19, 2008).

"Unesco Warning on Tower of London." BBC News Website. *news.bbc.co.uk/2/hi/uk_news/england/london/6072580.stm* (accessed April 19, 2008).

"USDA Forest Service, Rio Grande National Forest. History and Culture of the San Luis Valley Area." U.S. Forest Service Website. *www.fs.fed.us/r2/riogrande/about/history/index.shtml* (accessed April 19, 2008).

Vembos, Thanasis. *opoi Dynames stin Ellada.* Thessaloniki, Greece: Ekdoseis Archetypo, 2005.

Voss, Jerome A. "Antiquity Imagined: Cultural Values in Archaeological Folklore." *Folklore,* Vol. 98, No. 1 (1987): 80–90.

Wade, Nicholas. "DNA Boosts Herodotus' Account of Etruscans as Migrants to Italy." *New York Times* Website. *www.nytimes.com/2007/04/03/science/03etruscan.html* (accessed April 19, 2008).

Waldman, Carl. *Atlas of the North American Indian.* New York: Checkmark Books, 2000.

Walhouse, M. J. "Ghostly Lights." *Folklore,* Vol. 5, No. 4 (December 1894): 293–99.

Wallrich, William Jones. "Five Bruja Tales from the San Luis Valley." *Western Folklore,* Vol. 9, No. 4 (October 1950): 359–62.

———. "Some Variants of the 'Demon Dancer'." *Western Folklore,* Vol. 9, No. 2 (April 1950): 144–46.

Wellard, James. T*he Search for the Etruscans.* London: Cardinal, 1973.

Wenli, Zang. *The Qin Terracotta Army: Treasures of Lintong.* Hong Kong: London Editions, 2007.

Westwood, Jennifer. *Albion: A Guide to Legendary Britain.* London: Book Club Associates, 1986.

———. "The Rollright Stones. Part I: The Danes." *3rd Stone,* No.38 (Summer 2000): 6–10.

———. "The Rollright Stones. Part 2: The Witch." *3rd Stone,* No.39 (Winter 2000/2001): 62–66.

Westwood, Jennifer, and Jacqueline Simpson. *The Lore of the Land: A Guide to England's Legends, from Spring-heeled Jack to the Witches of Warboys.* London: Penguin Books Ltd., 2005.

Wright, Thomas. "Legend of the Rollright Stones." *The Folk-Lore Record,* Vol. 2 (1879): 177–79.

Zanger, Michael. *Mt. Shasta: History, Legend & Lore.* Berkeley, Calif.: Celestial Arts Publishing, 1992.

Index

About the Author

Born in Birmingham, England, author and researcher Brian Haughton studied European Archaeology at the University of Nottingham. After working on archaeological projects in England and Greece, and also at the Warwickshire Museum, he received a Masters in Philosophy in Greek Archaeology at Birmingham University in 1998. Soon after, he left England for Patra, Greece, where he currently lives and writes. Haughton's book *Hidden History: Lost Civilizations, Secret Knowledge, and Ancient Mysteries* was published in January 2007, and has already been translated into seven languages. Brian has written about the folklore of the supernatural and historical mysteries for numerous print and internet publications including the BBC's *Legacies* Website, *Paranormal Magazine, Doorways* magazine, *Awareness,* and *All Destiny.* His research into the Princess Caraboo hoax has been used by the BBC on a number of occasions. Haughton's *Mysterious People* Website (*www.mysteriouspeople.com*), devoted to human enigmas, has received around a million visits since its inception at the end of 2002.

Haughton is a member of the Folklore Society (England) and serves as a consultant for UK-based research and investigative organization Parasearch. His special subjects include the sacred landscapes and monuments of prehistory and the folklore of the supernatural. He long ago fell for the lure of the ancient and the supernatural, initially inspired by visiting the Neolithic chambered tombs of the Cotswolds (UK) and prehistoric archaeological sites on Crete, and by reading the ghost stories of Sheridan Le Fanu and M.R. James.